Frédéric Le Play
ON FAMILY, WORK, AND SOCIAL CHANGE

THE HERITAGE OF SOCIOLOGY
A Series Edited by Morris Janowitz

AUDREY COHEN COLLEGE
50664000140774
Le Play, Frederic, 1/Fr*ed*eric Le Play
HM22 .F8 L435 1982 C.1 STACKS 1982

```
HM      Le Play,
22        Frederic, 1806-
F8        1882.
L435        Frédéric Le
1982    Play on family,
        work, and social
```

DATE DUE

COLLEGE FOR HUMAN SERVICES
LIBRARY
245 HUDSON STREET
NEW YORK, N.Y. 10014

Frédéric Le Play

On Family, Work, and Social Change

Edited, translated, and with an Introduction by
CATHERINE BODARD SILVER

THE UNIVERSITY OF CHICAGO PRESS
Chicago and London

CATHERINE BODARD SILVER is professor of sociology at Brooklyn College and the Graduate Center of the City University of New York. She received a Licence de sociologie from the Sorbonne and a Ph.D. in sociology from Columbia University. She is the author of *Black Teachers in Urban Schools: The Case of Washington, D.C.*

THE UNIVERSITY OF CHICAGO PRESS, CHICAGO 60637
THE UNIVERSITY OF CHICAGO PRESS, LTD., LONDON

© 1982 by The University of Chicago
All rights reserved. Published 1982
Printed in the United States of America
89 88 87 86 85 84 83 82   1 2 3 4 5

Library of Congress Cataloging in Publication Data

Le Play, Pierre Guillaume Frédéric, 1806–1882.
  Frédéric Le Play on family, work, and social change.

  (The Heritage of sociology)
  Bibliography: p.
  1. Le Play, Pierre Guillaume Frédéric, 1802–1882.
2. Sociology—France—History. 3. Sociology—France—Methodology. 4. Labor and laboring classes—France—History. 5. Family—France—History. 6. Social change.
I. Title. II. Series.
HM22.F8L435   301'.0944   81-23125
ISBN 0-226-47266-3   AACR2

To my mother, Pierrette Fromentin,
to the memory of my father, Albert Bodard,
and to my sisters, Françoise Bodard and Nicole Moll

CONTENTS

	Preface	xi

INTRODUCTION, *by Catherine Bodard Silver*

1	Le Play and Social Science	3
2	The Life of Frédéric Le Play	14
3	Le Play and the Sociological Orientations of His Time	28
4	The Science of Society	41
5	The Monographic Method	58
6	Family Types	76
7	Theory of Social Mobility	81
8	Theory of Social Change	97
9	Le Play's Followers	115
10	Conclusion	125

FRÉDÉRIC LE PLAY
ON FAMILY, WORK, AND SOCIAL CHANGE

I. The Apprenticeship of a Social Scientist

1	Discovering the Science of Society: From Engineering to Social Science	137
2	Social Ills and the Science of Society	142

II. The Nature and Scope of the Science of Society

3	The Use of Direct Observation	151
4	Statistics versus Direct Observation	155
5	The Comparative Study of European Workers	159
6	The Subject Matter of the Science of Society	163
7	Defining "Workers," "Associations," and "Social Systems"	166

III. The Monographic Method

8	The Study of Working-Class Families	171
9	The Rules of Social Investigation	175
10	The Monographic Method	179
11	Monograph on the Miner of the Upper Harz Mining Corporation	184

IV. Theory of Social Mobility

12	Constructing a Social Hierarchy	209
13	Intragenerational Mobility	214
14	Comparing Occupational Styles	217
15	Conditions of Social Mobility	230

V. Theory of Social Change

16	Social Systems and Social Change	239
17	An Analysis of Social Trends	245
18	The Three Ages of Work	248

VI. Family Organization

19	Family Types: Patriarchal, Stem, Unstable	259
20	Family Organization in the Four Social Systems of Europe	263
21	Inheritance Laws, Family Organization, and Social Reform	267

VII. Social Reform

22	The Science of Society as a Theory of Social Reform	283
23	Proposals for Reform	288
	Notes	299
	Bibliography	327

PREFACE

My interest in the work of Frédéric Le Play grew out of a seminar held at Columbia University by Professors Robert K. Merton and Paul Lazarsfeld on the history of ideas and methods in sociology. I am grateful to both for creating an intellectual milieu in which new ideas were developed. In addition, Paul Lazarsfeld gave me much encouragement in the early stages of the research. I am especially indebted to Morris Janowitz, the editor of the Heritage of Sociology series, for his continuous intellectual and emotional support. I would like to thank Allan Silver, Sam Sieber, Sidney Aronson, Symour Spilerman, and Chaim Henoch for their intellectual stimulation, encouragement, and comments on earlier drafts. I would also like to thank Evelyn Ledyard for her patience in typing and retyping several chapters of the manuscript and Helen Danner for her editorial assistance. Finally, I would like to acknowledge the help of Philippe Perier who gave me access to the Le Play library at the Institut Catholique in Paris.

All the translations from Le Play's work, which has not appeared in English except in very limited excerpts, were carried out by me with the collaboration of Diana Wolfe Levy—then an assistant professor in the French Department at Columbia University—and Thomas Mathewson, a student at Columbia University. We attempted to make Le Play's nineteenth-century prose as clear as possible without altering the original flavor and, to help the reader, have often added the French term after the English translation of it. The research and translations were made possible by grants numbers 1731, 10121, and 11814 from the PSC-CUNY Research Award Program of the Research Foundation of the City University of New York and a fellowship from the Social Science Research Council.

CATHERINE BODARD SILVER

INTRODUCTION
by Catherine Bodard Silver

1

LE PLAY AND SOCIAL SCIENCE

Frédéric Le Play (1806–82) was the first social scientist to undertake field research of the "monographic" type, to collect his own data specifically to test hypotheses, and to undertake systematic, comparative cross-national research. A French industrial and mining engineer—for many years one of the most eminent in Europe—and a major figure in the development of elite technical education in France, he was also centrally involved, as practitioner, teacher, and consultant, in the industrialization of Russia and other European countries. As a conscious agent of the social change that stemmed directly from industrialization, particularly the introduction of the railroad and the development of large-scale markets and bureaucratic forms of organization, Le Play rejected both the rational individualism of capitalism and the newly self-conscious traditionalism of conservative political thinkers. As a Catholic, he supported social hierarchy and stability, but never clericalism or reaction. His scientific training in geology, mining, and chemistry disposed him to apply empirical and inductive methods to emerging social problems, instead of the speculative and deductive methods that characterize Comtean positivism. His education also led him to reject the purely reformist, essentially empiricist research being carried on by his British contemporaries and by such French contemporaries as Villermé.

Le Play believed that the "science of society" was an applied science, like metallurgy, whose discoveries were only first steps toward accomplishing certain tasks. Its main task, he believed, was to rediscover "the secret of happiness" of societies.

Le Play saw a direct link between understanding and social action, between the roles of social scientist and social reformer. He directed his energies toward discovering the types of social and economic arrangements that could best promote social stability and economic progress. He saw "duty toward the suffering classes" as a patriotic mission to educate the nation's elites to meet the new requirements of an emerging social and economic order.[1]

My task in this study is to demonstrate the originality and importance of Le Play's work, which has been neglected by most historians of sociology,[2] while taking a fresh look at some important sociological questions. First, we need to reexamine the social and intellectual roots of modern sociology and the history of its value orientation. One perspective particularly needing reassessment is the view that nineteenth-century liberal ideologies led to modern empirical research, but that conservative ideologies, based on neo-Catholic ideas about hierarchy and stability, offered only a return to a past golden age. Empirical social research, according to this point of view, was stimulated by certain individuals who articulated the central government's need for more complete and accurate information, society's need to find solutions to problems created by the industrial revolution, and the establishment's need to justify the bourgeois liberal organization of society. Thus, it is argued that liberal ideology stimulated empirical research, which was meliorist and empiricist in nature, whereas conservative ideologies fostered only reactionary and antiempirical research.[3] An analysis of Le Play's work, however, shows that a great deal of empirical research in France was actually the product of subtle interplay between conservative and liberal ideologies.

Sociologists in the latter half of the twentieth century are operating in large measure with essentially nineteenth-century ideas and assumptions, which are often so completely taken for granted that their origins are forgotten.[4] We tend to apply these concepts to our own time mechanically, without being aware of their relationship to the values, group interests, and general socioeconomic conditions of the nineteenth century. For example, such concepts as "cooperation," "association," and "paternalism" are products of distinctive features of the first half of the nineteenth century. It is useful to recall the original meanings of these concepts and to understand how they were used by thinkers as different as the socialist Proudhon, the positivist Comte, and the neoconservative Le Play.

Historians of sociology have concentrated on the ideas of the social thinkers and system-builders and have paid less attention to the empirical researchers. This oversight has led to misconceptions about the intellectual history of sociology. For example, it has been widely claimed that nineteenth-century French sociology was theoretical and global, in contrast to the empiricism of the Anglo-Saxon tradition. This view, however, cannot account for the work of Quetelet, or for the appearance in 1855 of Frédéric Le Play's *Les Ouvriers européens* (European Workers).[5] This work represents the first instance of large-scale empirical research based on a standardized method that combined both qualitative field observation and quantification. Le Play's method of family monographs, which used data collected directly from persons through what today would be called participant observation and interviews, provided a comparative framework for the study of family structure and work relations in different types of societies.

A new interest in the history of empirical social research has emerged in the last two decades, stimulated in part by the work of Paul Lazarsfeld and of his students.[6] Several authors have discussed the role of empirical research during the nineteenth century and have convincingly demonstrated that it played a role as important as that of general theories of society in sociology's growth as an intellectual discipline.[7] Sociology probably owes as much to Frédéric Le Play as to Auguste Comte (1798–1857). But while Comte, the social theoretician and system-builder, is acclaimed as the father of sociology, Le Play, the social researcher, is largely forgotten.

Le Play's empirical work was accomplished astonishingly early: between 1829 and 1855, when *Les Ouvriers européens* first appeared—thirty-eight years before Durkheim's *The Division of*

Labor. The elaboration of these ideas in later years in many publications—*La Réforme sociale* (Social Reform) (1864),[8] *L'Organisation du travail* (The Organization of Work) (1870),[9] *L'Organisation de la famille* (The Organization of the Family) (1871),[10] and the second edition of *Les Ouvriers européens* (1877-79)—has caused many to misdate his work, so that Le Play's striking originality has been obscured by the most elementary chronological confusion.

Les Ouvriers européens has not been translated into English, and the first edition (1855) is seldom read or even referred to.[11] It is one of those classics known principally through references to it in the secondary literature. It contains thirty-six monographs (the second edition has fifty-seven) on individual families scattered throughout Europe in the first half of the nineteenth century, families whose members included British factory workers and artisans; Russian, Spanish, and French peasants; a Swiss clockmaker; and a Parisian rag-picker. In each monograph Le Play supplemented the family data with a mass of information on local economic conditions, associations, historical traditions, relations between workers and employers, and ecology. In short, he presented a series of detailed case studies of European communities. It is no exaggeration to claim that this is the first time in which the largely silent and illiterate masses of Europe were studied in a scientifically intelligible way, with methods that essentially resemble modern-day sociological and anthropological procedures. Like Comte and de Tocqueville, Le Play was concerned with the problem of social stability and change in a time of rapid economic and political development. However, Le Play translated his concerns into field observation and tested basic ideas about the functioning of society. With a few contemporaries, Le Play made the decisive leap into what later became known as empirical sociology.[12]

In *The Rules of Sociological Method,* Emile Durkheim wrote several pages criticizing the monographic approach in terms which made clear that he was referring to Le Play's school, although he did not mention Le Play's name. He argued that while direct observation, exhaustiveness, and inductive reasoning give the method a scientific appearance, a truly scientific approach needs more than an accumulation of facts; it needs a general principle that will guide the selection and interpretation of "crucial facts."[13] Durkheim's criticisms reflect important methodological considerations, but they also make it clear that he was not familiar with *Les Ouvriers européens*. It is worth noting that Le Play did use complex classificatory devices, combining the traditions of H. Conring and W. Petty, to collect the information in his family budgets. These devices, which were intended to help the researcher to be as systematic and objective as possible, fit Durkheim's description of the monographic method. However, Durkheim missed the goal of the elaborate classification scheme in which the first edition's thirty-six monographs are located. This tableau was conceived by Le Play as a way to define all the families in a two-dimensional property-space. The horizontal axis presents four different types of society, and the vertical axis seven types of workers. Each monograph, therefore, is located at one of the intersections of these two dimensions and represents a type of worker within a type of social organization. Le Play wrote that he had made sure that for three of these types of societies at least one family monograph would be found in each of the tableau's "cells." In other words, the monographs in the first edition of *Les Ouvriers européens* were derived from a general sociological model that Le Play constructed.[14]

With this classification scheme, Le Play set up typologies of workers and societies. While his classifications are admittedly somewhat crude (they are neither exclusive nor exhaustive), they are unquestionably more than simple descriptions of reality or mere accumulations of facts. His typologies are abstractions from reality, created for the purpose of sociological analysis, and constitute a real methodological advance.[15] As we shall see later in some detail, these typologies are the basis for Le Play's theories of social mobility and social change. Starting from the observation of a variety of social institutions, he arrived at principles of organization which could be used both to describe social systems and to construct social theories.[16]

Le Play used empirical observation not only to construct his own theories but also to test other people's ideas. As a social scientist, he strove to convert purely ideological aspects of both conservative and liberal beliefs into a set of testable propositions.[17] For example, he clarified the general reformist belief in the social value of education by distinguishing between the social and moral "training" that takes place in the home—what he called "primary education"—and the education that takes place in schools. Le Play's family monographs convinced him of the overwhelming importance of "primary education" in the search for social order and economic progress. Like other contemporary sociologists, he was clearly influenced by the ideological perspectives which he brought to his work, but he was unique in using these perspectives to form an interpretative scheme which both guided and depended upon empirical observation.

Le Play's contributions have been known in the United States largely through the work of selected sociologists and social historians. Sorokin hails Le Play as one of the greatest and most creative social thinkers of the nineteenth century, a founding father of sociology, but he does not present a comprehensive exposition of Le Play's ideas and concentrates mainly on the contributions of Le Play's followers, Demolins and de Tourville.[18] Zimmerman and Frampton offer an important introduction to Le Play, which includes the first excerpts from his work in English. They recognize the importance of Le Play's theories about social change and the family, but their interpretation is too narrow and they tried to defend Le Play's moralizing enterprise.[19]

Nisbet's assessment of Le Play's contribution, both as methodologist and social theorist, is noteworthy. He locates Le Play within the development of sociology and demonstrates the influence of conservative ideas on Le Play and, equally important, Le Play's ability to transform these insights into research propositions. He presents Le Play as the first real social scientist:

> Fourier, Saint-Simon, and Comte had used the terminology of science, had rung changes on the themes of a science of society. Still others, such as Quetelet, proceeding from 18th century "political arithmetic," had compiled, or would compile, quantities of social statistics, pointing to correlations, or "patterns," and preening themselves on the quantitative exactitude of their handiwork. Le Play went much further, however, in that he set up a clear problem and through a

rigorous, if sometimes extreme method, reached objective conclusions.[20]

Nisbet considers Le Play the first researcher to carry out a truly scientific study of communities and the first to use the comparative method as a way to understand the concrete processes of change rather than as a way to promote general theories of societal development or "progress."[21] As Nisbet points out, Le Play realized that real comparison requires both a definite time period and constant dimensions against which the facts can be compared. Nisbet's analysis of Le Play's work is valuable and well informed, although he exaggerates the conservative influence on Le Play.

Goldfrank, more than anyone else, clearly shows the ambiguities and contradictions in Le Play's ideas and the resulting difficulty of locating him in any one tradition. Unlike most of Le Play's commentators, Goldfrank bases his reevaluation of Le Play on a careful analysis of his empirical work.[22] Paul Lazarsfeld's analysis is part of his general interest in the history of quantification; it presents a detailed analysis of Le Play's ideas and empirical work but pays little attention to the relationship between theory and research and overlooks some of Le Play's contribution in the first edition of *Les Ouvriers européens*.[23] Jesse Pitts offers a short but insightful analysis of Le Play's life and work, Philip Abrams analyzes Le Play's ideas in the context of the emergence of the English meliorist tradition, and Michel Dion analyzes Le Play's empirical study of the relationship between religion and family structure.[24] The fullest and most useful biography of Le Play in English is by Michael Z. Brooke, a British engineer. However, Brooke stresses Le Play's significance as a successful engineer, social reformer, public official, and ideologist, at the expense of his role as an early sociologist.[25]

In France, the image of Le Play is based largely on views which he expressed in his later years[26]—views found in his frequent attacks on the ideas of the Enlightenment and the "dogmas" of the French Revolution, his obsessive invocations of the Decalogue, his distrust of *lettrés* (academics), his rampant anti-intellectualism, and, finally, his professed antidemocratic ideals.[27] These ideas (or misinterpretations of them) have influenced an odd assortment of liberal economists, reactionaries, and social Catholics.[28] In 1947 the economist Louis Baudin presented a collection of excerpts from Le Play's work, for which Baudin also wrote an introduction. This introduction, making little attempt to discuss Le Play's empirical work, proposed ways to rebuild French society after the Second World War along the lines of an authoritarian state; the excerpts from Le Play's work were chosen because they seemed to support these proposals.[29]

French sociologists, on the other hand, have generally ignored or dismissed Le Play.[30] The ideological preoccupations of Le Play's later years must have repelled Durkheim and hidden from him the important affinities between his own and Le Play's ideas about social stability and change, for, in a review of the work of nineteenth century sociologists, he commented:

> As for Le Play and his approach, we have said nothing, because the concerns expressed are much more practical than theoretical. They rest upon religious principles and accept as an axiom the supremacy of the Pentateuch. His concerns have no scientific foundation whatsoever.[31]

Socialists and Marxists, on the other hand, saw him as an apologist for the emerging capitalist regime and a defender of "bourgeois" interests. Proudhon, for example, described Le Play's system as "the scientific organization of servitude."[32]

Le Play was also distrusted in his own time by both traditionalists and capitalists. Traditionalists criticized him for not supporting the church and for attacking the clergy;[33] capitalists criticized his paternalistic and moralistic orientation and saw his proposals as attempts to interfere with the free forces of the market.

All of the authors mentioned above based their analyses of Le Play's empirical work on the enlarged second edition of *Les Ouvriers européens*, which was published in 1877–79, almost a quarter of a century after the first edition. The second edition reflects a change in priorities: by 1877, Le Play was primarily concerned with spreading the "truth," attacking "false doctrines," and preventing what he perceived as an impending social disaster. In short, the second edition is full of the ideological polemics which have alienated later sociologists. Social analysis and research had become secondary to him. This may be why he completely omitted the classificatory tableau he had used in the first edition, in which he had formulated his theories of social change and social mobility.

These differences between the two editions help explain the interpretations of Le Play's work which stress its ideological and antiscientific characteristics. In my own discussion of Le Play's ideas, and in my selections of excerpts from his writings for this volume, I have drawn heavily on the first edition of *Les Ouvriers européens*, thereby stressing his contributions as a social scientist at the expense of his political and ideological views. This is an attempt to do justice to a historical figure whose contribution has too often been distorted or simply dismissed.

During his lifetime, Le Play was never able to secure long-term support for his vision of an empirical, policy-oriented social science, despite his commitment to social order and the sanctity of property. He and his followers organized what was probably the first private research foundation in sociology: La Société internationale des études pratiques d'économie sociale (International Society of Applied Social Economy). Its list of contributors shows us that, to a surprising extent, Le Play drew his support from scientists, small businessmen, lawyers, senior civil servants (regarded as professionals in France), and publishers. There were also a number of political figures, mayors, members of the National Assembly, senators, and others. But neither the old nor the new order—neither churchmen and aristocrats nor bankers and industrialists—is extensively represented on these lists.[34]

The backgrounds and occupations of Le Play's supporters suggest that the emerging empirical sociology of the nineteenth century cannot be simply identified with traditionalism or capitalism, the two opposing forces which many scholars have seen as the only two significant influences on sociology's early growth. An analysis of the social groups that supported Le Play's work reveals that he associated himself with some groups—small property-owners and squires—which were rapidly losing their influence after the middle of the nineteenth century and represented an economic and political force very much in decline. Both Le Play's own career and the nature of his public suggest the importance of the scientific professions (along with the older trades which bridged the gap between precapitalist and capitalist society) in sustaining the perspectives of a new kind of sociology animated by ideological and class interests but sufficiently detached from them to permit theoretical understanding and, above all, empirical research.

The revolutions of 1830, 1848, and 1870 had an important impact on Le Play and other early French sociologists. These social upheavals, which Marxists saw as models and portents of the great proletarian revolutions to come, disturbed the early French sociologists and prodded them to search for sources of social order. Indeed, the revolution of 1830 stimulated Le Play to combine his career as an industrial engineer with empirical sociology. His work reveals that his quest for social order was, in fact, a product of peculiarly French conditions, born neither of English empiricism, nor of England's intellectually unelaborated conservative tradition, nor of the radical sociology of such emigrés and refugees as Marx, Engels, and their followers, who were committed to no single national society.

The eclipse of Le Play's work seems to be a function of the general antiempirical orientation of French sociology, as well as the failure of Le Play's school to find a place within French academic sociology. Le Play did create a course in industrial administration and management at the Ecole des Mines with a recognizably sociological point of view, which he taught for twenty years, but it did not help him win recognition in the universities.[35] Unlike the Durkheimians and Marxists, who have become entrenched in the university system and have won state support for their research, the Le Playistes stayed outside the universities and did not seek financial support from the state. This situation was in part created by Le Play's own intransigent attitude toward the university and the state bureaucracy.

In some ways, Le Play's work bears out one of Karl Mannheim's ideas about the contribution of different types of ideology to social knowledge. In *Ideology and Utopia,* Mannheim suggested that while reactionary perspectives led to a focus upon fictive reconstructions of idealized golden ages, liberal ones promoted a sense of the discrepancy between a present state of affairs and a goal-state by which the present is evaluated. Thus, liberal perspectives evaluated the present state of affairs but gave no basic directives for altering it, since progress toward the goal, in classic liberal ideology, is a "natural" and inevitable consequence of the social process. Hence, the liberal Guizot's endorsement of empiricism in early nineteenth-century social research was designed to show how the imperfect present was gradually being ameliorated by the new commercial society. Mannheim's idea also explains the reactionary de Bonald's indifference to empirical observation and his evaluation of the present according to norms which he derived from the best elements of the traditional past.[36]

Le Play, however, might be described in Mannheim's terms as an authentically conservative figure—that is, one who is led by his concerns to analyze closely the detailed functioning of institutions in the present as the best means of grasping society's past, present, and future. Hence, Le Play's enormous comparative undertaking in *Les Ouvriers européens* was historical, for he sought in his research to understand how the past actually functioned; and comparative, in that he sought to understand the state of the disorganized urban and rural masses by analyzing a variety of families, communities, and economic systems chosen according to a taxonomic scheme. This systematic historical approach did not accommodate idealized conceptions of earlier social systems like the Middle Ages. On the contrary, Le Play believed it was impossible to escape into the past from the problems that accompanied the development of laissez-faire capitalism, and the goal of his method was to confront and solve those problems.

2

THE LIFE OF FRÉDÉRIC LE PLAY

Le Play was both witness to and an agent of far-reaching changes in France during his lifetime. He qualified as a mining engineer in the 1820s, on the eve of the French industrial age. His work was a direct response to the social and political events of his time. Le Play himself made a special point of stressing the connection between his life and his work in his own biography.[1] He believed that his scientific method and the conclusions he reached stemmed from his personal experience and, consequently, were not based on a priori ideas and abstract concepts.[2] His conception of the role of a social scientist stressed a direct link between scientific work and an active commitment to change society. Le Play did not see any contradiction between his belief that this research did not reflect a priori ideas, personal values, or group interests and his belief that his research method was a product of personal experience.[3]

Le Play brought social activism and scientific principles together in his own life in ways that made him an original and imposing figure in the eyes of his contemporaries.[4] Sainte-Beuve described him as follows:

> He is from a new generation. He is the modern man par excellence. Brought up in the midst of changes in the sciences and their application, he is in the same tradition as Monge and Bertholet.... However, unlike them, he sees social suffering and tries to understand it; he foresees dangers and reads signs of decay that should be attended to. Not only does he tell us about these dangers as a good citizen, but

as a practical man he proposes ways of correcting and stopping them based on his research and scientific knowledge.[5]

Ironically, this combination of moral and scientific concerns later led social scientists to dismiss Le Play's contributions.

In his autobiographical account, Le Play divided his life into three periods.[6] The first covers his childhood and adolescence from 1806 to 1829. By his own account, his youth significantly influenced his later understanding and interpretation of society. Having become an engineer, he set out during the second period of his life, 1830 to 1855, to create a new science—"the science of society"—on the model of the science of metallurgy, and carried out field research which led to his publication of *Les Ouvriers européens* in 1855. The third period of his life, from 1856 to 1882, was completely devoted to teaching the "truths" found in his empirical studies. Le Play then became a reformer and an activist, trying to convince his contemporaries to adopt his conclusions and organizing ways to implement what he called "Social Reform," that is, the acceptance of a way of life based on cooperation and social harmony.

Pierre Guillaume Frédéric Le Play was born in 1806 in a small fishing village in Normandy near the port of Honfleur. He spent part of his childhood and adolescence in that province, which was noteworthy for its economic backwardness and its conservative and royalist tradition.[7] His father was a minor customs officer with little education. After his father's death, his mother, a devout Catholic, was unable to support him, so she sent him to Paris, where he lived with a rich uncle from 1811 to 1818. This uncle was at the center of a group of conservative Catholics, landowners, and royalist emigrés who had come back to France under the Restoration. They often met at the uncle's home, and Le Play later recalled overhearing discussions that were to influence his adult opinions about social problems.[8] When his uncle died, Le Play returned to his mother's home and attended a lycée in Le Havre, where he pursued humanistic studies.

Le Play later recorded detailed and happy (perhaps slightly idealized) memories of small town life in a traditional French province before industrialization. This experience later convinced him of the superiority of rural traditionalism over urban progressivism. His vision of an ideal society reflects the features of the rural commune that he witnessed during his adolescence and youth: economic self-sufficiency and isolation, local administration, cultural "autonomy," and a dense network of interpersonal relationships.[9] The recollection of his past later became a basis for his interpretation of social change. Le Play could have found work in his native province—a family acquaintance offered him a job as a land surveyor, which he turned down. He also became close friends with an engineer who had graduated from the Ecole Polytechnique and who urged Le Play to take the same route. Despite this close friendship and his attachment to provincial life, Le Play decided to leave Normandy.

The second phase of his life started with his decision to return to Paris to study and prepare for the strenuous and highly competitive entrance exams for the *grandes écoles*. In 1825, after a year at the Lycée St Louis, he was admitted to the Ecole Polytechnique, perhaps the most prestigious institution in France, training military and civilian elites. Le Play disliked the school because of its military discipline and its emphasis on abstract and purely theoretical instruction.[10] He left it and entered the Ecole des Mines, where he distinguished himself by graduating after two years—instead of the normal four—with the highest honors the school had ever given. At these two schools, each of which had a completely up-to-date science curriculum, Le Play received the best engineering training that Europe had to offer at the time. He later said that his study of metallurgy at the Ecole des Mines first convinced him that social problems also required a scientific approach:

> While I was carrying out my apprenticeship as an engineer, I did not know where I would find the remedy to the ills of society; but after acknowledging the sterility of preconceived ideas, I was sure of one thing: that in the science of society, as in the science of metallurgy, I would not believe that I had found the truth until my ideas could be based on the direct observation of facts.[11]

When Le Play attended the Ecole Polytechnique and the Ecole des Mines, they were centers of debate about Auguste Comte's and Saint-Simon's proposals for reorganizing society (both

Saint-Simon and Comte had attended the Ecole Polytechnique). In 1829, when Le Play was at the Ecole des Mines, Saint-Simon's disciples, Bazar and Enfantin, gave a popular series of lectures presenting their interpretations of the master's ideas.[12] There is no doubt that Le Play was aware of these events and of the ideas discussed at that time. He believed that Saint-Simon's abstractions and a priori conceptions were useless to a scientific approach to social problems, he rejected Saint-Simon's belief that the state could play no part in directing society, and he attacked Saint-Simon's conception of social classes, particularly the "struggle which has always existed among the parts of the social body."[13] Le Play later recalled that as a student he tried to avoid these "fruitless" debates, which interfered with his scientific work. He could not take seriously ideas which had not been verified by direct observation. Le Play resolved to test Saint-Simon's ideas when he set out on the long field trip which the Ecole des Mines required of all graduating students.

Le Play and Jean Reynaud, a Saint-Simonian friend, traveled over 6,800 kilometers on foot through the German provinces of Hanover, Brunswick, Prussia, and Saxony. Their assignment was to visit several mines, study their organization and their metallurgical techniques, and write an essay about them. Le Play discussed at length the relationship among workers, employers, and managers. He observed and talked to the workers themselves, trying to learn the metallurgical techniques that had been transmitted from generation to generation over centuries by apprenticeship and imitation.

When he returned from Germany, Le Play became a teaching assistant in the laboratory of the Ecole des Mines and edited the school's publication, *Les Annales des Mines*. When the revolution of 1830 broke out he was recovering from injuries he had suffered in a lab explosion. Much later, in 1878, he recalled the impact that the events of 1830 had had on his career:

France had had ten governments since 1789. Each had been ushered in and subsequently overthrown by violence. This state of instability and suffering is unprecedented. Thousands of statesmen and writers have searched in vain for a remedy. I myself, although a stranger to politics and literature, was moved to find the secret of a government which would not begin and end in bloodshed.... When I saw the blood spilled by the July Revolution [of 1830], I dedicated my life to the restoration of social harmony in my country.[14]

After the revolution of 1830, the French government tried to modernize the country in a number of ways, including the creation by the Ministry of Public Works of a permanent Bureau of Statistics for metal resources. Le Play, appointed director of this agency in 1834, prepared annual reports on the organization, output, and conditions of the metals industry. His reports were ingenious, particularly his presentation of statistics. Le Play did not object to the use of statistics at this stage of his career. In fact, when he began his career and was a strong believer in a science of government, he suggested that courses on statistics and political institutions be added to the liberal arts curriculum in the universities and *grandes écoles*. But, at the same time, he thought that study of the "public sphere" and study of the "private sphere" required different approaches. Because official statistics only provided information about the public sphere, Le Play had to invent his own method for studying citizens' private lives, particularly their family life. Also, it should be noted that Le Play was not politically active during either the Restoration or the July Monarchy. He only became active in politics during the revolution of 1848 and the reign of Napoleon III, as a result of his research.

The French government, which customarily offered the services of its civil engineers to foreign governments attempting to modernize their countries, sent Le Play abroad to study mineral resources and the organization of mines. Between 1834 and 1844, he visited Spain, England, Scotland, Ireland, Belgium, Germany, Switzerland, and Russia at least twice. These scientific studies, published in the *Annales des Mines*, show that Le Play was interested in much more than purely technical research. They include long analyses of workers' families and of the social and economic conditions of communities. An example of such studies is his book, *Observation sur le commerce des matières premières* (Observations on the Commercial Trading of Raw Materials) (1834).

In addition to his services to the French government, Le Play also administered privately owned mines. For example, he did a study on the mineralogical resources of a vast domain in Russia's Donetz Valley belonging to the Russian Count Anatolii Demidov, who was so pleased with Le Play's work that he asked him to organize and administer his gold and silver mines in the Urals. Le Play became Demidov's partner and from Paris successfully administered a mining operation with over 45,000 workers.

In 1848 Le Play was nominated inspector for the whole Ecole des Mines. His teaching career at the school (which lasted from 1830 to 1855) provided him with both the time and the right working conditions for his sociological studies. He was free to create several new courses, which concentrated on the administrative and social aspects of engineering rather than on the more technical subject matter of traditional courses.[15] He used his courses to develop his monographic method of investigation and to discuss with his students the results of his field research. He may have been the first social scientist to combine research and teaching over a long period of time. Throughout Le Play's twenty-five-year teaching career at the Ecole des Mines, the Ministry of Public Works awarded him six months of paid leave every year to carry out field research on mining. These leaves enabled him to do research on hundreds of workers' families throughout Europe, England, Russia, and parts of Asia, research which provided the groundwork for the massive *Les Ouvriers européens*. At a time when it was difficult to find sources of financial support for research aside from personal wealth, statistical societies, and commissions from the Académie des Sciences Morales et Politiques, Le Play's position was exceptional.[16]

While the revolution of 1830 was the starting point of his search for "the secret of social happiness," it was the revolution of 1848, his participation in the provisional government, and pressure from political elites that finally convinced him to publish *Les Ouvriers européens* in 1855, through the Imperial Press of Prince Napoleon.[17] Le Play clearly perceived this work as the definitive solution to society's ills: "It contains social facts which establish the truth, the scientific method which allowed me to discover them, and the plan of reform that I derived from them."[18]

Le Play participated in the provisional government of 1848 in order to demonstrate his belief that his monographic method could solve social problems and restore peace and prosperity. He firmly believed that political antagonists could resolve their differences by studying the evidence gathered by his method: "The time has come for France to substitute for the struggles stemming from the vices of the ancien régime, and the errors created by revolutions, a fruitful cooperation based on the methodological observation of social facts."[19] Le Play later claimed that he had even succeeded in convincing François Arago, prime minister of the provisional government of 1848, on a number of policy issues. He advised Arago—presumably by appealing to facts established by his method—that society's problems could be solved by making employers responsible for the social and economic well-being of their workers. He argued that neither state intervention nor the unregulated play of economic forces could accomplish this.[20]

Several of Le Play's proposals for reforming working conditions were discussed before the Luxembourg Commission, whose members were workers, employers, and experts, and whose chairman was the socialist Louis Blanc. The commission recommended a reduction in the number of working hours in a week, and set up committees—Conseils de Prud'hommes—to settle disputes that arose between workers and employers. Le Play also took part in two other commissions set up by his old Saint-Simonian classmate and friend, Jean Reynaud. One studied metallurgical problems and the other made plans for a new school of civil servants which would teach a scientific approach to social issues.[21]

Le Play's active participation in the provisional government and his role as a private adviser to Napoleon III demonstrated his views on the role that social scientists could play in the formulation of policy. He saw the British Royal Commissions as the best example of the way social scientists and governmental elites should cooperate. However, his conception of the social scientist's role in the formation of policy did not include direct political involvement: "I absolutely did not want to become politically involved in the realization of a social system. My studies of society should only be brought to the attention of those of my friends who are in a position to implement them."[22] In Le Play's own career, the distinction between advice and political involvement became less and less clear, although he argued that none of his official positions were political in that none of them were elective offices. He took the traditional stand of high civil servants who commit themselves to working as experts, regardless of what government is in power, and who see themselves as neutral and detached agents of the nation-state. Consequently, he was convinced that the results of his research did not reflect the views of any one political group.

During this period of his life, Le Play agreed with the socialists Blanqui and Cabet about the need to control market mechanisms and to create work cooperatives and voluntary associations, including unions. In a letter to G. R. Porter, the head of a British statistical institute, he wrote:

> I believe that no definite organization of society has been reached by the English political economy and that such delicate problems as wages, competition, and international exchange are not sufficiently resolved by leaving the greatest possible freedom to private interests. I believe that these questions can be settled in a way suitable for humanity only by means of a certain organization of labor, industry, and of exchange.[23]

These opinions misled some people (Dion and Duroselle, for example) into thinking that Le Play was a socialist. On the contrary, he held the fundamentally paternalistic and antidemocratic view that while the government should try to improve the lot of the working class, this task should never be entrusted to the working class itself.[24] For Le Play, the purpose of workers' associations was not to promote the interests of a particular class. He valued these institutions because he thought they would facilitate agreements between workers and employers and thereby promote social stability.

In 1856, a year after *Les Ouvriers européens* was published, Le Play was appointed to the Conseil d'Etat.[25] After this date he did little research of any importance (even abandoning a metallurgical treatise he had been working on for several years) and devoted all of his energies to the dissemination of the "truth" which his earlier research had uncovered. His friends saw "a new man, full of fire, ready for action."[26] Le Play wrote:

> From now on I want to devote myself with the help of men of good will to the propagation of Reform. My behavior will become practical and action-oriented; the custom of working by myself in confinement will change through daily contacts with true reformers.[27]

In this final period of his life, Le Play took on several administrative and educational responsibilities. He demonstrated his great organizational ability as commissioner-general of the Universal Exhibitions of Paris and London in 1846, 1855, 1862, and 1867. He invented a turnstile to count the number of visitors to the exhibitions, he promoted a new way of presenting merchandise, and, most important, he publicized important innovations in working conditions. In this spirit, he designed a section of the exhibition to enable workers to present their own proposals for innovations in work arrangements. In 1861 he brought a group of workers to the exhibition in London in order to promote an exchange of views between English and French workers. Le Play went beyond paternalism by inviting trade unions, which were still illegal, to nominate their own panel to produce their own report on the exhibition.[28] Finally, in 1862, Prince Napoleon appointed him Senateur d'Empire, one of the highest distinctions in the political realm. By then Le Play had become an active participant in a highly antidemocratic regime.

While he served in the Conseil d'Etat, Le Play was asked to carry out a number of studies on proposed legislation. These governmental studies covered such topics as the housing conditions of the poor, the national lottery, paternity, technical education, the state of the rural provinces, the role of nonresident property owners, decentralization, and local government.[29] These studies, in contrast to Le Play's previous research, did not use a systematic approach and relied heavily on second-hand information collected by state officials. For a social scientist who had stressed direct observation and a standardized method, this may seem surprising. But the monographic method was not suited to these studies, and Le Play never tried to devise a new method, perhaps because by now he was exclusively preoccupied with getting his own proposals made into laws.

His record in promoting new laws was not impressive. The Conseil d'Etat debated only one piece of legislation that was based on Le Play's research, a bill that would reform French inheritance laws. Le Play saw the laws passed after 1789, which mandated the equal division of inheritance, as a source of social instability and national decline.[30] He proposed a return, not to the law of primogeniture, but to the freedom of testation practiced in Anglo-Saxon countries, but the National Assembly rejected his proposal.

This setback made him skeptical about the value of legislation for promoting social reform. Seeking a new way to teach the French elite the importance of reform, he created the Société internationale des études pratiques d'économie sociale in 1856. Villermé was its first president, and its members included such well-known scientists and social reformers as Adolphe Focillon, Jules Michel, Victor Brants, and Emile Cheysson. Its intent was to teach the monographic method and to apply it to an ambitious program of research aimed at providing a complete "social photograph of France,"[31] and to acquaint the elites with their responsibilities toward the working classes. Le Play's idea that raising the consciousness of an elite can help to bridge the gap between classes presents an interesting contrast to Marx's idea that a shared consciousness—an awareness of common economic interests—is an indispensable condition for collective class action. Despite the differences, it is worth pointing out that in both cases we are dealing with a process of recognizing one's dependence on others through personal experience.

Le Play wanted to make the French elite aware of the conclusions of *Les Ouvriers européens*, but the book itself proved a formidable obstacle to this effort. In its first edition he had refrained from spelling out solutions, assuming that the facts would speak for themselves and enable the reader to draw the correct conclusions. Unfortunately, this style made the book much too technical and difficult to read. When Prince Napoleon suggested that Le Play write books more accessible to the French elite, Le Play must have agreed, for he then wrote *La Réforme sociale*

(1864), *L'Organisation du travail* (1870), and *L'Organisation de la famille* (1871). These books did not use new empirical findings but summarized the conclusions of *Les Ouvriers européens,* leaving out methodological and empirical considerations and adding general observations of an ideological and polemical nature. For example, it is in these books that Le Play repeatedly denounces "the fundamental errors of our time, the false dogmas of the revolution," and preaches a return to religion, local sovereignty, traditions, and parental authority.[32]

La Réforme sociale is the best example of Le Play's attempt to propagate "the truth." Reprinted eight times in his own lifetime, it became his best-known book. In it he criticized the working classes for their lack of foresight, temperance, and industry, but reserved his harshest judgment for the political elites, whom he accused of selfish indifference to the working classes. Montalembert considered *La Réforme sociale* "the most original, courageous, useful, and powerful book of the century."[33] He compared *La Réforme sociale* favorably with de Tocqueville's works, arguing that while both authors understood the consequences of the trend toward equality in French society, only Le Play suggested concrete ways to direct them. In *La Réforme sociale* Le Play repeatedly warned that society would be doomed unless it reformed itself.

After the Commune of 1871, which seemed to Le Play to confirm his earlier prediction that violence and social disintegration would ruin society, he searched for new strategies for carrying out social reforms. Despairing of the efficacy of legislative and national leadership, he turned to local communities, urging them to carry out needed reforms under the leadership of their "social authorities." Reforming society now had a more urgent and sweeping meaning for Le Play: it meant reforming each individual's moral values. To this end, he founded Unions de la Paix Sociale (Unions of Social Peace), which were grass-roots organizations—a type rarely found in France—whose function was to mobilize public opinion. To help these "unions," Le Play wrote a pamphlet in the form of a series of questions and answers. It asked questions such as "What should be the role of the upper classes?" and "What should the government's role be in the nation's economy and social organization?" The answers to these questions were cast as formulas. For example, the question "Did the revolution improve the position of the working class?" drew this answer: "No, it made it worse, for from it unrest and danger emerged. The revolution has destroyed the state of mutual dependence—in other words, the state of solidarity—which in all prosperous nations unites individuals, families, and classes."[34]

In his last years Le Play published the second edition of *Les Ouvriers européens* (1877-79) and also wrote *La Constitution d'Angleterre* (The English Constitution) (1875) and *La Constitution essentielle de l'humanité* (The Essential Constitution of Humanity) (1881), a discussion of the principles and customs which lead to prosperity or suffering among nations.

In *La Constitution d'Angleterre* he tried to apply the monographic method to a whole nation. Le Play saw England as a "model" society because of its ability to undergo change without bloodshed and without destroying traditional institutions. He attributed English social stability to several causes: freedom of testation, an aristocracy responsive to economic change, widespread family organization of the "stem" type, and the British preference for oral traditions and customs over a written constitution.[35]

In *La Constitution essentielle de l'humanité,* Le Play proposed a general theory of social change. He analyzed "the three ages of work" and the conditions leading to prosperity or decadence among nations, distinguishing between "universal" and "variable" factors. This last book, which provides useful insights into Le Play's theory of society, has received little attention.[36]

It was during this final period of Le Play's life, his least productive as a social scientist, that he acquired the image that has persisted to this day and obscured his sociological accomplishments: that of a reactionary ideologue, as can be illustrated from the following conclusion to *La Constitution essentielle:* "There are seven elements which are indispensable to organizing society around peace and stability: paternal authority and the Decalogue, religion and sovereign power, the three forms of property ownership."[37]

Le Play's opposition to representative democracy, which by

the time of his death in 1882 had become entrenched, must have contributed to this image. He repeatedly refused to run for office, even resigning from the Senate when it became elective. Le Play criticized Thomas Jefferson for extending the franchise too quickly. In France he opposed universal suffrage.[38] He also continued to oppose the principle of a free market economy, stressing the need for continuity with the past and the strengthening of ties between social classes. He believed that the rural society that he had witnessed as a child, if it were blessed with a moderate rate of technical progress and a high degree of moral commitment, could provide the basis for an enduring social order.[39]

After Le Play's death, his disciples continued his work. One group, called La Réforme Sociale (created in 1855), promoted the purely ideological and reformist aspects of Le Play's work. Another group, La Science Sociale, founded by Demolins in 1886, set out to improve the master's research method, test his conclusions, and refine his classificatory devices. Some of Le Play's disciples, whose work among social scientists is better known than his, significantly extended and enriched Le Play's contribution to social science.

Le Play was not only aware of the links between his life and work that I have herein traced, but he also discussed them frankly to convince his readers that social science was based on real-life experiences instead of a priori ideas and, consequently, was more authentic. At the end of his life he wondered, in the best tradition of the sociology of knowledge, why he—and not one of his contemporaries "with greater intellectual gifts"—had been the first to discover the science of society. Le Play traced the causes to his rural upbringing, which emphasized the role of the family in the socialization of the young, and to his education in private, non-boarding, schools, particularly the guidance he had received from wise teachers. These factors, he believed, had enabled him to resist the evil influence of the urban centers which had spawned the false dogmas of the Revolution. Le Play went on to explain that these factors had strengthened his ability to resist the encroachment of public powers and the attraction of fashionable ideas.[40]

Le Play's works are full of scientific concerns and ideological statements which may be difficult to reconcile. But the apparent contradictions may simply reflect a different idea of social science, conceived during the first half of the nineteenth century, when the discipline was just emerging. Le Play was a man deeply committed to changing society, who saw his scientific discipline as an important means to that end, and who saw it as his duty to teach the "social truths" his work had revealed. He never hid the connection between his scientific research and the moral beliefs he wanted his research to serve. His frankness may partially explain his exclusion from most lists of sociology's founding fathers. Sociology has struggled to increase its capacity to operate as an "objective science," free from personal values and class interests. In the contemporary scene, however, the difficulty of achieving a "value free" sociology is recognized, and even more to the point, the concern with policy implications of social research parallels Le Play's early outlook on these issues.

3

LE PLAY AND THE SOCIOLOGICAL ORIENTATIONS OF HIS TIME

To appreciate Le Play's originality, we must view his work against the backdrop of the dominant intellectual modes of his time. In fact, his work does not fit any of our existing images of nineteenth-century sociology. It would be a mistake to identify him with either the liberalism of Bentham and Mill, the utopianism of Fourier, the radicalism of Marx or Proudhon, the reactionary tradition of Burke, de Bonald, and de Maistre, or the visionary positivism of Comte.

It would also be a mistake to compare Le Play with such giants in the field of sociology as Marx, Durkheim, and Weber, whose ideas appeared at a later point in the development of sociology. We can understand Le Play better if we compare him with those of his French contemporaries—Saint-Simon, de Tocqueville, Comte—who have been credited as founders of sociology. These men witnessed the early nineteenth-century's great scientific advances (especially in chemistry and physics),[1] French technological and economic changes, and its major political upheavals.[2]

Le Play's interpretation of society combined conservative and liberal ideas about the social order and social change within a problem-solving perspective. It is this combination of ideas that makes his work original and unusual. The conservative ideology which emerged after the Restoration in 1814 provided Le Play with an interpretive scheme and concepts such as community, authority, status, and the sacred—all important elements in French sociological thought and central to Le Play's work.[3] Throughout his books, he quotes de Maistre and de Bonald, as well as Burke. He adopted the conservatives' belief in the primacy of the group over the individual, along with the belief that society is an entity and a system in itself, not merely a collection of individuals. For Le Play, as for de Bonald, society is made up of families, and the family is the "moral cell" of society. He also adopted their emphasis on studying institutions and the social needs and functions they serve. Finally, like the conservatives, he turned his attention to the study of social change through historical analysis.[4]

At the same time, many of the issues which Le Play addressed were important to those notables and bourgeois who formed the nation's political elite during the July Monarchy and the Second Empire.[5] He shared with the liberals of that time a paternalistic attitude toward the working class and a belief that the virtues of industry, thrift, and education would lead to the moral improvement of the masses. Like Comte and Saint-Simon, Le Play believed in the ownership of property as a source of social stability, in an ideology of cooperation between social classes, in opportunities for social mobility among the working classes under the leadership of the bourgeoisie, and, at the same time, in the need for limited intervention by the state in economic and social affairs. These ideas appealed largely to small entrepreneurs, small businessmen, small rural landowners (who formed the majority at the time), and to professionals, all of whom were uneasy about big banks and big business.[6]

An understanding of the sociohistorical context in which Le Play's work emerged is essential to an understanding of his sociological concerns and his links to social thinkers such as de Bonald.[7]

Early sociologists studied societies which were strikingly different from fully industrialized nations. The society that the French founders of sociology observed was not yet dominated by national enterprises, and large manufacturers were not widespread. French society was organized around rural communes and small cities. In many ways it was closer to the traditional model of a preindustrial society than to the model of an industrial capitalism. It was also a society which saw the emergence of a multitude of associations, from mutual aid societies to trade unions. Le Play's analysis of the role of individual initiative and mobility among the working classes and his study of the new bases of social solidarity reflected fundamental changes which took place in French society during the first half of the nineteenth century.[8]

Sociologists have interpreted sociology's emergence as a response to changes caused by the French Revolution of 1789 and the industrial revolution (beginning in 1850 in France, according to Henri Sée).[9] The "industrial revolution" usually means the introduction of manufacturing, major migrations from the countryside to large cities, mechanization of industry, and concentration of workers in large manufacturing towns. These changes had far-reaching consequences for society and led to a variety of interpretations by social thinkers. In trying to understand Le Play's work, one must also consider the process of transition from a premarket to a market society, because industrialization began late in France and grew slowly.[10] This transition between two modes of social and economic organization was characterized by a series of specific transformations that occurred prior to the introduction of large-scale manufacturing:[11] the breakdown of local economies, the expansion of commercialization on a national scale, the collapse of traditional geographical and local legal barriers, and the introduction of the steam engine. These changes had been occurring gradually in France over several decades, and were nearly complete by the 1850s. It is important to note that the social consequences of this transition were not all negative. For example, throughout the first half of the nineteenth century, the number of property owners and of family farms increased.[12] The acquisition of property by a large number of peasants and artisans—and by a smaller number of workers—represents a phenomenon just as important (though less noticed) than the pauperization of the urban working classes. Le Play, who had close links with rural France, was reacting more to such changes than to the impact of manufacturing per se on society or the creation of an urban proletariat. In France, the first half of the nineteenth century, which was such a period of transition, was characterized by the emergence of new institutional arrangements, the revival of localism, and a reinforcement of personal ties.[13] The interpretation of later changes, namely large-scale urbanization and industrialization and their impact on the social structure, should be analyzed with this prior context in mind.

De Bonald's analysis of the stages of France's transition to a modern economy directly influenced Le Play's own understanding of the period. For de Bonald, the gravest consequence of this transition was the subordination of social and personal relationships to economic considerations and the resulting dehumanization of society.[14] The growth of the modern, centralized, bureaucratic state also disturbed de Bonald, as did the rise of a new and selfish industrial aristocracy and the isolation and eventual pauperization of the working classes. De Bonald thought that these changes had caused the destruction of the old links of dependency and mutual obligation that had formed the fabric of traditional society, subordinating these social relationships to market relationships based on competition and conflict. Not unlike Marx, de Bonald showed how industrialism changes personal relationships into monetary relationships.[15] He believed these conditions would inevitably lead to social antagonism. One of Le Play's key concerns, which derived directly from de Bonald, was the analysis of the causes and consequences of the social isolation and economic vulnerability of workers. His empirical research was aimed at determining how to promote new links of mutual obligation between workers and employers and how to ensure economic security and promote mobility for working-class families:

> The bonds of *patronage* have been broken and individualism has a free hand; commercial competition has become a struggle for existence and rages unchecked by the traditions of former years. Only the strongest can resist its assaults; the others succumb. Outstanding individuals advance to the front ranks: they rise higher and higher and reject the troublesome obligations which the old regime imposed on them with regard to the weak; and the feeble, left to their own resources, sink lower and lower. Thus, social inequality develops, dragging after it a cortege of selfishness, suffering, hatred, and envy.[16]

Le Play and de Bonald were not primarily concerned with the social problems caused by the introduction of large-scale manufacturing. These problems—the creation of a new and destitute urban working class and the rise of prostitution, alcoholism, and crime in its midst—mainly engaged the attention of liberals and meliorists.[17] Le Play and de Bonald were more concerned with what they took to be deeper and more pervasive conditions of social instability, whose causes they traced to the isolation of workers and social antagonisms in three places: the family, the workshop, and the local community.[18] Both men believed that authority, stability, and cooperation must be restored in all these places before social harmony could be achieved in society as a whole. For Le Play, France's social ills were the consequences of the corruption of the ancien régime, the influence of *lettrés,* the growth of the public sphere, the loss of traditions, and encroachments by the state on paternal authority.[19] One of his goals was to find the conditions under which "social harmony" could be achieved in the family, community, and society.

Conservative thinkers of the ancien régime had not seen the family as an important source of social stability. Rather, they had emphasized institutions such as guilds, parishes, corporations, and lineages. After the Revolution dislodged these institutions, the family took on a new importance for de Bonald and other conservatives of the Restoration.[20] De Bonald thought that the family, which he called a "partnership of the dead, the living, and the unborn," could provide the continuity that is essential to maintaining the social order. To this end, he proposed a return to inheritance laws based on primogeniture. Le Play reformulated de Bonald's idea by stressing the importance of continuity between generations, which minimizes a sense of isolation and vulnerability for the individual, but he stopped short of insisting on primogeniture. He favored the English system, which was based on freedom of testation, that is, the father's right to choose an heir as he wished.[21] Like de Bonald, Le Play believed that the erosion of paternal authority attributable to the revolutionary inheritance laws was the most important cause of the social instability of his time.

Le Play, however, did not accept the conservative tradition unconditionally. For example, while he did adopt de Bonald's analysis of "industrialism," he rejected de Bonald's conclusion that this change was a "decline" which could only be arrested by restoring the monarchy. In contrast to these conservatives' uncritical attachment to the past, Le Play believed that history's lessons must be carefully analyzed and evaluated. The most important difference between Le Play and the conservatives was Le Play's insistence on empirical research. As Nisbet said, "Le Play transformed the moral insights of the conservatives into a set of concrete problems calling for rigorous field investigation."[22] Le Play's commitment to empirical research led him to conclusions which were unacceptable to conservatives. For example, his research showed him that, contrary to conservative beliefs, religion was not always a crucial factor in the development of stable, socially successful families.[23] As we shall discuss later, Le Play, long before Durkheim, understood the secular sources of social solidarity.[24]

In other cases, Le Play modified conservative views by combining them with liberal ideas. For example, he thought that the best way to achieve the conservative goal of social stability was to promote a new order based on merit. He believed that hierarchy and social position should only reflect differences in age, sex, intelligence, wisdom, and moral values. A strong commitment to the principle of social mobility must have come naturally to a man who, in spite of humble birth, had attained high positions in academia and politics. With his liberal contemporaries he believed that social mobility should be promoted: "Raising the largest possible number of individuals from lowly origins to the ranks of the bourgeoisie is a legitimate goal and one of the noblest that modern civilization can pursue."[25] It should be noted that professional and social mobility were realistic goals in France at that time, as later social historians have shown.[26] The crystallization of French society into opposing camps only emerged after the Commune of 1871.[27] Le Play believed that social mobility was a sign of the successful exploitation of virtues such as temperance, discipline, thrift, and industry, as well as reciprocity and tolerance. He thought the family could do the best job of teaching children these values and thereby help to assure the stability of the new social order.[28] His concern about the disruptive impact of an individualistic economy on workers' lives went hand in hand with his concern about social mobility. In his empirical research he sought institutions which could provide both freedom and security. His family monographs revealed that Anglo-Saxon countries provided the best combination of mobility and security.[29]

Le Play also combined de Bonald's belief that the family was the "moral cell" of society with the emerging bourgeois ideal of the family, based on norms of privacy and domesticity.[30] Love and affection among family members became one of the indicators of social happiness and a most important means of teaching bourgeois morality. In his field research, Le Play paid special attention to the ways in which all of these bourgeois values—which he called "moral" values—were acquired. Like the liberals, Le Play acknowledged the inevitability of technological progress. But unlike the apologists for the French Revolution, he did not see Freedom as an abstract, universal principle. For him, there were freedoms—concrete rights—such as the right to acquire property through work[31] or freedom in religious choice.

Although he admired the Middle Ages, he rejected medieval institutions, such as the corporations and guilds, as models for modern society because he believed they provided security but no freedom.[32] He offered his concept of the "stem" family as the best way to maximize the interests of both the individual and the group. Fathers of these families, enjoying freedom of testation, could at once assure the continuity of the family line and provide a variety of opportunities for their children. One socially useful option was to help children who could not stay on the paternal property to start new families in underpopulated areas of the world.[33] Le Play also thought that the institution of "patronage"—based on the employer's responsibility for the economic and social welfare of the workers—and mutual aid societies could offer both freedom and security, and consequently should be encouraged by elites engaged in modernizing society.[34]

The conservatives whose ideas influenced Le Play disdained, for the most part, empirical methods of investigation, but they were the only nonempirical theorists whose ideas Le Play did not reject out of hand. Unlike other social scientists who studied at the Ecole Polytechnique, Le Play particularly disliked systems of abstract ideas which purported to explain all of humanity and to systematize all branches of knowledge. He also rejected formulas for restructuring society which were based on a priori notions. Although Le Play shared with Saint-Simon a general belief in a society based on "order and progress," in the importance of technology, and in the need to effect (in Saint-Simon's phrase) "the moral and physical improvement of the largest and poorest portion of society,"[35] he thought that Saint-Simon's program for a complete reconstruction of society and the creation of a new religion was based on nothing but speculation and abstract ideas. In the same spirit, he explicitly rejected three schools of social thought which he characterized as "revolutionary," "positivist and evolutionist," and "naturalist, materialist, and nihilist."[36]

For Le Play, the "revolutionary" schools consisted of those social thinkers who accepted "the three false dogmas of the French Revolution: systematic liberty, providential equality, and the right to revolt."[37] Le Play believed that the authors who spread these ideas were responsible for social antagonism and instability; thus he described de Tocqueville's *Democracy in America* as the most dangerous book written in the century.[38] He did not disagree with de Tocqueville's analysis of an "irreversible trend" toward equality, but he feared that excessive equality would create social disorder by weakening traditional bonds. In his view, the trend toward equality should be kept in check and the abstract principle of "Equality" should not be presented to the masses as an absolute right. He condemned de Tocqueville's failure to speak out against the forces that he had analyzed so well. "De Tocqueville lacked the courage to speak the truth which he knew, and to attack the errors which he perceived."[39] It was this omission that Le Play set out to correct when he wrote *La Réforme sociale*.

He denounced democracy as the most dangerous political system:

> the word "democracy" pleases first of all those who see in equality an absolute principle, and who wish this principle were sanctioned by a system of government. According to their false doctrine, every man would have a right to govern! This kind of conception is at once chimerical and unjust. Its first application would inevitably provoke the emigration of

the elite. It could be said to decapitate any nation subjected to it and debase it to the utmost degree. It is important, therefore, that Europeans stop encouraging such dangerous errors by the use of a vague and useless word.[40]

Le Play traced the belief that the three dogmas upheld universal, inalienable rights to the view that men were born free and good. Rousseau's doctrine of the social contract and of man's original perfection contradicted Le Play's own belief in original sin.[41] He cited passages from St. Augustine's *Confessions* to refute the view that man was originally perfect.[42] He also did not believe in the fundamental innocence of children, describing them as "little barbarians with an innate penchant for evil."[43] Consequently, he devoted a good deal of his research to understanding ways in which children could overcome their evil nature and acquire good moral habits. His belief in original sin accommodated his personal philosophy that everything valuable in life must be acquired by personal struggle and sacrifice. Consequently, he did not see equality, liberty, and happiness as principles upon which society should be based but as benefits which each individual must earn. Accordingly, Le Play did not see suffrage as a universal right but as a privilege which each individual must earn. Citing the example of the United States, he argued that property ownership guaranteed the responsible use of this privilege.

Le Play also saw the "three false dogmas of the Revolution" as descendants of the ideas of the Enlightenment, which he generally distrusted.[44] He believed that the philosophers of the Enlightenment had tried to disseminate a conception of science, derived from Newton and Locke, that they had misunderstood. He would have agreed with the historian Ruggiero that

> the object of reverence and even worship [among the philosophers of the Enlightenment] was not at all the idea of science as representing a collective labor scarcely begun and moving forward with deliberate and cautious steps. It was rather science as the symbolic incarnation of reason, a universal dimension, capable of wiping out in one broad stroke human prejudice in every field.[45]

Le Play thought that the Enlightenment's exaltation of pure reason was a way to avoid the difficult task of acquiring scientific knowledge through empirical investigation. Like the conservatives, he saw this tendency toward generality and abstraction as an escape from the study of concrete social problems. In Mannheim's words, liberal ideas of the Enlightenment were no more to Le Play than "mere opinion, a bare image, a pure possibility behind which one takes refuge, saves oneself and escapes from the demands of the hour."[46] For him, the belief in general principles became an obstacle to the study of concrete issues and to the solution of pressing social problems.

Le Play thought that the defects of the "positivist and evolutionist" school of social thought also derived directly from the ideas of the Enlightenment, especially the tendency to formulate general theories of humanity on the model of the physical sciences, to seek general laws of development, and to depend on deductive reasoning. In his work, he never mentioned Comte, but he seemed to be referring to his ideas in the following statement: "I will not even allow myself to be dazzled by the lessons at the Collège de France, where eloquent professors have discredited national customs and presented the development of the human mind as civilization's supreme goal."[47] Le Play rejected both the idea of the unity of the human mind and the positivist definition of sociology as the understanding of the necessary, indispensable, and inevitable progress of the mind.

> In the thoughts of those who incessantly call for progress, this word has reference to an order of chimeras which have no connection with reality. It is referred to as an occult force, a blind destiny which builds up nations the way the circulation of the blood develops the human body. By virtue of this force, improvement will incessantly go on by itself, and people can profit by it without being subjected to those severe sacrifices which labor and the practice of virtues require. The fatalism of the good is no less dangerous than the idea of creating a destiny indifferent to both good and evil... this error is naturally presented to the minds of the ignorant classes, who hear and repeat it incessantly.[48]

Le Play did not believe in abstract rational constructs or in the view that all change is for the better. He argued that change will not necessarily bring about improvements and that its movement is not linear but spiral. He strongly objected to the idea of social inevitability and determinism. To Le Play, the acceptance of such ideas meant the rejection of the role of human volition—especially the acquisition of moral qualities through suffering—and the role of human action in guiding the forces of change. Finally, he rejected the idea of a universal principle of organization applicable to all humankind. For example, he believed that "positivist thought" could not be applied to the realm of morality or religion. Le Play distinguished between the material and moral spheres in society, claiming that progress can only take place in the material sphere, whereas in the moral sphere one deals with "eternal truths" which are constant in time and space.[49] By introducing this distinction, he was rejecting the positivist belief in the fundamental unity of the physical and social worlds. The idea of progress also implied the rejection of past habits or old institutions. Saint-Simon believed that habits are bad because they have been learned in a state of affairs which no longer exists and that progress can only occur if one can dismiss these obstacles to change.[50] Le Play, on the contrary, claimed that progress can occur only if it is an outgrowth of past institutions and tradition. One of his fundamental ideas is that change must not be accomplished without maintaining continuity between the past, present, and future. Unlike liberals, he believed that everything that existed was of value because it came into existence slowly and gradually.

Like Comte and the positivists, Le Play stated very clearly and forcefully that he wanted to create a "science of society" on the model of the natural sciences. He believed that direct observation according to the scientific method was the only way to reach reliable conclusions about the organization and functioning of society. But, unlike the positivists, Le Play put the understanding of human volition at the center of his analysis, believing that free will is what distinguishes humans from animals. The existence of free will in human beings means that they cannot be treated as "objects." Le Play also did not believe in the search for general causal laws. He sought generalizations of a different type by studying the way institutions function; he wanted to determine which institutional arrangements were most likely to lead to social happiness. Finally, he believed that the science of society must be directly linked to policy-making, and that a sociologist must be simultaneously a scientist and a reformer, actively engaged in analyzing and changing society.[51]

The third school of thought that Le Play rejected consisted of "naturalists, materialists, and nihilists."[52] He never defined what he meant by these terms nor did he indicate who he included in these groups (he seldom mentioned names). The core of his criticism was that these thinkers assimilated human society to animal society, emphasizing the role of the instincts and denying the role of free will in human behavior. He thought that by denying free will they dismissed society's basic moral problems, a conclusion he rejected as "mechanistic." He explicitly criticized Darwin and his "naturalist" theories and the German materialism of Ludwig Buchner.[53] He also rejected Spencer's individualistic premises and evolutionary views. Le Play attributed to these authors the belief that either nature or man can surpass God. His criticisms of all three schools of thought are very general and often misleading. It seems that he did not read carefully any of the authors whom he was criticizing.

Though he rejected some tenets of positivism, he used scientific methods to study society and applied these methods to collect data, test ideas, create typologies, and reach generalizations. These features of a research enterprise are closer to modern social research than to the grand theories of French positivism. Le Play's insistence that moral questions are not reducible to scientific questions and that sociology must somehow confront both types of questions may explain why sociologists have neglected his empirical work. Le Play was a positivist, if we understand by that the French tradition which began with Comte and culminated in Durkheim's theories, as well as the British tradition of empirical research. However, Le Play had closer affinities with the statistical movement of the 1830s organized around the Statistical Society of London and the English meliorists. Unlike the meliorists, however, he was not content with organizing social surveys. As Philip Abrams observed, "he offered a sociological theory of social reform. The reforms Le Play proposed were strictly derived from a generalized analysis of the integration and malintegration of social institutions."[54]

Le Play's originality stems from his eclectic mind and his ability to combine the ideas of the French ideologues of the Restoration with the methods used by British empiricists in the analysis of social questions. Perhaps no internally consistent scheme of analysis, either reactionary or liberal, could have produced the kinds of concerns and tensions to which Le Play's groundbreaking empirical and comparative sociology was a response. Of course, this very eclecticism, without which his contribution would have been impossible, also accounts for his later eclipse by the great systematic social theorists of the century, and it also underscores his continuing relevance in a period concerned with policy analysis.

4

THE SCIENCE OF SOCIETY

About the time Auguste Comte was developing his conception of "sociology" and Adolphe Quetelet was developing his "social physics," Le Play was working out his own "science of society."[1] Le Play did not, however, adopt Comte's biological model of society as a kind of "organism"; nor did he share Quetelet's preoccupation with the search for social "laws" along the lines of the laws of nature which physicists seek. Instead he drew on metallurgy and statistics, the two disciplines he knew best. His scholarly training in statistics and his experience as the head of a government statistical agency from 1830 to 1848 taught him the need for a rigorous empirical method to study social issues. He derived a "practical" approach to the science of society from his earlier work as a mining engineer: he believed that the social scientist's job was to make society work, on the basis of direct observation.

In his early studies of society Le Play drew on two seventeenth-century approaches to social research: the British tradition of "political arithmetic" developed by William Petty (1623–87), and the German tradition of "descriptive statistics" developed by Hermann Conring (1606–82).[2] These early approaches influenced Le Play's notion of a "science of government," according to which a nation could be well administered only if it systematically collected enough information about its human and natural resources to keep its policy-makers well informed. He also believed that such data would bring about consensus among political parties and ultimately banish prejudice and a priori ideas:

> Harmony among political theories will be restored as soon as the observation of society is sufficiently perfected and as soon as the facts are sufficiently illuminated so that it will no longer be possible for educated men to be ignorant of a single important fact, nor for reasonable men to interpret the same fact in two different ways. This is the lofty mission reserved for statistics as soon as that science is definitively established, and as soon as it fulfills its proper role as an instrument of education and of government.[3]

During his travels in southern Germany before 1850 Le Play met scholars using "descriptive statistics," which was still being taught in the universities. This tradition was carried out in its most refined form at Göttingen, whose scholars taught an approach called "university statistics." Le Play adopted the Göttingen school's view of statistics as a mixture of geography, history, law, political science, and public administration. (Not until the 1850s would statistics become a strictly quantitative discipline.) Although Le Play did not get his idea that researchers must do their own observations from these scholars, they did teach him the practice of making field trips to study statistical records. Le Play seems to have been influenced by the work of Aschenwall and Schlozer, two Göttingen scholars who had made Conring's system of data classification a more "reliable" (by which they meant exhaustive) technique for comparative research. These classificatory devices were not simple compilations of facts but consisted of categories which were systematically derived from general principles of organization.[4] They ensured that no important fact would be overlooked, and served as efficient administrative tools even in the hands of mediocre bureaucrats. Finally, Le Play may have thought that "university statistics" could do for France what it had once done for Germany. The system had emerged in the 1680s, after the disruptions of the Thirty Years War, to meet the urgent need for rational and efficient administration of the German states. Le Play thought that France in his own time, similarly devastated by wars and revolutions, should teach the German classificatory system. To this end, he created two courses at the Ecole des Mines and helped to found the well-known Ecole Nationale d'Administration, which trained high-ranking civil servants.

In Le Play's statistical treatise of 1840, *Vues générales sur la statistique* (General Considerations on Statistics), he argued that the science of government could be improved by creating new classificatory devices, and he presented a model of the type of information he thought the French government should collect. This model consisted of hundreds of categories and subcategories in the manner of the German statistical tradition. He urged researchers to go beyond traditional demographic and economic information and to record the age, sex, level of education, profession, and place of residence of each member of the population. He also wanted information on a number of the population's intellectual and moral characteristics, including:

> commitment to worship and to religious instruction; state of general and professional education; general laws on marriage, widowhood, single life; on prostitution, legitimate and illegitimate births; on abandoned children; summary of the judgments of various courts; principal laws covering individuals unclassified in society's ranks and without known professions.[5]

Later, in his family monographs, Le Play would use the same type of information when studying the level of moral well-being in families and communities.

Furthermore, Le Play categorized positions and occupations for all of French society. For the public sphere, he described the structure of the French state bureaucracy; for the private sphere, he presented what we would call today a system of social stratification whose categories included: "Owners of capital, industrialists, the liberal professions, workers, the poor (including cripples), dangerous classes (prostitutes, arrested persons), and foreigners."[6] He urged researchers to study the relationship between the private and the public sector and also relationships among the groups in each sector. Le Play was the first researcher of his time to distinguish clearly among workers, the poor, and the criminal class. These distinctions, as well as his classifications of moral behavior, figured importantly in the development of his monographic method.

Le Play's discussion of a science of government in his statistical treatise of 1840 introduced concerns that would figure prominently in his monographic method and remained with him throughout his career: the role of categorization and an overriding interest in the relationship between social, economic, and geographical factors, a stress on society's "social capital," and an attempt to define social behavior in terms of consumption and production patterns. However, the nation and not the family was still the unit of analysis and the treatise said nothing about how to collect data or how to insure accuracy—two problems he later saw as crucial.

Le Play's science of government also reflected a French tradition of national surveys sponsored and administered by the state which dated back to the official inquiries of the ancien régime. The first administrators to use civil servants and military authorities to collect information about the population had been Colbert (in 1657–63) and Vauban (in 1707), whose main concerns had been justice, finance, and administration.[7] Le Play acknowledged his debt to this tradition by quoting Fontenelle's praise of Vauban in the foreword of *Les Ouvriers européens*.[8] Official and administrative surveys took on a renewed importance in France under Napoleon with the creation of the position of "préfect," an official who represented (as he does today) the central government in each of the provinces of France and had considerable power. Prefects were required to carry out extensive and regular surveys of the local population.

For a long time Le Play believed that the prefects were reliable agents for collecting data, probably because he accepted the traditional French conception of civil servants as totally independent of any political party or regime. However, after the revolution of 1848 the National Assembly agreed to the creation of a commission to organize a national social survey of the condition of the working class, a problem then called *la question sociale*. The commission was accepted in place of a more politically threatening idea: the creation of a Ministry of Labor which would organize labor and limit the effects of competition.[9] The idea of an official survey obtained the support of the conservative elements of the National Assembly because it was presented as a political weapon against socialist ideologies and as a way to promote the views of the liberal bourgeoisie on *la question sociale*. This was made clear in a statement by Auguste Thiers reported in *Le Constitutionel* on May 13, 1848:

> The major goals of the official survey are the following: on the one hand to use it to rectify the exaggerations and unwarranted opinions of several researchers on the condition of the working class which conclude that the situation has worsened and that the real causes of the misery of the working class come from the very structure of industrial society. On the other hand, the official survey must find ways to ameliorate the conditions of the working class which can be put into practice without making any major changes and without hampering economic laws like that of competition.

Some of the survey's twenty-two questions sought specific information about working conditions in different industries: the hours, the number of workers, the wages, the number of women, the number of children under sixteen years of age, the percentage of literate workers. A second group of questions addressed the state of the industry and the workers' standard of living. Other questions attempted to determine the relationship between workers and managers.[10] Unfortunately, most of these questions were vaguely formulated, and the prefects received no instructions about how to collect the data or even about whether the workers themselves should be consulted. In fact, very few workers actually participated, because of fear, ignorance, or illiteracy. Not surprisingly, the survey's results reflected the manufacturers' views much more than it did those of the workers. The survey was postponed several times for fear of social unrest, and in Paris and other turbulent areas it was cancelled.

The official survey of 1848, so clearly created out of fear and for political purposes, may have compromised the use of surveys in France as a legitimate tool of social research.[11] Even though Le Play does not refer to this survey in his work, its failure must have accounted for his later rejection of official surveys and for his even stronger belief that information should be collected directly from the workers themselves.

> Statisticians do not make firsthand observations and they must rely on observations which were not scientifically made. Their comparisons cannot deal with the most essential aspect of social activity, for these areas always lie in the private realm, even in those nations where government activity is most extensive. The attempt to fill these gaps by appealing to the good will of the individuals or companies involved has usually been in vain, along with attempts to demand that agents of public authority directly collect the information in the routine exercise of their official functions. These studies have rarely led to reliable results, either because the agents employed lacked the good will or aptitude or because they did not have the necessary authority to overcome the difficulties occasioned by these studies.[12]

Le Play's dissatisfaction with published statistics was one reason for his rejection of "moral statistics," a new approach to statistics which replaced "descriptive statistics" and "political arithmetic" during the second half of the nineteenth century. This new approach was elaborated by the Belgian scholar Adolphe Quetelet, whose major work, *De l'homme et du développement de ses qualités: Physique sociale,* was published in 1835. Quetelet was less interested in collecting data than in using already available information to study the distribution of physical and moral characteristics among groups and nations and to analyze averages and rates over time. By comparing statistics such as those on crime and marriage rates, Quetelet tried to establish regularities or "laws" of social behavior on the basis of which he proposed a concept of the "average man."[13] This innovative method was partly stimulated by his association at the Ecole Polytechnique with the well-known mathematicians Laplace and Fourier. In France the champion of Quetelet's approach was Ange-Michel Guérry, who analyzed the new crime statistics that were collected during the 1830s and 1840s.[14] Quetelet's findings of regularities over time in the crime and marriage rates of certain groups created a heated debate about whether there are social forces independent of human will.

Le Play objected to "moral statistics" on several grounds.[15] First, he thought that the data base was not reliable, coming from the ever-growing pool of information gathered by government or public institutions on such topics as health, literacy, and alcoholism. Second, he thought that rates and averages, like a priori ideas, were useless to social scientists because they did not account for historical and institutional differences among countries:

> Suppose, for example, we measure criminal offenses in two countries of equal size by comparing court records from these countries, and use these data to study the relative morality of the respective populations. Our conclusions would be quite unreliable. Evaluation of this kind, based on a single comparison of figures, inevitably leads to errors. The extent of these errors becomes obvious through direct observation. Observation would reveal the differences between the institutions and customs of the two countries, the differences in the effectiveness of the methods of repression, in the corruption of judges, the influx of criminal elements from abroad, etc.[16]

Third, Le Play objected to Quetelet's approach because it conflicted with his conviction that individual action, based on free will, was history's prime mover. The acknowledgment of social "laws"—particularly Comte's laws of social development and Quetelet's statistical laws—was, for Le Play, an acknowledgment of man's powerlessness before the forces of history. Le Play, whose ultimate commitment was to social reform, saw no use for Quetelet's results.

In his search for an approach to empirical research which was compatible with social reform, Le Play looked to the British statistical societies of the 1830s. Their research on the impact of the industrial revolution often resulted in reform legislation. These societies directed their efforts in several directions. First, they helped prepare and collect data for the censuses.[17] They also provided information to royal commissions and select committees studying social questions. Finally, they sponsored independent social research and gathered data about the new urban masses by investigating hospitals, prisons, local factories, and police records.[18] After 1840, the statistical societies apparently lost some of their influence and limited themselves to analyzing government statistics rather than securing their own data, but they had already done much to institutionalize social research. The statistical societies' research impressed Le Play for three reasons: it flourished on private initiative and support; it presupposed the elite's traditional moral commitment to the amelioration of society; and it succeeded in combining this commitment with political action because most of the men involved in doing or promoting research were also active in political bodies.[19] Le Play was also impressed by the flexible research methods of the British royal commissions, which were small teams of experts who carried out detailed analyses of specific questions, collecting the information from any source they deemed important. However, Le Play thought that these research methods should be combined with greater rigor and precision in data collection, an improvement that he tried to carry out in the quantitative section of his family monographs.

During his lifetime, the French never managed to combine policy concerns and research as successfully as had the British. Even though most of their statistical institutes, unlike their British counterparts, were sponsored and directed by government ministries or other official institutions, they did not encourage as much policy-oriented research.[20]

Because the goal of Le Play's "science of society" was social reform, he saw the conclusions of his monographs as a first step in the formation of social policy. He proposed a simple division of labor: social scientists should study reality and offer solutions, and government should implement these solutions:

> The statesmen of the Continent, following the example of those in Great Britain, must see to it that the facts are established at all costs. This is the only way to correct the evils which exist at the present time, to ward off the perils that the future may hold, to mend the social fabric and to satisfy all interests, within the limits set by reason and justice. Curiosity and scientific interest are not the only reasons for conducting a comparative study of the condition of European workers. These studies will furnish statesmen with a solid basis for resolving social questions.[21]

Because Le Play saw the lack of responsible leadership as a main cause of France's social ills, he placed great emphasis on educating the nation's elites.[22] Le Play urged them not only to study family monographs but also to undertake such work themselves in order to learn more about their community. To this end, he revised and reprinted *La Méthode sociale* (The Social Method), a book whose subtitle reads:

> ... intended for the ruling classes who, in accordance with the tradition of the great races, desire to prepare themselves by systematic journeys to fulfill in worthy fashion the obligations imposed by the supervision of domestic households, rural and manufacturing workshops, neighborhoods, local government and the great national interests.[23]

This training, Le Play thought, would teach the ruling classes the gravity of their responsibilities to the "suffering classes." It seems never to have occurred to Le Play that placing his science of society at the disposal of this group might advance their views and interests, and thereby compromise his method.

Le Play's unusual conception of the science of society as both a scientific endeavor and public policy, whose purpose is to make society work, implied a further conception of social reform. He believed that only when all individuals, workers as well as members of the elite, lived according to the principles of the science of society, would true reform—Le Play capitalized each word of the phrase "La Réforme Sociale"—be possible.[24]

By the time Le Play published *Les Ouvriers européens* in 1855, he was convinced that social research should focus on the private lives of citizens, especially their family lives, rather than on population characteristics or national resources. Furthermore, he came to believe that in order to gain access to the private lives of workers, researchers must rely on the systematic use of direct observation.[25]

Only by comparing *Les Ouvriers européens* with research by Le Play's contemporaries can we see just how original his methods and concerns were. In the first half of the nineteenth century, the study of the conditions of the working classes was mainly initiated by aristocrats, philanthropists, economists, and physicians, who were concerned above all with the state of morality that existed among the poor. The study of the "dangerous classes"[26] (a common way of describing the working classes in the nineteenth century) was a direct response to the social conditions under which many workers lived in the new manufacturing towns. The discovery by the bourgeoisie and the upper classes of a "nation within a nation"[27] reflected not only their bewilderment at modes of life completely foreign to them but also a sense of danger. The conditions of working-class life were seen as dangerous not only because they promoted crime but also because they led to social unrest. Most of these studies, whose authors described themselves as "concerned citizens," were vivid descriptions of the physical and moral condition of the urban masses, with the poor, criminals, and the unemployed being treated as one group. These studies were concerned primarily with the problem of urban poverty and its consequences: prostitution, alcoholism, promiscuity, and the general disintegration of the family. Some of these authors proposed private philanthropy and public welfare programs as solutions to the problem of poverty. Others thought that the solution required the successful control of the greatest vice of the dangerous classes—laziness. Still others indicted the industrial system as a whole. Although there were a few efforts to get information from workers themselves, they were not very successful. These studies were characterized more by their humanitarian concern and moral outlook than by an interest in the systematic collection of accurate information.[28]

In contrast, Le Play never used the term "dangerous classes" in referring to industrial workers; rather, he used the term "improvident workers," pointing to a different set of issues. His concern was not confined to the problems of the urban poor. Instead, he wanted to discover the social and economic conditions which could ensure "social happiness" for all types of workers—miners, artisans, craftsmen, peasants, and industrial workers. His concerns were linked to an understanding of the social structure—family, associations, and community—in which the worker was embedded, as well as to the long-term trends that might be at work in the society.

Le Play was not only concerned with *la question sociale*. Rather, his analytical framework led him to study and compare workers in different types of families and in different types of societies in order to reach generalizations regarding the conditions under which social order and economic progress could best be achieved. He undertook to study these conditions through the use of a method—the family monograph—that allowed for precise information collected directly from workers themselves.

Direct observation and interviewing were used for the first time as a tool of research by two of Le Play's contemporaries. Parent-Duchâtelet, a physician and member of the Académie de Médicine, undertook one of the best inquiries about prostitution in Paris. His results, based on police files, field observation, and interviews with prostitutes, were published in 1834 in a two-volume work entitled *De la prostitution dans la ville de Paris* (On Prostitution in the City of Paris). Parent-Duchâtelet asked the prostitutes about their regional and social origins, their attitudes toward marriage and the family, the conditions which led them into prostitution, and the conditions that might help them get out of it.[29] Another physician, Louis René Villermé, who was commissioned by the Académie to study the condition of the working class in three manufacturing towns, published the results of his study in 1840, also in two volumes.[30] To study the lives of the workers Villermé used official statistics available in the *départements*, he collected information about the workers from a variety of people, he interviewed workers in the silk mills, and he shared in the workers' lives by joining them in their workshops, bars, and homes.[31] Le Play praised Villermé's research, which he saw as an important contribution to the understanding and solution of social problems in the tradition of the British royal commissions. Villermé's findings were instrumental in the passage of a new law in 1841 regulating child labor and the introduction of the *livret* in 1845.[32] Nonetheless, they did not offer any appropriate tools for systematic and reliable collection and analysis of data.[33]

Le Play, in contrast, undertook to study social issues by using a monographic method that provided both precise and standardized information and a framework for interpreting it. For Le

Play, the systematic use of direct observation represented a whole conception about the nature and subject matter of the "science of society":

> In scientific matters, only direct observation of facts can lead to rigorous conclusions and their acceptance. This principle is acknowledged today in the physical sciences, but it is still unrecognized in social science. The practitioners of social science are generally inspired by preconceived ideas which perpetuate antagonisms and which cannot serve as a basis for systematic action. People imbued with such biases tend to disdain the facts and the conclusions which can be inferred from them. Social science thus remains in a situation comparable to the physical sciences when they were based on the conceptions of astrology and alchemy; social science will not be established until it is founded on observation.[34]

Le Play first presented his conception of the role of direct observation as a tool of scientific analysis in his *Description des procédés métallurgiques employés dans le pays de Galles* (Description of Metallurgical Procedures Used in Wales) (1848).[35] In studying the copper mines, he realized that neither the owners nor the managers knew or understood the techniques used by the workers. The workers, of course, knew the technical processes for obtaining high-quality copper, but they did not understand the chemical operations involved. Le Play felt that their techniques, which had evolved through a process of trial and error and had been transmitted from generation to generation, could only be understood by observing what the workers were doing and by talking to them. Thus, Le Play recognized that in order to understand these metallurgical procedures, he had to study people, a project which required extensive contact between the researcher and his subject. It was necessary, he thought, "to enter the minds of the workers." He believed that "practical knowledge of workers opens new possibilities to science and nothing can replace carefully detailed and philosophical observation of their work, even from a purely scientific point of view."[36] Without this interaction, Le Play thought, the researcher simply could not gain access to the kind of information he needed. He did not realize that along with its advantages, this kind of interaction presents the researcher with special difficulties which the metallurgist does not have to face.

Le Play believed that the discovery of the secret of "social happiness," like the discovery of the Welsh miners' techniques, was basically an act of "remembering." The social scientist, according to Le Play, can only discover how to make society work after he has understood the practices and traditions which have made it work in the past. His research led him to rediscover traditions that he called "universal truths,"[37] by which he meant that they had been very widely practiced for centuries. By insisting that there was nothing new to invent in the science of society, he was also rejecting the view that this science should be used to promote new systems of social organization. His suspicion of the abstractions contained in the jargon of some of his contemporaries made him very careful about creating new words. Thus, in discussing the science of society, he could say: "If the term is new, the idea is old. It makes up the oldest knowledge."[38] He believed that the science of society should use everyday language whose meaning he specified in a "social vocabulary."[39]

Le Play's historical concerns, which I have already mentioned, also figured in his science of society. Histories of extraordinary events or great men were of little use to him. In order to rediscover "social truths," he needed to study the history of regions and social institutions, a kind of history which did not yet exist. He argued that the social scientist was in a better position than the historian to begin this kind of research because the social scientist actually could do studies on social institutions which belonged to different historical periods but which could be found at the same time in different parts of the world.

> If we want to recapture the mentality of the past and thereby gain a thorough understanding of the present situation of the working classes in the West, the best way to proceed is to study conditions in countries where the agricultural and industrial techniques, the organization of labor and the natural relations of the various social classes remain like those which existed in France in past centuries.[40]

By distinguishing the "requirements of all social systems" from their "variable traits," Le Play hoped to learn what combination of factors would work best in a given social context. He thought these investigations might uncover valuable institutions which had been either wiped out by violent upheavals or forgotten. He knew, however, that discarded institutions might not serve the needs of his own time, and he warned against trying to revive the "corporation," an institution which had played an important role in traditional social systems by ensuring for the worker a certain level of security and well-being. He thought corporations were incompatible with the new spirit of freedom and innovation, and he sought to understand what institutions had replaced them.

Le Play emphasized the importance of the knowledge and wisdom of "social authorities" in rediscovering society's traditions. His "social vocabulary" describes them as

> individuals whose private lives can be considered models; who demonstrate an outstanding propensity for good, regardless of race, condition, and social system; who by the example of their households and their workshops (as well as through strict observance of God's law and the customs of social harmony), win the affection and respect of all those who surround them; and finally, who make well-being and peace reign in the community.[41]

Le Play's reliance on these men may seem to contradict his commitment to the scientific method. But he saw the experience and expertise which they had acquired as leaders of their communities—along with their proven moral excellence—as sources of the most valuable kind of knowledge. Because he thought that they embodied the principles of the science of society and represented the traditions of the community, Le Play called them "the true masters of social science."[42] He believed that social authorities can be found in any society and in any social class and that they are the men who make society work.

Le Play's general suspicion of theories based on a priori ideas, like his belief in direct observation, can be traced to his experience as a mining engineer. This training taught him to evaluate an operation or an investigation according to its effectiveness, in the way a manager would. It also taught him that mining operations which relied on practical knowledge did better than those which relied on theories.

> The people who wish to subjugate the industries of thirty centuries' duration to the dominion of a theory scarcely hatched are not only powerless to improve present conditions, but they too often lead industry astray, either by directing it toward chimerical goals, or by exciting it to misunderstand the resources it has acquired. It is only in this way that so many industrialists ruined by imprudent undertakings have been able to affirm correctly that practice is worth more than theory. This just condemnation of false science cannot be extended in principle to the theory that true scientists strive to create: this, resting immediately upon experience, accepting and explaining all the facts, can never be found in contradiction to practice.[43]

Le Play's important distinction between "false" and "true" science shows that, far from rejecting the role of theory, he endorsed scientific theories based on facts. He thought that such theories did not yet exist in the social sciences and that his mission was to provide them.

Le Play's managerial perspective also led him to see the "science of society" as an applied science—that is, a science directed, like metallurgy, toward practical goals. Le Play fits Friedrich von Hayek's description (in a discussion of Polytechnique graduates of the first half of the nineteenth century) of an "engineering type of mind, which conceives the study of society as a series of practical problems whose solution requires a plan like an engineer's blueprint."[44] The practical problem which Le Play set for himself was to find ways to improve society's functioning.[45] His science of society concentrated on understanding *how* to improve society under specific conditions as much as on understanding *why* society was the way it was.

C. Wright Mills has criticized this practical approach to society's problems as a disguised apology for a certain vision of society, as both "propaganda for a philosophy of technique and an admiration of administrative energy disguised as part of the natural history of science."[46] Le Play did believe that evaluation of a mining operation and evaluation of a society required the same logic: in each case, the investigator must determine by direct observation whether the standards for success have been met. It could also be said that Le Play believed that the most successful societies, like the most successful mining operations, were the ones which "functioned" best. Just as the best mining operation produces the best metals, so does the best society produce the highest level of well-being.

Putting aside his usual suspicion of a priori ideas, he believed that his science of society required special premises, or first principles:

> In my approach to the social sciences, by contrast to metallurgy, I was obliged as a human being to obey one sentiment: a prior belief in the worthiness and legitimacy of mores and institutions which would put an end in my country to conflicts leading to bloodshed.... The science of society is based on love for one's fellow man just as geometry is based on the axioms of extension.[47]

Le Play's standards for a successful society, in sharp contrast to those of his positivist contemporaries, were clearly moral ones. But his discussion of his standards of morality shows that he also offered ultimately testable criteria for determining when these standards are met:

> We will not hesitate to state that of two social systems set up in analogous conditions, the one to be preferred is the one which best guarantees the morality and well-being of the workers' families, as well as mutual affection between workers and masters.... In order to eliminate all vagueness from these evaluations, we will take as a measure of morality and well-being selected facts whose importance is universally recognized. We shall affirm that the conditions of family life are good when the head of the family is moderate in his taste, just and affectionate toward his dependents, when he finds an assured means of subsistence in regular work; when the woman of the house, faithful to her duties as wife and mother, sees that order and cleanliness prevail in both household and clothing; when the children respect their parents; when finally, all bestow upon the aged, the

infirm, the ill, the respect, affection, and care they deserve.[48]

These ideas affected Le Play's interpretation of empirical results and also his decisions about what to study in the first place. His acknowledgment of the moral premises of the science of society led commentators to claim that he used a scientific method to prove a priori ideas—the same criticism that he had leveled at the positivists. Le Play apparently never understood the contradictions which his different positions about a priori ideas implied. At any rate, the explicit acknowledgment of his moral premises brings him closer to the critics of the positivist approach who have insisted that personal values and beliefs underlie all sociological research. Le Play's work must be understood within the limits created by these premises.

5

THE MONOGRAPHIC METHOD

Le Play based his science of society on the monographic method, which was more than a technique for collecting data. In this chapter I will try to show that it provided a particular approach to the study of social facts and that the monograph's family budgets provided a frame of analysis for interpreting that data. For Le Play,

> The monographic method provides a guideline: it directs observers through the labyrinth of facts; it gives them a standard measure of accuracy and directs them toward conclusions which will be accepted as general laws, once they are sufficiently verified by observation.[1]

Furthermore, he argued that workers and families were particularly good subjects for social research. Because he conceived of the family as the basic unit of society, he believed that social happiness depended on familial happiness.[2] He also believed that happy families, like happy societies, were the ones which satisfied the two basic needs: "daily bread" and the "moral law."[3] He concluded that his monographic method "provides a living portrait ... in which we can see the principles which ensure a people's progress or decline."[4] Accordingly, he believed the method was able to "capture all the nuances of social happiness" by studying the physical and moral condition of different families. He also used the method to study the institutional arrangements—especially work relations, land tenure, professional organizations and voluntary associations—which might account for a family's success or failure in satisfying these two basic needs.

Le Play chose to study working-class families exclusively in his monographs because he thought they—more than any other group—offered the researcher a clear view of the workings of society as a whole. He defined workers broadly as

> those individuals who work with their hands to provide for a society's usual needs. These persons take a major part in providing the basic means of subsistence...they vary widely according to location, race and historical period. It follows that the material and moral organization of the working population and the nature of its labor form one of the characteristic traits in the constitution of societies. In short, we have observed and included in the present study under the generic term "worker" only those persons who perform manual labor other than that in the personal service of a master, whose principal means of existence is remuneration received for their labor, and who may also own or manage some personal property.[5]

This definition includes not only industrial workers, what Marx called *prolétaires*, but also peasants, artisans, craftsmen, and shopkeepers; it excludes intellectuals, academics, politicians, writers, managers, and others who do not work with their hands.[6] Le Play's distinction between the workers and the bourgeoisie resembles Saint-Simon's distinction between the productive and unproductive classes. However, unlike Saint-Simon, Le Play believed that these two groups could cooperate with each other.

Le Play's definition reflects some of the unique characteristics of the working population during the first half of the nineteenth century. The French working class at this time was far from homogeneous. It was difficult to distinguish between peasants and industrial workers, especially those in small factories who usually cultivated a small plot of land on the side and generally had a peasant mentality.[7] The urban industrial working class formed only a minority of the working population. The majority consisted of artisans, shopkeepers, and craftsmen who worked at home or in small workshops. Georges Duveau, the social historian, has shown that artisans in small workshops, who were better educated, more family-oriented, and more likely to save money than other workers, formed the elite among the working classes.[8] In Le Play's mind, these workers qualified as models for other workers because they maximized economic security and social stability without jeopardizing the individual's prospects for advancement. Social historians have noted with interest that during the first phase of industrialization there was more mobility within the working classes—many peasants became artisans—than there was between the working classes and the bourgeoisie. Le Play's study of mobility reflects this social reality.[9]

In Le Play's mind, workers offered the researcher special methodological advantages. Because workers formed the majority of a nation's population, he believed they were the best representatives of its traditions, customs, and mores. He suggested that the researcher should start by studying peasants, who had changed the least and therefore had kept their nation's traditions intact. Furthermore, he argued that workers, unlike the bourgeoisie, lacked the means to modify their physical and social environment. This implied that the impact of the environment on workers was uniform.

> The workers' means of existence are thus essentially subordinated to the combined influences of the soil and of the climate. These influences, together with the modifications introduced by human industry, are usually constant over a large area inhabited by the same race and subject to the same natural conditions.... In this way, the laboring classes lend themselves to methodological observation.[10]

Le Play's claim that the conditions of working-class life were basically constant was essential to his argument that researchers could "apply facts established for a small number of families to entire populations or at least to an entire category of workers."[11] Commentators have criticized him strongly on this point, seeing in his method an unwarranted leap from case studies to generalizations about society. Few have recognized his awareness of variations in the working classes or his emphasis on selecting families which were representative of the region and occupational group to which they belonged. He believed that "if you study the living conditions of a certain number of families of average size, age composition, wealth, and morality, who live in the same area and are employed in the same occupation, you will generally arrive at uniform results."[12]

We may well ask how Le Play decided that the families he selected were representative in these ways. Statistical information based on the family as a unit of analysis did not exist, and the few statistics on local communities were often misleading and inaccurate. Le Play sometimes tries to give a sense of how representative a family is by comparing it to other families in the same community. For example in the monograph "Maître-Blanchisseur de Clichy" (Master Laundryman of Clichy), Le Play found that "out of 100 families in the same occupation, 25 are property owners as the family studied, 50 others without becoming owners are able to be well-off, and only 25 have gone into debt and fallen in position to the point of having to work for someone else."[13] Le Play relied primarily on "social authorities," by which he meant persons who had achieved social recognition and respect in their community (today we would call them informants), who helped him select "average families" and win the trust of the families he studied. It never occurred to him that social authorities were a group with specific interests. In his mind their eminence depended on universal recognition of their merit, an endorsement which guaranteed the "truth" of certain traditions. Le Play believed that the social, political, and economic power which these personages achieved merely reflected their moral excellence. His critics were not persuaded of the neutrality of these men and suspected that by helping him select families the social authorities steered his research toward foregone conclusions. Le Play's emphasis on understanding the conditions of social happiness sometimes led him to depart from the selection of representative families. Instead, sometimes, in poor economic settings, he chose deviant cases—that is, prosperous, successful families—in order to demonstrate clearly how families can overcome environmental obstacles.[14]

I have already mentioned the family's pivotal role in Le Play's theory of social happiness. But the family also offered methodological advantages as a subject for study because, first, it provided an excellent "experimental" setting. By comparing children in the same family, Le Play tried to understand the role of individual characteristics in accounting for success or failure in improving one's economic position. Second, the family was small enough to permit a researcher to observe directly how it functioned as a whole and how each member contributed to the family's physical and moral well-being. Third, the family's clear boundaries made it possible to study the relationship between it and the other institutions in the community.[15]

Let us briefly examine the organization and content of the monographic method.[16] The method's standardized format, based on classificatory devices, told the researcher what information to record and how to record it with the help of a "question-book." This format guaranteed the accuracy and consistency of the researcher's observations, thereby enabling him to base comparative analyses of different families on these findings. The method, Le Play thought, could therefore be used by different researchers without fear that personal bias would distort the results.

The monographic method has been described by Le Play's followers as an attempt to combine quantitative and qualitative approaches.[17] In all family monographs the first and third sections offer qualitative analysis, while the second consists of a quantitative analysis of the family budget. A complete understanding of family monographs requires a study of all three of these closely related sections, although Le Play's commentators have singled out the budget as his major contribution and have analyzed it apart from the two other sections.

The first part of the monograph, which Le Play called "Preliminary Observations," described the major physical and social characteristics of the family's environment, the type of work done by the head of the family, and each family member's contribution to the household economy. An important function of the monograph's first section was to teach the researcher how to cope with the special problems presented by interviews and direct observation, which were new field techniques during Le Play's time. First Le Play thought the researcher, after being introduced to the family by a social authority, should tell them about the research, "letting them know the public usefulness of its goals and the spirit of self-sacrifice which inspires the observer."[18] The message to be conveyed was that the researcher wanted to understand the family's living conditions in order to help them improve their lot. In his list of ways to capture and hold the family's attention, Le Play mentioned "compensating them financially for the loss of time which the investigation imposes on them, discreetly praising the wisdom of the men, the grace of the women, the manners of the children... judiciously distributing little gifts to everyone."[19] He never discussed the impact that this kind of flattery might have on research.

Second, Le Play urged the researcher to let the worker volunteer as much information as possible and to encourage him to talk first about memories that he might enjoy recounting. Le Play thought this approach would make the worker feel comfortable and more willing to answer detailed and tedious questions later:

> Questioning should be conducted in the order indicated by the method. Nevertheless, this order must not be followed too rigorously. The working man will naturally tend to elaborate on certain subjects. He will enjoy relating memories of his youth and telling his family history. It is important not to interrupt the worker, so that useful information will not be lost. Too many questions will tire him—if they do not bore him or make him suspicious—and they will be a constant reminder that he is being questioned. It is much better to listen than to ask questions, especially—as is often the case—when differences in dialect or native language make understanding questions and answers difficult for both parties.[20]

Le Play thought that the worker's lack of sophistication would make many of his statements unclear, a problem that could only be corrected by direct observation: "The observer should use every means possible to spare the members of the family unaccustomed intellectual efforts which they are not used to and which might spoil the accuracy of their statements."[21] At the same time, Le Play also used direct observation to verify statements about workers by members of the "directing classes," since many of these persons had little or no accurate knowledge of the living conditions of the workers in their communities, and also because they would be more likely to present a distorted picture of working-class life. Le Play never questioned the honesty of the working classes. Although he was not unaware of the interviewer's effect, he believed that both the researcher's and respondents' personal biases could be corrected by safeguards built into the method of observation itself.

Le Play not only told the researcher how to collect his information, he provided a detailed and standardized guideline telling the researcher what information to collect (see table 1).[22] By listing what to study and what to observe in great detail, Le Play was trying to standardize the format of his monographs in order to guarantee the accuracy (i.e., exhaustiveness) of their results. This guideline for observing a family's life, perhaps the first guide for field research in sociology, shows how detailed and original Le Play's method was. Under "Religious habits" (no. 3), for example, we find the following items: "Religious affiliation and beliefs of the members of the family, as well as those of the general population; private worship, prayers, holy images, ceremonies at marriage, birth, and death, places of worship, and religious holidays." Under "Morality" he distinguished between "domestic" virtues, "social" virtues, and "moral habits." He counted as "domestic" virtues

TABLE ONE
Guideline for the Collection of Data in Part I of the Family Monograph

A. **Description of the place, the work organization, and the family**
   1. state of the soil, industries, and population
   2. civilian status of the family (age, names, sex, kinship relations)
   3. religious and moral habits
   4. hygiene and medical services
   5. the family's rank among the seven types of workers

B. **Means of subsistence**
   6. property
   7. subsidies (additional benefits, aside from wages)
   8. work and domestic industries

C. **The family's style of life**
   9. diet and meals
   10. lodging, furnishings, and clothing (inventory of all furniture)
   11. recreation

D. **History of the family**
   12. principal phases of its existence
   13. customs and institutions assuring the family's physical and moral well-being

all behaviors and feelings which occur *in the home,* including affection between married couples, the influence accorded to women in domestic matters, the care and deference accorded to elderly parents, the ways in which dead parents are remembered, the affection and care given to children, and the care given to servants, slaves, and animals.[23]

Le Play used these items to determine what he called the "moral well-being" of family members. The importance which he assigned to the quality of family relationships and family life is impressive, particularly at a time when most researchers concentrated primarily on economic well-being. In his discussion of "social virtues" he was referring to "behaviors and feelings" occurring outside the home, between family members and such elite members of the community as employers, priests, and other authorities. These virtues included charity and self-sacrifice, a propensity for hospitality, a spirit of conciliation in disputes, politeness and harmony in social relations, deference of family members toward employers, and tolerance—especially toward people of other religions. The list of moral habits includes:

> propensity toward cleanliness in one's home and one's clothing; inclination toward simplicity and temperance; propensity for thrift; a set of habits whose goal is to put savings to good use and to provide a piece of property for one's family; means of transmitting acquired property when one dies or reaches old age; inclination to stay in one place or to emigrate permanently or temporarily.[24]

Le Play's originality stems as much from his method as from the questions he investigated, a method that was directed to collecting information on the social and emotional aspect of human relationships within a specific socioeconomic and geographical context.

His analysis of "moral factors" shows that he was not content to assert general principles but always emphasized the concrete social behavior to be studied. Many commentators have mentioned the importance of morality in his work without explaining how he defined the term and operationalized it, and they have thus misunderstood his basic purpose. For Le Play, "morality" refers to social behavior which enhances the happiness of the family. Information about "moral" behavior served not only to corroborate the findings in the budgets but also to provide valuable qualitative indicators about family life. One such indicator was a forty-year-old worker's refusal to answer questions before consulting his father—a sign of respect for paternal authority.[25] The joy that one father and mother experienced in giving their child a gift served as evidence of intimacy and affection among family members.

Another indicator of caring in the family was whether or not animals were treated properly. Le Play assumed that anyone taking good care of animals would be more likely to take good care of humans.[26] The Parisian ragpicker's avoidance of the familiar pronoun "tu" in conversation suggested his sense of deference. The fact that he did not associate with other ragpickers showed that he had higher social aspirations than they had.[27] Le Play interpreted one family's failure to find a priest in an emergency as a sign of religious indifference.[28] He noticed that one cabinet-maker's wife was buying sugar every week, rather than every month at a wholesale price. He loaned her the money to buy a month's supply in order to teach her how to save. The result of this small experiment was unexpected: the wife was unable to refuse additional sugar to her children, who consequently consumed more than before; the wife quickly returned to her previous habits. Le Play concluded that this family, lacking self-discipline and restraint, would not easily move up the social ladder. However, he praised the wife's generosity and contrasted it to the callous and selfish behavior of some workers who had achieved higher social positions.[29]

Le Play also attempted to create what we call today contextual variables, to evaluate the state of a community as a whole, although he never offered the kind of guidelines for this purpose that he did for family life. For example, a high number of illegitimate births indicated low morality.[30] The widespread custom of adoption in one community was a sign of strong moral commitment, despite that population's lack of religious feelings.[31] The fact that seats in one church were not assigned indicated to Le Play that there was harmony between social classes;[32] by contrast, the introduction of seating arrangements in churches—"contrary to the true spirit of Christianity"—was a sure sign that close relations were deteriorating.[33] Thus a close scrutiny of the items listed by Le Play under the thirteen subsections of the first part of the monograph provides a clear enough picture of the variables and qualitative indicators that he selected and of the relationships that he wanted to study.

In accordance with his assumptions regarding the nature of the science of society, Le Play explicitly selected items reflecting social harmony and cooperation at the expense of items reflecting social conflict and antagonism. This selectivity clearly influenced Le Play's conclusions, as critics have pointed out, but it cannot be equated with simply using research to test preconceived ideas.

For many readers, the form of Le Play's presentation—especially the long, seemingly shapeless list of topics—has proven confusing and frustrating. Not all of the subsections have a clear purpose. Even when Le Play did indicate the purpose of certain data, his explanations were often buried in the endless lists of items to be surveyed. He was more concerned about offering researchers a detailed field guide than he was about stating his research purposes. Ironically, even though Le Play was studying relationships between variables—between morality and mobility, for example—he never put forward working hypotheses for fear of unduly influencing his readers and of being accused of using preconceived ideas. He thought that stating his ideas before collecting the data would contradict his opposition to a priori ideas and his belief that "the facts should speak for themselves." As a result, when readers stumbled on the family budget in the second section they were often overwhelmed by a mass of carefully organized information which they did not know how to use.

Many consider Le Play's family budgets his most important innovation. Actually, William Petty had introduced family budgets in the seventeenth century, and some of Le Play's contemporaries—Villermé, Pelletier de la Sarre, E. Engel, and Ducpétiaux[34]—used them to analyze economic aspects of family life. Le Play, however, was the first to use budget data to analyze the structure and functioning of the family. He derived his ideas about the budget from his training in chemistry and mineralogy:

> The surest way an outside observer has to know the spiritual and moral life of people is very similar to the procedure which a chemist uses to understand the nature of minerals. The mineral is known when the analysis has isolated all the elements which enter into its composition and when one has verified that the weight of all these elements adds up exactly to that of the mineral under analysis. A similar numerical verification is always available to the student who analyses systematically the social unit represented by the family.[35]

Le Play thought that by matching the totals of a family's budget of receipts with the totals of its expenditures he could verify scientifically that he had accounted for every aspect of family life. He also compared this kind of equivalence with the equivalence accountants seek in double-entry bookkeeping. He was convinced that

> every fact about the existence of a worker's family ends up more or less directly in a receipt or an expenditure. There is scarcely a sentiment or an action worthy of mention which does not leave a clear trace in the budget of receipts or that of expenses.[36]

Consequently, all details of family life—anything produced, consumed, or spent over the course of a year—had to be recorded according to a complex classification system. The quantification of the information in the budget was meant to guarantee objectivity and accuracy. He believed that by finding the value of every family's receipts and expenses in francs, the researcher could compare workers in a variety of social settings. Le Play decided to compile annual budgets instead of monthly ones because the production and consumption patterns of most workers—especially peasants and artisans—varied from month to month.

In the first edition of *Les Ouvriers européens,* Le Play presented the budgets of receipts and expenditures on facing pages in order to provide a "social photograph" of family life (tables 2 and 3 give a schematic presentation of one such pair of budgets).[37]

The reader was not so lucky with the second edition, some of whose budgets ran on for twenty pages.[38] His early presentation was intended to help readers compare subtotals and to look at different relationships between budget items and draw conclusions from them.

The budget of receipts was designed to show the variety of ways in which workers' families made a living.[39] It included all sources of revenue (cash revenue and revenue in kind) and the value of all property owned. Under "Work Performed by the Family" Le Play distinguished the types of work done by family members and the number of days each member spent at such jobs. Le Play found great uniformity in the working family's expenses as contrasted with its sources of income. The five sections of the budget of expenditures reflect what he called the "five universal needs"; "food, dwelling, clothing, moral needs (including health and recreation), and financial expenses."[40] To calculate a family's expenditures for food, he computed the quantity consumed by the family in kilos, the average price per kilo on a yearly basis, the amount of cash spent, and the value of the food acquired in kind (either as payment in kind or as produce from the family's own garden).

What did Le Play do with all his budget data? Lazarsfeld has distinguished between "analytic," "synthetic," and "diagnostic" uses of budget data.[41] The synthetic approach, which was used extensively by Charles Booth, consists in organizing budget data to create types.[42] Le Play created worker types in his social hierarchy, and family types, although unlike Booth he used budget data in a very loose form. Le Play relied most heavily on the "diagnostic" approach, which involved interpreting budget data as indicators of values, opinions, and expectations, much as he had done in the qualitative section of his monograph:

> Often a single figure says much more than a long discourse. Thus, for example, one cannot doubt the degradation of a Paris worker after one has learned from studying his budget that each year he spends 12 percent of his income to get drunk, while he does not devote a cent for the moral education of his children, who are between the ages of four and fourteen.[47]

TABLE TWO
Monograph on the Miners of the Upper Harz Mining Corporation, Budget of Annual Receipts

Receipts		Approx. Value (in francs)		Value of Goods Received in Kind (in francs)	Cash Receipts (in francs)
FAMILY PROPERTY[43]			SECTION 1: INCOME FROM PROPERTY[44]		
1. Real property		2,340,00	1. From real property	62,93	39,67
2. Personal property		12,00	2. From personal property	0,60	—
3. Right to allocations from mutual aid societies		50,40	3. Allocations from mutual aid societies	—	—
TOTAL		2,402,40	TOTAL	63,53	30,67
SUBSIDIES			SECTION 2: INCOME FROM SUBSIDIES		
1. Property received as usufructs		—	1. Value of property received as usufructs	—	—
2. Rights of usage for communal property		74,52	2. Value of rights of usage	6,21	—
3. Allocations of goods and services		1,034,76	3. Value of goods and services allotted	95,22	14,41
TOTAL		1,109,28	TOTAL	101,43	14,41
WORK PERFORMED BY FAMILY	Days Worked		SECTION 3: WAGES[45]		
1. By the worker			1. Worker's wages	16,74	471,88
primary work	318	7,059,60			
secondary work	29	269,70			
2. By the wife			2. Wife's wages	73,89	64,53
primary work	110				
secondary work	217	2,076,30			
3. By the eldest son	312	1,043,55	3. Eldest son's wages		69,57
TOTAL		10,449,15	TOTAL	90,63	605,98
TRANSACTIONS AND BUSINESSES UNDERTAKEN BY THE FAMILY			SECTION 4: BUSINESS PROFITS		
1. Profit from work		222,60	1. Additional wages from secondary work	—	22,26
2. Tasks undertaken for family's benefit		143,40	2. Profits from family businesses	4,91	9,43
TOTAL		366,00	TOTAL	4,91	31,69
OVERALL TOTAL		11,986,83	OVERALL TOTAL	260,50	682.75
			TOTAL YEARLY RECEIPTS		943,25

The following examples will shed more light on the diagnostic use of budget data: the tendency of a gunsmith at the semirural factory of Solingen to spend money for "useless or dangerous leisure activities" like drinking and smoking meant that he would never

TABLE THREE
Monograph on the Miners of the Upper Harz Mining Corporation, Budget of Annual Expenditures

Expenditures	Weight (in kilos)	Average Price Per Kilo	Value of Goods Grown or Created in Household (all prices in francs)	Cash Expenses
SECTION 1: EXPENDITURES FOR FOOD[46]				
1. Food consumed in the household:				
grains	889.0	0,277	70,32	176,86
fats	24.4	1,402	—	34,22
dairy products	118.5	0,161	—	19,11
meat and fish	85.5	0,817	—	69,85
fruit and vegetables	873.0	0,083	25,14	47,15
condiments and stimulants	43.5	0,338	—	14,71
fermented beverages	173.0	0,164	—	28,30
2. Food consumed outside the household			25,53	
TOTAL			120,99	390,20
SECTION 2: EXPENDITURES PERTAINING TO THE DWELLING				
1. Lodging			79,15	1,24
2. Furnishings			—	7,29
3. Heat			24,66	1,71
4. Light			—	20,24
TOTAL			103,81	30,39
SECTION 3: EXPENDITURES FOR CLOTHING				
1. Worker's			4,65	67,24
2. Wife's			2,32	33,62
3. Children's			2,33	33,62
4. Laundry			—	13,32
TOTAL			9,30	147,80
SECTION 4: EXPENDITURES PERTAINING TO MORAL NEEDS, RECREATION, AND HEALTH CARE				
1. Religion			—	1,96
2. Education			9,00	5,12
3. Charities			—	—
4. Amusements			—	9,72
5. Health services			4,20	1,80
TOTAL			13,20	18,60
SECTION 5: EXPENDITURES PERTAINING TO PROFESSIONAL WORK, DEBTS, TAXES, AND INSURANCE				
1. Professional work			—	—
2. Interest and debts			—	93,60
3. Taxes			—	—
4. Insurance			13,60	2,16
5. Mutual aid societies			—	—
TOTAL			13,20	96,76
ANNUAL SAVINGS			—	—
TOTAL ANNUAL EXPENDITURES			943,25	

save enough money to advance socially;[48] the high dues that one tinsmith paid to a labor union indicated his hostility toward the upper class;[49] a London cutlery worker's annual expenditure of 50 francs for the care of a bird indicated his lack of foresight, though Le Play also acknowledged that it was the worker's only source of amusement.[50]

Lazarsfeld has claimed that Le Play relied exclusively on the diagnostic approach, but Le Play also used budget data analytically, that is, he studied the relationship of particular expenses to each other and to the total budget. For example, he discovered the following relationship:

> When urgent circumstances compel a simplification of the diet, grains become so predominant that they absorb half of a family's expenses. As affluence increases, other foods—particularly fats, meats, and fermented beverages—take a larger place in the diet. It is thus that in certain cases, the portion of a family's total outlay that is spent on grains is reduced to one-eighth; in other cases, to one-twelfth, sometimes, finally, to one-thirteenth.[51]

Le Play presented his finding almost in passing as an interesting observation. In fact, this "observation" anticipated the economist Ernest Engel's law of consumption, which states that the proportion of income spent on food increases as total income decreases. In a similar vein he analyzed the relationship between a worker's salary (cash revenue) and his total income and also the relationship between home industries and savings. He found that the greater the proportion of income from a worker's salary, the more vulnerable the family is to economic fluctuations; the greater the importance of home industries in the family's income, the greater the savings.

Le Play never discussed the logic used to reach his conclusions or the computations he undertook. This led the sociologist Goldfrank to state that "the budgets themselves seem superfluous since whenever they are mentioned it is within the context of lengthy qualitative passages."[52] It is true that Le Play frequently used budget data as mere illustration, but it would be unfair to say that he never used them analytically.

The third part of the family monograph presents qualitative information also, but it differs from the first qualitative part in two ways: it does not follow a standardized format or present a detailed guideline for collecting information; and it is not closely linked with the family budget. Instead, the third section, which consists of a series of short essays, focuses on the institutions, customs, laws, history, and geography of the community. Here Le Play paid special attention to institutions which maintain workers' security. He also recorded his observations about family structures, inheritance laws, and emigration patterns—observations which later figured in his theories of society.[53]

Le Play's monographic method has encountered three main types of criticism. The first is the complaint I discussed earlier: that monographs are purely descriptive with no theoretical orientation. The second is that family monographs simply do not provide a basis for inferences about society as a whole. The third criticism of Le Play's method concerns the reliability of his data. As mentioned above, the biases of local social authorities must have played a role in the selection of some of the families Le Play studied. Some critics have denied Le Play's claim that he successfully standardized his method. He believed that anyone with a practical sense of a worker's life and needs could do successful monographs.[54] Critics, however, have argued that researchers who lacked Le Play's perceptiveness and sympathy failed to make the monographic method work. They found this problem especially in the later monographs, in which Le Play delegated more responsibility for data collection to his disciples.

Some of Le Play's own disciples questioned the reliability of the data in the family monographs. In 1897 Eduard Julhiet, a contributor to Le Play's journal *La Réforme sociale*, reexamined the region of the Harz Valley where Le Play had studied a family in 1845. In Le Play's mind, this community had represented a type of social organization which was most likely to promote social harmony and economic security. Julhiet, however, thought that Le Play had idealized the workers' situation—especially the relationship between employers and employees—and exaggerated their general level of satisfaction. His own research seemed to show that mine workers in the Harz Mountains often compared their situation unfavorably to that of urban workers.[55]

The first attempt to replicate one of Le Play's monographs was undertaken by Reuss, who went back to a German community in 1913 to assess Le Play's work.[56] Reuss interviewed two surviving members of the family that Le Play had studied in 1851. He compiled extensive information on the social and economic situation of the community by analyzing historical records and local newspapers. Like Julhiet, he found that Le Play had chosen facts which emphasized social harmony and cooperation between social classes and had failed to report conflicts and antagonisms in families and in the community. For example, when Le Play had recorded the amount of money spent on "drinking" outside the home in the budget of expenditures, he had not mentioned the local custom of conducting political debates and other activities in taverns. This omission may reflect Le Play's belief that political activity was dangerous and futile for workers. Reuss also saw Le Play's conclusion in the same monograph—that the integral transmission of family property benefited all family members—as a distortion of social reality. According to Reuss, Le Play minimized the conflicts that this practice created between parents and children and the bad consequences that the younger children had to bear.

It should be pointed out on Le Play's behalf that he did acknowledge these difficulties in other monographs. In one he wrote:

> In a region where vineyards are cultivated, children hope for the death of their parents in order to stop paying the life-annuity [*rente viagère*], while parents are often selfish toward their children, forcing them to pay a rente [*rente usuraire*] for using and continuing their business.[57]

Le Play also pointed out the possibility that the child chosen by the father might do a poor job of administering the business, thereby inflicting financial losses on the other children. However, if Le Play acknowledged these situations they were never analyzed in terms of social conflict.

In 1950 Eliot and Hillman tried to assess the changes which had taken place in Norwegian families by comparing Le Play's monograph on a worker in a cobalt foundry with their own study of contemporary foundry workers from the same town.[58] They found serious discrepancies between their own research and Le Play's. Historical records showed them that riots erupted two years after Le Play's monograph was published, giving the lie to his portrait of social harmony. Furthermore, these researchers were unable to trace the family Le Play had studied, and suspected that it might have been an idealized combination of several families.

In spite of these defects, Le Play's monographs have been valuable sources for a number of social historians who have studied the life-styles, values, and habits of workers in the first half of the nineteenth century. Georges Duveau used Le Play's monographs in his study of French workers during the Second Empire, even though he criticized Le Play's negative evaluation of the morality of the workers.[59] Louise Tilly and Joan Scott relied on Le Play in their analysis of the role of women in the domestic economy of preindustrial times.[60] One should mention, among economists, Ernst Engel and his use of the family budgets collected by Le Play and Ducpétiaux to elaborate his famous consumption law. Among sociologists, Maurice Halbwachs, a disciple of Durkheim, also used Le Play's family budgets in his book *La Classe ouvrière et les niveaux de vie* (The Working Class and Standards of Living) (1912).

Despite the real shortcomings of the monographic method, Le Play's methodological queries and research tools are evidence of a much greater continuity than we have acknowledged between this early pioneer in social research and modern sociology.

6

FAMILY TYPES

Of all of Le Play's contributions, the elaboration of family types has received the most attention from followers and commentators.[1] Le Play created these types from information collected in his family monographs[2] and later used the types in analyses of social mobility and social change. Here we will examine the three family types elaborated by Le Play.[3]

The "patriarchal family," sometimes called the "traditional family" or "community," encompassed a large group of people, including the patriarch, his wife, all of his unmarried children, and the families of his married sons.[4] They all lived under the same roof, though sometimes the married sons settled a short distance away and continued to work together on a piece of property which they owned in common. Ultimate authority belonged to the father, who represented the interests of the family as a whole. Because he combined the "triple functions of property-owner, king, and high priest,"[5] his power was at once social, political, and religious.

Le Play described the head of a patriarchal family among the seminomadic shepherds of the Asian slopes of the Urals:

> This leader exercises absolute authority over all the partial households united in one house; he distributes jobs, makes purchases and sales, and handles common funds. He determines before his death his choice of successor and the distribution of property in the community.[6]

In patriarchal communities there was no private property and therefore no private accumulation of wealth. Savings took the form of surplus that the community stored to cope with natural disasters. The distribution of resources among family members provided enough for everybody's needs without introducing inequalities.

Because societies with patriarchal families had no other significant social organizations, Le Play called them "family-based societies." Patriarchal communities, which were found among the nomadic and seminomadic tribes of Asia, required large uninhabited tracts of land and abundant natural resources. Le Play called families in regions with limited amounts of land "quasi-patriarchal." These families did not have several generations living under the same roof, although they did hold resources in common and all members of the household worked as a unit under the supreme control of the head of the household. Quasi-patriarchal families tended to be found among settled peoples in Russia and Central Europe. Le Play always admired the patriarchal family but did not see it as a model to be followed by "the most advanced nations of the West," because it was dominated by a spirit of tradition which stifled change.[7] Change occurred only when the natural growth of the population put pressure on the land. When that happened, the patriarch prepared a group for emigration. Le Play spoke of "swarms" that went off to start new patriarchal communities headed by a man chosen by the patriarch.[8]

The second type elaborated by Le Play, the stem family, consisted of the parents, the unmarried children, and one married child chosen by the father to continue his work when he died or retired.[9] This child was not necessarily the oldest, but the one whom the father considered best qualified to take over the family property. This integral transfer of family property perpetuated paternal authority. The father's choice was neither arbitrary nor determined by the doctrine of primogeniture; it was based on a judgment formed during the years when he had worked in close cooperation with his sons. When the father retired, the chosen son was obligated to pay a "life annuity" *(rente viagère)* to his retired parents and to provide cash or dowries for his siblings who would settle outside the family. Those who left the household could always rely on the heir in case of hardship; he, in turn, could also call upon them for help. Members of stem families were encouraged to work and save in order to help children settle outside the paternal home. All families were considered equal and shared their resources according to each family's needs; consequently, there were no poor. The stem family also encouraged these children to seek opportunity abroad in underdeveloped countries, a tendency Le Play saw as healthy for the nation as well as the children. He concluded:

> This system satisfies both those who are content in the situation in which they were born and those who boldly wish to rise in the social hierarchy through their own initiative. It strikes a just balance between paternal authority and the freedom of the children, between stability and the improvement of social conditions.[10]

The stem family, Le Play reported, was found among settled populations who owned private property, in places where resources—especially land—were limited. In the stem family, moral and economic needs were intertwined more than in any other family type.[11] In order for the family to function well, all of its members had to cooperate. Le Play viewed specialization of tasks in the household or in the family trade as a source of malfunctioning and antagonism among family members. Every member of the stem family at one time or another participated in every family task. Furthermore, living and working in the same place created a valuable sense of solidarity and self-sufficiency within the family. In addition, Le Play suggested that families of the same region should depend on each other, helping each other at harvest time instead of hiring outsiders. These characteristics of the stem family encouraged frugality, love of work, thrift, and personal dignity.

Le Play was aware that the stem family existed only in isolated rural provinces in the low mountainous regions of Western Europe.[12] He also acknowledged the weakening of the stem family during his own time, a condition that he blamed on the laws passed by the revolutionary government of March 1793. Le Play believed that those laws, which mandated the forced partition of inheritance among heirs, had led to a number of devastating consequences: an increase in the number of hired hands and the proletarianization of the countryside, the weakening of paternal authority, the destruction of the family as a moral and economic unit, and a reduction of the birth rate.[13] Furthermore, Le Play believed that the stem family as a mode of social and economic organization could counteract the devastating effects of large-scale industrialization, while encouraging gradual economic change and individual mobility. He was also aware that the increasing industrialization and commercialization of France could only further weaken the stem family. Nonetheless, he was convinced that a nation's "happiness" was based on its ability to promote the stem family.[14]

He argued that England and the United States, which had retained freedom of testation, had promoted the stem family and with it prosperity, stability, and opportunity.[15] "It is obvious to everyone familiar with the customs and economic systems of the two great Anglo-Saxon nations that their happy combination of individual freedom and paternal authority is the principal cause for this race's success wherever it has settled."[16] He was convinced that if France failed to follow the English and American examples it would fall into ruin.

Le Play clearly used his concept of the stem family to present his picture of an idealized society of small, rural property-owners, where economic change would be less important than social stability. His analysis of the stem family minimized conflicts between family members, particularly the jealousy that emerged when the father selected his heir. He acknowledged only minor conflicts between the individual and the family over small expenditures.[17] Some of Le Play's followers have shown how overoptimistic he was about the transfer of inheritance. Cheysson, for example, studied a stem family—the Melouga family—over several generations and showed that it failed to survive because of conflicts over inheritance.[18] More recent studies of the importance of the stem family in Europe have shown that it was never widespread and that harmony among family members was more a myth than a reality.[19]

Le Play characterized the third family type, the "unstable family," as follows:

> It establishes itself by the union of two free adults, grows with the birth of children, shrinks with the successive departure of the members of the new generation, and dissolves finally, without leaving a trace, with the early death of the abandoned parents.[20]

Le Play perceived this type of family as a "frail shrub" compared to the "vigorous and admirable stem family." He found that unstable families, which were most common in Western manufacturing centers, had suffered a serious erosion of paternal authority. Because the father no longer could keep the family property intact by bequeathing it to one child, he could not provide the traditional safeguards for members who lacked the necessary moral qualities. Once the children moved away, their retired parents were left to fend for themselves; once the property was divided and the family was dispersed there was no source of collective support. When Le Play spoke of "unstable" families, he was referring not to individual behavior but to a type of family structure which did not allow for family continuity and which therefore made well-being and mobility more difficult to achieve for certain individuals. Thus, he concluded:

> Unskilled or morally delinquent workers fall even faster to a wretched condition, unable to claim any assistance. Unfortunately, this state of affairs tends to perpetuate itself once it occurs, either because parents can no longer contribute through savings to the establishment of their children, or, more likely, because the children are left without supervision and succumb to their evil inclinations or are perverted by bad examples at an early age.[21]

Le Play's family types show his ability to create conceptual tools. In the next chapters, we will demonstrate how he used them to interpret social reality and propose social theories.

7

THEORY OF SOCIAL MOBILITY

Le Play's analysis of social mobility concentrated on the processes by which successful family members acquired property, thereby gaining economic security and also a sense of dignity and personal freedom.[1] Like many of his contemporaries, Le Play believed that the gradual acquisition of property was the only solution to pauperism, which he saw as the foremost social problem of his time. Unlike his contemporaries, however, Le Play sought empirical tests for this widely held belief. Because he saw the emancipation of the working classes as "the supreme task imposed on man's efforts by the divine will,"[2] he hoped that the study of social mobility would lead to reform. It is important to note that Le Play never used the term "mobility" but rather a variety of terms, including "betterment," "improvement," and "changes in social conditions." In this discussion I have used the term "mobility" because I feel that Le Play's ideas are an early expression of this concept.

Le Play never organized his ideas about social mobility into one definitive presentation. Instead, his findings, which are scattered throughout the first edition of *Les Ouvriers européens,* reflect two main approaches to the problem. One is evident in the informal study of the "History of the Family" which appears in the first qualitative section of his monographs. Here he gives an account of the stages in a worker's life, the social and economic changes that he and his family underwent, and the factors and institutions which might account for his success or failure. For example, he described the mason who, like other long-term migrant workers, managed to save more money than settled Parisian workers did—even though Parisian workers usually made higher salaries.[3] Le Play attributed this propensity to save to the migrant worker's lifelong aspiration to buy property in his native province and return home to retire. The geographic characteristics of the mason's native Auvergne, particularly its economic isolation and impoverished soil, gave him an early incentive to seek a successful trade outside the community. His family structure and social environment also improved his prospects for advancement. Most families in Auvergne owned small properties in communities with communal pastures. Before they were six years old children in these families were learning the importance of work, contributing to the household economy mainly by tending the animals. Around the age of sixteen, the boys selected their future occupation, and would-be masons became apprentices to a master, who was usually a family friend already working in Paris. At twenty-five, the young mason completed his apprenticeship and married a woman from his native province (who was likely to work harder and save more money than Parisian women, who generally spent more money for luxuries). The mason worked in Paris for about twenty years, curtailing his expenditures as much as possible. At forty-five, when he retired to his native province and bought a home with a vegetable garden and domestic animals, he was able to "enjoy the ease and consideration which he had achieved through hard work and foresight."[4]

In these workers' life histories, Le Play analyzed the conditions under which work habits were most successfully learned at each stage of the worker's career. Concentrating on obstacles to social mobility, he reached four fascinating insights. He found, for one thing, that education was more of an obstacle than an aid to social mobility because children who went away to school for long periods of time often had trouble learning the skills required to manage a farm or a business. When the laundryman from Clichy sent his children away to a better school, he found that they could not learn the family trade, and also that they had adopted new values and had begun to look down on manual labor. As a result, the children failed to take over his business and failed to maintain even his modest status.[5]

Le Play's second conclusion was that women who worked outside the home impaired their families' prospects for advancement. If women were not at home, they could neither raise their children properly nor supervise home industries—two roles which were essential to a working family's success.[6]

Third, Le Play saw the worker's aspiration to imitate the bourgeoisie as the most serious obstacle to his advancement. The Geneva clockmaker's expensive efforts to copy the dress, furnishings, and general way of life of the bourgeoisie seriously hampered his efforts to acquire property.[7]

Finally, he found that improvident workers, though lazy and prone to debauchery, also showed the "noblest sentiments: compassion, selfishness, and enthusiasm."[8] Unfortunately these virtues, which Le Play considered indispensable once workers had acquired property, proved to be additional obstacles to mobility for the improvident because they made economic planning and calculation all the more difficult.[9]

Le Play's study of family histories revealed a pattern of variations in ability to save over the course of the family life. He found that middle-aged workers, who had been through the difficult periods of life and paid all the costs involved in raising a family, were in a better position to save money than younger workers. He concluded that these workers provided the best evidence about real ability to save.[10]

A second, more systematic, approach to the study of social mobility led Le Play to compare seven types of workers located in different socioeconomic positions in order to understand the forces which enabled some of them to move up the social ladder.[11] He defined these positions by combining the remuneration given for work and the nature of a family's possessions. He set up a "social hierarchy," on the basis of a continuum which showed how economically independent from his employer each type of worker was. Table 4 shows what these classifications were.[12]

Le Play made his broadest distinction—between workers who were not heads of households and workers who were—because domestic workers made up no less than 35 percent of the working population of France in the first half of the nineteenth century, as a recent study has shown.[13] Among workers who were heads of

TABLE FOUR
The Seven Principal Positions That Workers Can Occupy in the Four Social Systems to Raise Themselves from the Lower Ranks of the Workers' Hierarchy

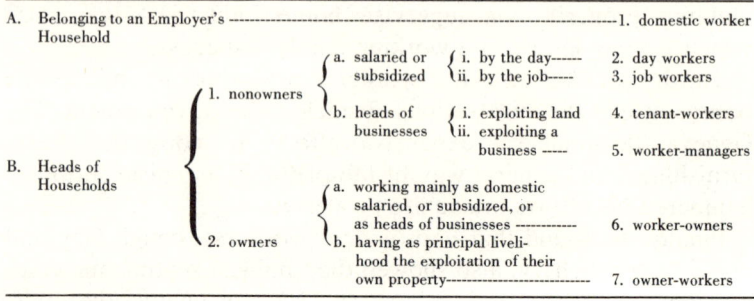

households, Le Play distinguished between those who owned a home and those who did not. Within each group, he introduced further distinctions regarding the type of remuneration and the worker's position vis-à-vis his employer. Le Play's classification is, if not the first, one of the first attempts at ranking workers on a socioeconomic scale.

The domestic worker had two essential characteristics: he owned no property, and he depended on a master for all his needs. Most agricultural workers fit Le Play's description of day workers, who occupied the next rung on the ladder. Like domestic workers, these workers owned nothing; but since they were heads of households they were a little more independent of the master. Job workers also owned no property, but their relationship with their employers at least enabled them to "negotiate a contract, which is advantageous to worker and owner alike."[14] Tenant-workers also owned no property, but made their living by exploiting a piece of rented land. This situation often required cooperation between the tenant and the owner, since the worker needed not only the landowner's tools but also his guidance in administering the property. The next category of worker, the worker-manager, rented a business which he managed for profit.

The two highest positions in this hierarchy of manual laborers belonged to property owners, who were almost of the bourgeoisie. The worker-owner owned his own tools and machinery, but was not totally independent because he worked for someone else. Only the owner-worker, who managed his own piece of property by himself and was fully responsible for his family's needs, had attained "true independence engendered by property acquired through work."[15] Le Play believed that a worker progresses through these different positions in order to attain the status of owner-worker. He thought that a worker who wanted to own property must first undergo a "property-owner's apprenticeship," consisting of a long learning process starting in childhood. Without this training, Le Play thought, the worker could never acquire those indispensable moral qualities—especially thrift and temperance—which enabled him to advance.[16]

Le Play made it clear that he meant to base his theory of social mobility on a comprehensive comparative analysis of the seven types of workers in each of the four social systems.[17] In fact, he never fully carried out this plan: he only used the seven worker types in one comparative analysis of budgets of receipts among sedentary populations and did the analysis in an unsystematic way, leaving most of the work to the reader.[18] He did, however, propose a number of empirical generalizations. For example, he found that as a worker achieved greater economic independence by moving up the social ladder, his budget of receipts grew more complex and varied, while his salary became a smaller portion of his total income.[19] The worker at the bottom of the hierarchy, who depended mainly on his salary, was vulnerable to price fluctuations and other economic changes and therefore less likely to improve his situation. As a worker acquired more property, he acquired the time and the means to secure additional revenues: he might rent out tools, buildings, or machinery; he might take a second job; or he might receive returns from savings or investments.

The supplementary sources of income in the budget of receipts to which Le Play devoted the most detailed comparative analysis were the domestic industries—that is, the ways in which families produced goods and services in the home.[20] Domestic industries provided the clearest sign of economic success: "For a given social organization, the number and importance of domestic industries increase in proportion as the worker rises higher in the series of stations which separates the simple domestic worker from the worker who owns property."[21] By providing additional revenues, they provided the family with greater economic stability, a requirement for long-range planning and further mobility. Domestic industries also served an important social function: they made family members depend on each other. This cooperation, in turn, made it easier for families to succeed. On the other hand, family members which lacked this cooperative spirit usually fell prey to serious antagonisms toward each other.[22]

Even more important than the economic and social functions of domestic industries was their moral function: they taught family members the virtue of foresight. Because they were based on thrift, they provided a training ground for the property owner's apprenticeship: "Domestic industries teach one to resist the force of the physical appetites in favor of a more remote advantage. The entire family is thus initiated in all the virtues which derive from foresight."[23] Le Play stated clearly that mobility was based on deferred gratification stemming from learning in the household the virtues of thrift and temperance. Each time a family saved money instead of spending it on immediate material gratification it was strengthening these virtuous habits and in turn encouraging home industries. The budget of receipts shows the exact contribution of the worker, his wife, and their oldest child to domestic industries, right down to the number of days worked by each and the value of that labor. This computation confirmed the insight that Le Play offered in the qualitative section of his monographs—namely, that women played a key role in domestic industries.[24] Finally, this study of domestic industries led Le Play to the following empirical generalization: "The rank occupied by the different types of workers in the social hierarchy is always related to the degree to which they have developed the virtue of foresight."[25]

Le Play rejected the view that "social and political laws" of a nation were a major influence on mobility. He pointed out that most provident workers came from localities characterized by poor soil, hard climate, and economic isolation, refuting those who attributed mobility to the economic prosperity of a particular region. He also ruled out mental ability as a determining factor, arguing that workers from rural and isolated regions, who tended to be less intelligent than workers "raised in the great centers of population and industry,"[26] also tended to be more upwardly mobile. Finally, Le Play rejected the proposals of reformers such as Napoleon III who believed that a redistribution of resources—particularly land—would encourage social mobility:

> An immense fraternal spirit which would lead to a redivision of Europe's available capital among all its working families would have no other result than to dissipate most of this capital through senseless consumption. The aptitude for ownership simply cannot be conveyed by a mere allocation of objects. It does not necessarily derive from more highly developed acquisitive instincts. Its only sources are temperance, which regulates physical needs by keeping expenditures smaller than income, and foresight, which preserves gains won by thrift.[27]

Except in his analysis of budgets of receipts, Le Play's seven worker-types did not figure importantly in his analysis. Instead, he described a more fundamental distinction between two broad types:

> If one tries to go to the heart of the matter according to the spirit of the method presented in his work, one soon finds that all these varieties of the working classes belong, on the whole, to two main types. The first type, still too rare in the present state of civilization, includes those workers who are sustained by their own providence and who, by saving, are constantly building up first properties and then revenues which augment the resources created by labor. The second type is far more common and includes all the individuals dominated by the opposite propensity; among them consumption is always greater than income and has no limits other than credit, no check besides necessity. As soon as a family's domestic life is analyzed and a budget is established, one or the other of these tendencies can be seen in every detail of family life.[28]

The key difference between provident and improvident workers was not the amount of money they earned but the way they spent the money. Therefore, Le Play based this comparative analysis primarily on his budget of expenses. This budget showed that improvident workers spent all they earned to fulfill immediate material needs and that provident workers curtailed expenses in order to use their money for productive purposes. The budget measured a worker's propensity to save by recording the amount he saved each year and the proportion of that amount that he poured back into equipment, training, voluntary associations, professional organizations, or his trade.

Fifteen of the thirty-six monographs in the first edition of *Les Ouvriers européens* are about provident workers. These monographs enabled Le Play to offer some generalizations. He found, for example, that provident workers were most common in the system of long-term work agreements. He also found that provident workers tended to come from low mountainous regions like Galicia in Spain, the Auvergne in France, or the Italian Piedmont. They usually migrated to cities and took up specific crafts, becoming mule-drivers, market-gardeners, mowers, linen-combers, stove-makers, blacksmiths, and masons. Le Play also found provident agricultural workers and fishermen, but he never foumd provident industrial workers in large urban centers.[29]

Le Play also classified provident workers by the purposes (i.e., goals) for which they saved. A first group saved in order to repay debts or loans, provide money for a daughter's dowry, or compensate children for giving up their claim to family property. The stem family from Lavedan, France, and the peasant communities of Bousrah in the Ottoman Empire (Syria) belonged to this group.[30] A second group saved money to acquire additional properties and revenues. The Geneva clockmaker who received interest from a savings account belonged to this group, as did the carpenter from the English town of Sheffield who used his savings to pay dues to a land society, who received interest from accumulated savings, and who bought tools to improve his work.[31] A last group used their savings to buy a house or a business. The master laundryman from Clichy, who used his savings to buy state bonds, industrial shares, and a house belonged to this group.³² Le Play assumed a progression among these three types of provident workers. The members of the third group occupy the two highest positions of his hierarchy. He called them "model workers" and urged other workers and policy-makers to study them in great detail.³³

Le Play's study of workers who did not save distinguished between improvident workers and those whose traditional societies did not require them to save. He was not primarily concerned either with workers who could count on the community to take care of their essential needs or with workers whose traditional ethos discouraged ambition. Improvident workers from industrialized urban centers did concern him, however, because modern society had no built-in protections for them. He devoted nineteen of the thirty-six monographs in the first edition of *Les Ouvriers européens* to such workers. He distinguished between those whose habits were "totally different from those of the bourgeoisie" and those who imitated the bourgeoisie, describing the first group as follows:

> They frequent places of amusement outside the city limits, near toll-gate walls or surrounding villages; they do not read newspapers and are not interested in politics except when events concern them directly. They are not jealous of their employer's influence; they desire only more time to indulge in their weekly debauch.³⁴

Le Play described this group as passive and deferential toward the upper classes, devoted to pleasure, inclined to associate with people from similar backgrounds, unable to engage in long-term relationships (e.g., marriage), and totally lacking in religious feelings.³⁵

The second group of improvident workers had achieved higher social positions and their tastes and modes of life resembled those of the "petite bourgeoisie." According to Le Play, "these workers constantly tried to copy the furnishings, clothing, and amusements of the lower middle class."³⁶ They frequented dance halls in the center of the city, went to theaters, were more educated, and associated with shopkeepers and other members of the lower middle class. Like the other group of improvident workers, they often also engaged in illicit relationships, but Le Play thought that their relationships were generally more stable. He saw the fact that they often demanded the same consideration for their mistress as for a legitimate wife as a sign of their higher morality. These workers were less deferential toward the upper classes, and their dissatisfaction with their wages and working conditions was a constant source of antagonism and danger to the social order. Le Play found that a majority of the workers who participated in the revolutionary events of 1848 belonged to this group.[37] Like the other improvident workers, these workers lacked religious feelings.

Having argued that moral qualities were essential to a worker's success, Le Play went on to question why some workers were able to develop the necessary moral qualities and others were not. He linked success in moral training to five causes: religious beliefs, family structure, parental authority, worker-employer relationships, and a worker's institutional affiliations.[38]

Liberal thinkers during Le Play's time frequently discussed religion in broad terms as a cure for workers' degradation, which they saw as society's worst affliction. Le Play, however, was the first to study the daily behavior of workers in order to "determine whether the development of religious feelings goes hand in hand with the development of foresight."[39] His monographs contained information on religious behavior, religious education, and religious feelings. He asked family members about church attendance and religious practices inside and outside the home and he measured religious feelings by the worker's contributions to charitable institutions and religious expenses.[40] In all family monographs Le Play investigated the relationship between religious feelings and thrift. For example, the family of the London cutler did not go to church, spent no money on religious ceremonies (paying for a mass, buying candles, honoring dead relatives), and gave no money to charity. Instead, most of the cutler's money went toward improving the family's diet and the material comforts of the household. Le Play inferred that because this worker's family had no religious commitments they could not control their material appetites and consequently were unable to save money.[41] By contrast, Le Play found a positive relationship between religious practices and the ability to save money in the case of the day laborer/tenant farmer of Laon, a practicing Catholic whose wife and daughters were particularly devout. His family spent money for religious obligations—church membership, collections, and offerings—and they gave money to charities. They also owned animals, working tools, and their home, and they eventually saved enough money to buy a potato field.[42]

In his observation of religious behavior, Le Play tried to isolate its most important features.[43] He observed the impact of different religious faiths on the ability to save. He did not make systematic comparisons, but he saw enough to notice that Protestant families—especially Calvinists—were more likely than other families to save money, an observation which anticipated Max Weber's findings of a century later. He also determined which of the daily activities that he recorded in his budgets was most closely connected to thrift: "The most decisive symptoms can be seen among populations who acquire the tendency to help, by alms and other assistance, individuals who are plunged into destitution."[44]

Le Play found a relationship between donations to charity and savings, even among workers who were not religious. For example, the family of the master laundryman did not go to church and had no religious education, but they gave money to charity and were still able to save enough money to buy state bonds. Le Play decided that the laundryman, and other nonreligious workers whose desire for gain had not "hardened their hearts," exhibited at least the "symptoms of religious feelings."[45] It should be noted that Le Play also tried to account for deviant cases. After examining the case of the swordsmith of Solingen, who was somewhat religious but not thrifty, he admitted that his well-being was probably due to the economic prosperity of the region.[46] Though he acknowledged these exceptions, Le Play concluded that there is a clear connection between religion and thrift: "Religion not only elevates societies to moral perfection, the ultimate goal of all civilizations; it is also, in the economic order, the strongest source of success."[47] Le Play thought that religion, aside from its ability to "restrain the gross instincts" of improvident workers, could also serve a different function for provident workers who had acquired property; by minimizing such negative consequences of thrift as harshness and selfishness, religion could train workers who had reached higher social positions in their new obligations to the lower classes.[48]

Another important factor in Le Play's theory of social mobility is the role of women in the household.[49] He distinguished two important types of work done by women. One consisted of household chores, the traditional tasks that a housewife performed for the family and its members. Among these activities he included preparing and cooking food, caring for young children, doing the laundry, mending linens and clothing, keeping the house and furniture clean, and caring for each member of the family. Because this labor did not create additional revenue, Le Play did not calculate its value, though he did record in the budget of receipts the number of days the wife spent at these tasks.

He did try to compute the value of the wife's "productive work"—that is, her efforts to make extra income by growing vegetables, gathering berries, candlemaking, canning, spinning, weaving, sewing, carrying foodstuffs to and from the marketplace, or looking after animals. He based these calculations on the daily wages of workers doing the same work. Le Play compared the relative importance of household chores and productive work done by women by comparing the number of days spent on each over a year.[50] He also estimated the wife's annual contribution to the household economy in a number of families and found that the more the wife contributed, the better the family's chances were for improving its social position.

Even more important than the wife's productive work was her moral leadership. Since the key to successful saving was not so much increasing income as curtailing expenditures, the wife's most important role was to conduct the property owner's moral "apprenticeship," teaching her children to be temperate and thrifty.[51] Over and over again, Le Play stressed that women are above all moral creatures and are at the center of the moral and material development of the family.[52] The wife of the laundryman, like many other women, developed these moral qualities before getting married, because she had to save money to acquire a dowry.⁵³ Le Play also noticed that women in the working classes were more intelligent, educated, and religious than the men.⁵⁴ For all of these reasons, women were better equipped to manage the household, to spend money wisely, and to raise children. Le Play concluded that the government should encourage them to contribute to the household economy instead of taking jobs outside the home; otherwise, he thought, the family's moral welfare would be endangered.⁵⁵ He criticized organizations, like the German corporations, which discouraged early marriage. He also opposed the English poor laws and other laws which caused families to break up. His concern for women also led him to investigate the criminal laws on seduction in the United States, England, and France.⁵⁶

Le Play's analysis of the impact of family structure, work relations, professional organizations, and voluntary associations on intragenerational mobility clearly shows that he understood the role of social structure and institutions. Few scholars, however, have acknowledged the role that Le Play's ideas on family structure played in his theory of mobility. In his analysis of family organization, he discussed how structural conditions interact with individual characteristics to affect a worker's material advancement. The structure of the patriarchal family, which promoted stability and the interests of the group at the expense of the individual, precluded any possibility of mobility. The stem family, by choosing the best qualified child to follow in the father's footsteps and providing money to help each of the other children to settle outside the family property, created economic conditions for both geographic and social mobility. Even more important, the structure of the stem family, whose self-sufficiency depended on solidarity and cooperation among family members, encouraged frugality, love of work, thrift, and personal dignity—individual characteristics whose contribution to mobility we have already seen. Of the three family types, the unstable family presented the best opportunities for social mobility, but also the gravest risk of failure. The skilled and thrifty individual who was no longer responsible for the needs of his relatives could use his abilities for his own benefit. Furthermore, "small families are relieved from the problem of maintaining solidarity among a large group of people."[57] Thus, in the unstable family, individual interest had finally prevailed over collective needs. At the same time, the individual no longer had the economic and social support that the other two family structures had provided for him. If he lacked the necessary ability and moral qualities, "he would fall below his family's position," becoming downwardly mobile.

Le Play also tried to understand how institutions and social relationships outside the family affected social mobility. He was interested in two problems: he wanted to know what types of social relationships would best help workers develop a sense of thrift and a positive attitude toward ownership; and he wanted to know what existing institutional arrangements could protect improvident workers from destitution.[58] This second problem particularly concerned him.

> No matter where we look in Europe today, the heads of most families lack foresight. Sometimes only an insignificant minority have developed this quality. Consequently each social system must provide special mechanisms to make up for this moral deficiency. These mechanisms are usually found in the relationships which link workers to masters, communities, and voluntary associations.[59]

Le Play attached the greatest importance to social relationships between persons in different hierarchical positions, particularly worker-employer relationships. Of the four types of work relations which figure in his theory of social change, Le Play decided that the one which served the worker's welfare best was the system of long-term voluntary work agreements, which he also called the "system of patronage."

Patronage as a social institution was a set of economic and social arrangements which flourished in France during the uncertain period between 1820 and 1850, when a full-fledged market economy was emerging.[60] By controlling prices and limiting production and competition, patronage provided stable returns for the employer and a stable income of fixed annual allocations for the worker. Because the employer did not have to worry about economic instability, he could provide housing, health care, education, and recreational facilities for the worker.[61] Thus, Le Play thought, while patronage did not restrict the worker's freedom as earlier systems of work agreements had, it retained most of their provisions for his well-being. Furthermore, the system encouraged workers to acquire property through a system of loans and subsidies designed to protect them against usurers. The social historian Tudesq has shown that the political and social leaders in the French provinces at that time *(les notables)* wielded personal authority which the workers recognized as legitimate, a distinctive characteristic of patronage. He also observed that patronage reinforced familial, regional, and personal ties, and thereby exerted some control over the forces of change.[62]

Le Play was so positive about patronage that he created a prize at the Universal Exhibition of 1855 for the most successful "patron." The prize was awarded to a small manufacturer in Mulhouse who had created for his workers a whole village with a school, playgrounds, and a small hospital. Le Play idealized patronage and prescribed it as a "model" for the rest of society to emulate, much as he did with the stem family. He strongly believed that patronage could mitigate the negative effects of industrialization, while providing employers with a stable and docile work force.[63] It was this idealized conception of patronage that angered Le Play's critics, who saw him as an apologist for the exploitation of industrial workers. By concentrating on the negative connotations which patronage acquired later in the century, they may have overlooked the social and economic reality under which it emerged and misunderstood the fact that it originally represented a form of control over the devastating effects of a market economy. For his part, Le Play may not have realized that in a fully industrialized society patronage had become obsolete.

Le Play's ideas about social mobility do not amount to a theory that has been systematically derived from general principles of social organization. By today's standards his approach is crude and his methodology inadequate to demonstrate causal connections, to analyze the interaction between variables, or to determine each variable's independent effect on mobility. His analysis is more illustrative than systematic. Nevertheless, he was a pioneer in his attempt to study empirically the ways in which family structure, religion, individual aspirations, and institutional arrangements influence mobility. The original techniques and modes of analysis that he did use—the combination of life histories with the comparative analysis of workers located at different levels of his "social hierarchy"—make his analysis of these relationships an important step in the history of empirical social research. Many of Le Play's ideas about mobility reflect the liberal bourgeois ideology of his time, particularly his selection of patronage and the stem family as "model" institutions. Nonetheless, his study of social mobility does have important insights regarding the role of solidarity and the work ethic, ideas which were later developed by such sociologists as Durkheim and Weber, neither of whom ever referred to Le Play's work.

8

THEORY OF SOCIAL CHANGE

Le Play's monographic method, along with his complicated views about a priori ideas, has encouraged the widespread opinion that he never used his research to elaborate theories of social change,[1] that he collected case studies without taking theoretical considerations into account.[2] I will try to show that, contrary to these opinions, Le Play was guided by a general scheme and did formulate theories based on facts, even though the relationship between his research and theories is not always clear. Le Play claimed that his theories derived from direct observation. He actually used the term "theory" in a number of ways: he presented empirical generalizations, made ex post facto interpretations, and built general theories unrelated to his empirical research.[3]

It has been noted that Le Play created the monographic method in order to answer a series of questions about the organization and functioning of society. His primary interest was to find out, through comparative analysis, how individual freedom and social stability could be combined in different types of social organization.[4] Le Play was not the first to base theories of social change on comparative analysis. Comte had already used a comparative approach to arrive at his law of the three stages of human development, but he had not based his analysis on his own empirical findings but on his philosophical notion of the development of the human mind. Le Play developed his theory of social change in a different way:

> I have thus observed types of workers who function in different kinds of social organizations; and by comparing these types, I have been able to formulate several conclusions....[5]
>
> It is only by comparing types of society that I have learned how a race can acquire, preserve, lose, and finally regain the two essential human requirements: daily bread and the observance of the moral law.[6]

To facilitate these comparisons, Le Play arranged his monographs in a two-dimensional property space (see table 5). One axis presented four types of society, while the other presented seven types of workers. Le Play placed at least one of his thirty-six monographs at all but four of these twenty-eight intersections.[7] His theory of social change stemmed from this general intellectual scheme, which allowed him to systematically compare different types of social organizations on the basis of family monographs.

A distinction needs to be introduced between Le Play's early studies of social change, in which he tried to identify social trends empirically, and later work, which represented a more theoretical and global, but also reductionist, analysis. Many commentators—Sorokin and Zimmerman, for example—have primarily discussed ideas that Le Play presented in his late works, thus conveying the image of a man obsessively concerned with the issue of social order and the role of moral laws (particularly the Decalogue) in social reform.[8] These critics have overlooked Le Play's earlier work.

In his analysis of social trends, Le Play used his monographs to elaborate and compare four types of society, which correspond to four stages of historical development. He defined each type of society in terms of the social and economic relationships between its workers and employers. He studied the changes that occurred between each type of society and the next—not so much to find the causes of change but to identify trends running through all four stages of development.[9] This interpretation of social change as a gradual, quantitative process contrasts with Marx's belief that societies can only reach the next stage of social development

TABLE FIVE
Definitions of Workers and Their Relationships to Masters, Communities, and Associations in the Four Systems of Social Organization of Europe

Definition of the Seven Types of Worker	Definitions of the Four Types of Social Organization in Europe[10]			
	Nomadic Population	Sedentary Populations		
	I	II	III	IV
The seven stages through which workers may pass from the lower ranks of the industrial hierarchy to the status of owner or proprietor in the four types of social organizations.	Nomadic systems of social organization	System of non-voluntary work agreements (feudalism, slavery, peonage)	System of long-term voluntary work agreements (patronage, guild, tenancy)	System of temporary work agreements or work without agreements (self-employment, industrial employment)
1. Domestic worker		monograph II	monographs XVI, XII	monographs XXI, XXIII, XXIV, XXV
2. Day worker	monograph II	monographs III, IX	monographs VI, XXVI, VII, XXV	monographs XI, XXVII, XXVIII, XXIV, XXIX
3. Piece worker		monograph IX	monographs III, XIII, XVII	monographs XVI, XVII, XIX, XII, XX
4. Worker tenant		monographs XII, XXXIV	monograph VI	monograph XX
5. Master artisan	monograph I	monographs II, IV, V, IX	monographs VI, XII	monographs XXX, XXXV, XXXIV
6. Worker-owner[11]		monographs IV, V, VIII	monographs X, XIV, XV, XXI	monographs XXX, XXI, XXXIV, XXV
7. Owner-worker[12]	monograph I	monographs III, IV, VI	monographs VI, XV	monographs XXX, XXXIV, XXI, XVI, X

through violent upheavals and the destruction of existing economic and social institutions.

Le Play's earliest theory of social change appeared in the 1855 edition of *Les Ouvriers européens*. He began his discussion by summarizing the observations of different communities that he had made during his travels around the world as an engineer and a mine inspector. He noticed that Eastern societies were characterized by stability and tradition, while the countries of the West were characterized by prosperity and innovation. Le Play explained these differences by calling attention to the ethos or "spirit" which prevailed in each type of society: the "spirit of tradition" which dominated Eastern societies had kept them at the lowest stage of social development, while the "spirit of innovation," by contrast, had propelled Western societies to the highest level of material, intellectual, and even moral development. Le Play suggested that a comparison of the means of communication, the number of books published, and the number of schools in the two types of societies would convince the reader of the "superiority" of the Western nations.[13] He concluded that these nations were "models" of social organization:

> The people of Europe were able to maintain firm order and stability without falling into the excesses of despotism or a caste system. They raised religious feelings to greater heights than had any other people, without bowing to a theocratic regime or hampering freedom of thought. While preserving the concepts of governmental authority and collective action, they granted much more individual freedom than had any other race. By favoring the development of democracy, they accelerated the progress of the popular classes and affirmed the influence of the middle classes without stifling the sources of greatness which flow from the aristocracy.[14]

Le Play—not unlike Durkheim—identified two parallel trends in this transition from the lowest stage to the highest: the growth of individual freedom and the growth of a new morality. With increasing individual freedom, the individual's moral values began to replace restrictive external laws as means of social control:

The rapid change and the complexity of modern societies require more extensive and energetic motives than those which sufficed for a simpler state of affairs. The external law which regulates actions can only become less repressive if the internal law of the soul becomes more so.[15]

Le Play attributed these trends, in turn, to the influence of Christianity, which he believed had formed the "European character."

His belief in the West's inevitable trend toward more freedom, like his belief in the inevitable improvement of the conditions of the working classes, seems to contradict his frequent objections to the social ills that resulted from industrialization, urbanization, and other kinds of modernization. These views may not seem so contradictory when we remember that Le Play saw the bad effects of industrialization—pauperism, social inequality, and unrest—as mere "blemishes" or "temporary consequences of human imperfection, accidental deviations from society's principle of self-preservation."[16] Social ills were only the consequences of excesses of individual freedom. Le Play's concern for social reform and his vision of the science of society as a practical science led him to criticize these vices of modern societies and to emphasize the positive aspects of traditional societies. By doing so, he was hoping to raise the consciousness of the elite about the need for reform.[17] However, this approach did not blind him to the excesses of the spirit of tradition in earlier societies. "Even though we have been obliged to praise various consequences of social systems based on tradition and authority, we are far from proposing such a system as a model."[18]

Le Play's acceptance of an inevitable trend toward greater individual freedom seemed to involve him in another contradiction. How can we reconcile this view with the criticisms of the idea of progress which I discussed previously? What Le Play rejected was the view—which he ascribed to the philosophers of the Enlightenment—that progress is a universal principle applicable to all aspects of human life, including moral principles. He accepted the inevitability of progress in the material order but not in the moral order. If moral progress were inevitable, it would follow that free will has no role to play in social change, a consequence which he considered unacceptable.[19]

Le Play also considered the Enlightenment's concept of progress so abstract and vague as to be useless for research. He directed the same criticism at the concepts of "Freedom and Equality," which he called the "false dogmas of the Revolution."[20] He thought that his empirically based concept of social trends would serve policy-makers better than these general ideas would. Thus, instead of speaking of "Freedom," he studied "freedoms," which he defined as modes of individual behavior that he could examine empirically.[21] He also gave new empirical meaning to Comte's and Spencer's idea of stages of social development by distinguishing and studying the social and economic structures corresponding to each stage. With this new approach he was able to analyze the ways institutions adapt, disappear, or reemerge in response to the most powerful social trend—the growth of individual freedom.[22] He also planned to use this analysis to discover additional manifestations of the trend.

In order to study the impact of social change on institutions, Le Play distinguished four types of social organization.[23] He called the first type the "nomadic" system, or the "system based on communities." No one mode of work agreement is found in this system, which adhered completely to the "spirit of tradition." Among settled populations, he distinguished three types of social organization, according to their work agreements: a system of nonvoluntary permanent work agreements; a system of long-term voluntary work agreements (or patronage); and a system of temporary work agreements (or work without agreements), also called the system of full-blown independence.

On the basis of his empirical observations, Le Play selected five dimensions to analyze these types of social organization. Three of these dimensions described aspects of the relationship between the worker, the employer, and the community; two described characteristics of the community. The first dimension identified the types of bonds that linked the worker to his employer and to social institutions. Some workers were attached only to a master; others to a master and a community; others to a master and a corporation;[24] and still others to a master and to voluntary associations. Le Play also indicated whether the bonds between the master and the worker were based on restrictive laws, customs, contracts, or a combination of these. The second dimension specified the length of the relationship between worker and master and the nature of their mutual obligations. The third dimension accounted for the individual's position within his social group by indicating whether the group allowed him to improve his social position and/or to move away. The fourth dimension described the extent to which resources were shared in the community and the degree of economic equality. The fifth dimension, by specifying how much cultivated land each type of society had, indicated what kind of demographic pressures its citizens faced.

Each type of social organization was described along these five dimensions. For example, organizational forms II and III take the following values:

II. System of nonvoluntary permanent work agreements
   1. Workingmen committed to a master (landed gentry, landowner, etc.) by law or by custom; also often committed to a community.
   2. Work agreements are generally incumbent upon both worker and employer; in a few cases obligations rest on only one of the parties.
   3. Outstanding individuals can improve their position while either maintaining or severing their obligations to their employers or the communities to which they belong. Moreover, these obligations gradually become less stringent in their infringements on individual freedom as individuals rise on a moral and intellectual scale.
   4. All individuals enjoy at least a minimal level of well-being.
   5. A small portion of the land is cultivated.
III. System of long-term voluntary work agreements
   1. Workingmen are committed to a master (owner, proprietor, merchant, etc.) by their own choice, guided by custom or obligated by long-term contracts; occasionally committed to a community or corporation.
   2. The moral obligation or written stipulation which guarantees the permanence of the work agreement weighs equally on the employer and the worker.

3. A few individuals gifted with the quality of foresight rise to a higher social position, including that of owner, proprietor, and *rentier,* due to the beneficial influence of employers, communities, or associations.
4. Due to the same influences, individuals lacking foresight are able to enjoy a certain minimum of well-being.
5. A considerable portion of the land is given over to cultivation.

For Le Play, these dimensions were interconnected and formed a system, so that a change in one would always lead to change in others. These dimensions of social organization, which describe aspects of the relationship between the individual and the group, anticipate many of Durkheim's ideas.

Le Play's study of social trends stems from his comparative analysis of all four systems of social organization according to each of these dimensions. In a crude way, he was analyzing social change by offering rough quantitative measures. For example, Le Play evaluated the relative importance of "communities" in different social systems by estimating how often individuals belonged to them: in the nomadic system "workers are *always** organized in communities"; in the system of long-term compulsory work agreements, "workers are *often* committed to a community"; in the system of long-term voluntary work agreements, "working men are *occasionally* committed to a community"; and finally, in the system of short-term work agreements, "working men are *never* committed to a community." This gradual shrinking of the role of communities as a mode of social organization constitutes a clear trend.

A comparison of the importance of social mobility in the different social systems, based on an estimate of how many and what types of individuals change their social position, reveals another trend: in the nomadic system, "*no one ever* leaves the group"; in the system of long-term compulsory work agreements, "*outstanding individuals* can improve their positions"; in the

---

*The italics in the quotations in this paragraph and the next are mine.–Ed.

system of long-term voluntary work agreements, "*a few gifted individuals* with the quality of foresight rise to a higher position"; finally, in the system of short-term work agreements, "*many individuals* gifted with foresight easily rise to a higher social position." Again, the trend is clear: social mobility plays a more important role as individual freedom increases, because the worker who no longer depends on his community and his master can rely on his own initiative. Le Play's comparative analysis also reveals a trend toward greater social inequality: in the nomadic system, "*all* members of the community enjoy *about the same* level of well-being"; in the system of long-term compulsory work agreements, "*all* individuals enjoy at least *a minimal level* of well-being"; in the system of long-term voluntary work agreements, "due to the beneficial influences of employers, communities or corporations, individuals lacking foresight are able to enjoy *a certain minimum* standard of well-being"; finally, in the system of short-term work agreements, "individuals lacking foresight...*usually* succumb to a kind of moral and physical degradation unknown in the other three social systems." Le Play did not specify how he measured well-being, although he gave indicators of what he considered a "prosperous society."

Le Play analyzed some relationships between these trends. For one thing, inequality grows along with individual freedom. Second, inequality, due mainly to workers' lack of foresight, could be eased in the intermediate social systems through the action of institutions linking the worker to the employer and the community. In the system of short-term work agreements there are no such institutions left, and the children of workers who lack foresight will experience "hereditary pauperism,"[25] to use Le Play's words. Short-term work agreements weakened the ties that had bound workers to employers under long-term voluntary agreements:

> In industrial centers, master and worker have become strangers. They are only remotely bound by short-term contracts and remain free of all reciprocal obligations. The worker is no longer tied to the workshop which employs him, to the house in which he lives, or to the land where he was born.[26]

Le Play called these economically vulnerable and socially isolated workers the "new nomads." Constantly confronting slack periods and a "recurrent cycle of misery and debauchery," they could no longer provide a stable life for their families.[27] The employer's authority, which was no longer personal, turned arbitrary and alienated the workers. As industrialization destroyed the worker's traditional relationship with his family, region, and employer, it severed his economic life from his moral and social life. He became, in Marx's words, a commodity in the marketplace.

In order to cope with the dangers of this new situation, the worker began to look for new institutions to replace the ones which had once protected him. He might join "communities," which were organizations like producer-cooperatives, "in which the interested parties pooled their instruments of labor and shared a piece of real property, a commercial enterprise, or a consumer market."[28] Or he might join "voluntary associations, whose purpose was to protect workers from privations resulting from illness, unemployment, shortages, fire, and excessive competition."[29] Le Play paid special attention to those voluntary associations (including English land societies and mutual aid societies), which managed workers' savings and retirement funds.[30] Because such associations helped workers without endangering the economic structure, they were sponsored by liberals and conservatives alike. Le Play perceived the emergence of voluntary associations as a response to the breakdown of traditional forms of solidarity:

> The principle of association never received great development as long as work organization was based on the solidarity between master and worker. Today, mutual aid societies are still unknown in the regions of the North and East, where such solidarity was maintained. They took an immense development in the manufacturing regions of the West, where institutions, mores, and the very organization of industry push toward independence between master and worker.[31]

Le Play's analysis of the secular bases of social solidarity in early industrial society preceded Durkheim's analysis in *De la division du travail social* by some fifty years. Le Play stressed the superiority of the traditional, hierarchical relationships, which were based on the reciprocal duties of workers and employers, to the new ones, which linked social equals and promoted solidarity based on "professional pride or a spirit of hostility toward employers."[32] He approved of the attempts of professional associations and unions to cope with the problems of unemployment and economic insecurity, but he also believed that workers' antagonistic feelings toward their employers must not disrupt a union's efforts to reach wage agreements. He concluded that unions should be created under the sponsorship of the employers.

Once again, Le Play used some of the empirical data in the family budgets as the basis for his comparative analysis. The budget quantified worker-employer relationships by computing, among the worker's sources of income, the subsidies he received in the way of cash, food, dwellings, rights of usage, etc. It also computed the costs and benefits of joining voluntary associations. Using this information, he compared the costs and the advantages received by the worker through employer's contributions with those received through voluntary associations in the four systems of work agreements. He suggested that in short-term voluntary work agreements workers who joined associations were more likely to acquire security and save money.[33] Although he discussed these relationships in his family monographs, he failed to present systematic computations, thereby blurring the link between his data and his analysis.

Thus, Le Play's analysis of social trends shows that they can have bad effects. The system of long-term voluntary work agreements seemed to him to strike the best balance between individual freedom and stability. Le Play concluded that during his own time stability should be encouraged while the trend toward freedom should be slowed down, since most workers had not yet acquired the personal moral values which the system of full-blown independence demanded. "In the workshop and the family the solution to the social problems confronting us today consists in procuring for individuals not so much the satisfaction of independence as the rewards of solidarity."[34]

Le Play also analyzed the relationship between individual freedom and family structure in the four types of social organization.[35] In order to accommodate the growth of individual freedom in the different stages of development, the family had changed from a communal organization in the nomadic system to a patriarchal group in the system of long-term compulsory work agreements; the stem family had arisen in the system of long-term voluntary agreements, giving way finally to the modern nuclear ("unstable") family in the system of short-term work agreements. Le Play thought these changes in family structure had had positive effects on some families and negative effects on others:

> Families possessing the necessary intellectual and moral qualities for achieving social success are able to rise in the social hierarchy. On the other hand, families lacking these qualities may be crushed in their isolation by miseries and degradations unknown to less civilized peoples.[36]

Le Play did not see these negative consequences as inevitable; rather, he thought that they reflected the lack of a strong religious spirit and the existence of laws encouraging independence and isolation rather than cooperation and security. He believed that unsuccessful modern families succumbed because their family structure did not provide the protection for aging parents and the moral training for children that the stem family structure had. The solution, he thought, was to arrest the decline in paternal authority that had occurred under the system of short-term work agreements. He was convinced that a father's authority depended upon his right to bequeath his property as he wished.[37] Le Play thought that freedom of testation had a number of positive consequences: it promoted social stability, it allowed for a better distribution of talents in society by selecting the best-qualified child to manage the family property, and it encouraged intimacy between a father and his children.

> The head of the family, bound by no single law or custom, freely following his heart and his conscience, finds the solution in each case by drawing on his profound knowledge of his property, his profession, his clientele, and by studying the character of each of his children: he can divide his estate equally among the children if each is capable of putting his

share of the inheritance to good use; otherwise, he can keep the family wealth intact to everyone's advantage.[38]

Le Play believed that the integral transmission of property gave more leverage to the father over his children. It also was more likely to promote the value of thrift, to teach children the value of hard work, to strengthen family relationships, to develop attitudes of obedience and respect, and, above all, to teach children not to rely on their inheritance but rather on their own efforts and qualities. Le Play strengthened his argument by contrasting England and the United States, two prosperous and democratic nations which allowed freedom of testation, to France—a faltering, declining nation which mandated the equal division of property.[39]

Le Play's analysis of social trends has shortcomings: his typologies are made up of dimensions which overlap, some of them incorporate a variety of unrelated factors, and some are poorly specified. Nonetheless, this analysis is the first attempt to study social change empirically through the elaboration and systematic comparison of types of social organization and with the use of quantitative indicators of change. Perhaps the most striking feature of this part of Le Play's work is the total absence of polemical language. We find no references to the role of "The Decalogue, Authority, Religion, or Sovereignty"—ideas which are central to his later works. Le Play did not present himself in these works as a prophet of doom, preaching redemption through suffering; more than anything else, he resembled a social scientist engaged in research which might help policy-makers.

However, none of the proposals for reform that he offered in the first edition of *Les Ouvriers européens* ever brought the country's elites to make legislative or administrative changes or to implement his social policies. Le Play's failure to affect public policies, along with the increasing spirit of antagonism and violence which developed in France after 1848 and culminated in the Commune of 1871, may explain why his ideas changed as he grew older. His concern for individual freedom and his analysis of social trends gave way to a greater need to understand the conditions of social stability.

Le Play presented his later theories of social change in *La Constitution essentielle* (1881), *La Réforme sociale* (1884), and in the second edition of *Les Ouvriers européens* (1878–79). He distinguished cycles of prosperity and decline in human history in an effort to find ways to arrest what he saw as the drastic decline of French society.[40] These theories, like his earlier ones, reflect ambitious analytical schemes but, unlike the earlier ones, they do not rest on his family monographs. Le Play's ideas about cyclical change were clearly influenced by the eighteenth-century Italian philosopher Vico,[41] who believed that change is essentially cyclical but that each cycle is an improvement over the preceding one. Le Play adapted part of this idea in his analysis of societies: "Simplicity, complexity, corruption, finally reform or ruin—these constitute the cycle from which up to the present no civilized race has been able to escape."[42] Like Vico, Le Play saw social change not only as a product of physical forces or of divine will but as a force stemming from individual actions as a result of man's free will and his conscious attempt to direct his own destiny.

St. Augustine's doctrine of original sin also influenced Le Play's analysis of cyclical change.[43] According to Augustine, man must struggle constantly to overcome his evil tendencies. Le Play believed that these corrupting tendencies also afflict societies and that social prosperity inevitably leads to inequality, political corruption, and, finally, to decadence and suffering.[44] His account of society's redemption is similar to Augustine's account of the individual's redemption: society can save itself only by willing to reform itself, and it can reach this insight only through suffering.[45] Once reformed, society would then begin the same process over again, starting each time at a higher level. Le Play's vision of history as a process of learning through suffering seems to reflect the Christian idea of progress set forth in the medieval notion of "concursus," or cooperation of God and man in history. According to this interpretation, "history assumes the role of an educational process, with man as student and God as teacher."[46]

Le Play suggested two ways to study cycles of prosperity and decline. One way was to compare prosperous and suffering nations, the other was to compare historical periods of prosperity and suffering.[47] By studying simpler, more traditional societies, Le Play was able to arrive at a preliminary definition of social prosperity:

I call "prosperous" those societies where peace reigns without the need for armed force; where the stability of the home, the workplace, and the community is guaranteed in each family by the independent judgment of the father; finally, where the conservation of the traditional order, based on the moral law, is the common will of the people.[48]

By contrast, decadent societies, whose leaders must frequently resort to armed force to protect their power, are afflicted by instability and antagonisms in the family and the workshop, by the abandonment of traditional attitudes toward authority, by the weakening of the private sphere of life, by chronic official corruption, and the increased role of bureaucracies.[49]

Having defined "prosperity" and "decline" in empirical terms, Le Play could then look for the "signs"—what we call today indicators—of prosperity and decline in each nation's history.[50] In French history, for example, Henri IV, whose Edict of Nantes restored religious tolerance and revived national traditions, opened a new period of prosperity. The reign of Louis XIV brought on another decadent phase, characterized by increased centralization, bureaucratization, and corruption. This process culminated in the Revolution of 1789 and the propagation of the three false dogmas of the Revolution. It was during this revolutionary period that the government passed laws mandating equal division of inheritance and laws prohibiting any form of associations (Loi le Chapelier).[51] The years between 1815 and 1851 saw a number of attempts to promote reform and social peace; after 1851, however, centralization, war, and corruption resumed, finally bringing on the events of 1870, which many say Le Play predicted.

Le Play urged the nation's political and social elites to learn to identify the signs of prosperity and decline and to introduce appropriate reforms, which turned out to be the same reforms that he had proposed in earlier works—strengthening regional and local customs; protecting the private sphere of life; giving greater responsibility for social order to heads of households; weeding out corruption in the public sphere—except for a new emphasis on the Decalogue.[52]

In *La Constitution essentielle* (1881), Le Play spoke of an "essential social order," which was based on "The Decalogue, Authority, Religion, and Sovereignty."[53] He presented these four vague features—which he ascribed to all "simple and happy" societies—as indispensable conditions of social prosperity.[54] In this discussion, as in much of his later work, Le Play seems to have forgotten his earlier warnings against abstractions and unwarranted generalizations. Thus, we learn about the struggle between "good and evil," and we read the repeated warning that adherence to the Decalogue is the only way to bring about prosperity.

Along with these "constant" features of society, Le Play also analyzed its variable features. By offering a new set of stages of development that were spurred by technological innovations, he tried to study the impact of "variable" traits—climate, demographic pressures, and economic resources—on each society's effort to realize its moral ideals, which he saw as "constant."[55] By comparing the "age of pastures" with the "age of machines" and the "age of coal," Le Play wanted to study how

> the science of society, on the basis of observed facts, can teach us how families which grew into larger units were able, without endangering the happiness of the race, to increase the production of daily bread through the transformation of their social relations and work organization.[56]

Le Play described these three "ages of work" in some detail.[57] He thought that the "simple races," including nomadic and seminomadic tribes of hunter and shepherds, belonged to the "age of pastures," where natural products abounded, work tools were simple, and domestic farm animals were unheard of. Physical strength and skill played a crucial role in this age. His comparative study of several societies belonging to this stage of development revealed important moral differences which he traced to differences in climate, means of communication, and family structure. Equatorial and other hot climates seemed to "destroy respect for women," while the northern climate managed to "moderate sensual appetites." These differences in sexual mores, in turn, served to explain the stability of the family among hunters and nomads of the north and the absence of family structure in the hot regions. Efficient means of transportation like canoes and dogsleds allowed group members to remain together during travel and expeditions, while societies which lacked these means of transport had to abandon the old, sick, and weak members of the group. Among simple societies social change was not likely to occur because the spirit of tradition was overwhelming. When change did occur, it resulted either from population pressure on the land, forcing families to emigrate and start a new group, or from contact with Western nations, usually through "foreign wars."

The second age of work, the "age of machines," started with the invention of the plow and the harnessing of animals, two advances which greatly increased man's power over nature. This age, which Le Play found among seminomadic tribes, represented a state of "ideal happiness," characterized by an abundance of food, family stability, social equality, and economic self-sufficiency. As these groups grew, they fought with each other over resources. To control these outbreaks of violence, they needed a local government. The whole period was characterized by a spirit of innovation and by constant material and intellectual progress. It was during that time that manufacturing, commercial industries, and means of communication developed. This period also saw an increase in both inequality and mobility, which during the age of machines resulted from a natural process of selection, according to which the most intelligent received higher earnings and higher positions. The growth and complexity of society led to the creation of a church and a national government to help local leaders in their task. The church taught the moral law, while government kept the peace with the help of the police and army, and maintained justice with a legal system. Leaders represented the "aristocracy of talent and virtue, providing happiness to the majority of the population, which was poorly endowed or accidentally destitute."[58] Finally, the age of machines achieved a balance between the spirit of tradition and the spirit of innovation, because production and competition were limited.

According to Le Play, the third age of work, the "age of coal," came into being through a number of major inventions, including the steamboat, the railroad, and the electric telegraph. These inventions, which changed the very nature of society and "transformed man himself,"[59] were dangerous because they brought on "too sudden an increase in wealth, intelligence, and power."[60] Le Play deplored the railroad's destructive impact on traditional and rural ways of life, the destruction of local economies, and the erosion of traditional social bonds. These changes in turn undermined the authority of the father, who no longer could hope to control the upbringing and future of his children. The technological innovation brought about changes in the economic and social structures which took society by surprise, destroying the traditional fabric of society. Le Play's task was to protect workers from the consequences of such drastic changes by demonstrating, through comparative analysis, the types of institutions which could help create new sources of solidarity.

In this analysis of Le Play's theories of social change, I have tried to show the shifts that took place between the two editions of *Les Ouvriers européens*. These shifts present a set of puzzling contrasts. His ultimate goal in both his early and his late research was social reform; but while his early works emphasized the need to understand change before trying to direct it, his later works concentrated on reform at the expense of his scientific method. The first edition's analysis of social trends—and the sets of dimensions and types of societies upon which it is based—constitutes a crude but original attempt to analyze change quantitatively. Le Play's ideas in the second edition, on the other hand, are much closer to the macro-theories of change expounded by such contemporaries as Comte and Spencer. The moral purpose of his later comparisons of societies and his investigation of the causes of change interfered with his scientific purpose: the essential condition of social happiness in his scheme turned out to be obedience to the Decalogue.[61]

Le Play's early work, which was clearly more scientific than any other nineteenth-century sociological approach (including Spencer's), has influenced a number of modern demographers, social geographers, and sociologists who have tried to study societal change.[62] By contrast, the moral preoccupations of his later work, including his emphasis on the Decalogue and on the concepts of free will and original sin, led him to be classed as a pre-positivist thinker.[63]

9

LE PLAY'S FOLLOWERS

Le Play's belief that the findings in his monographs could settle ideological disputes plays an essential role in his vision of the science of society. After the publication of the 1855 edition of *Les Ouvriers européens,* he strove to realize this dream by harnessing his scientific method to a program of social reform. For this purpose he founded La Société d'étude pratique d'économie sociale (Society for the Practical Study of Social Economics) in 1856 and worked hard—and quite successfully—to attract members to this group (I will refer to it as the Society). On the one hand, the Society trained a corps of observers in the use of the monographic method.[1] Students' monographs were published by the Society in its publication, *Ouvriers de deux mondes* (Workers of Two Worlds) and discussed in weekly meetings in Le Play's apartment.[2] On the other hand, the Society wanted to interpret the monographs' results, propose reforms, and take action to implement them. After the upheavals of 1870, for example, they founded Unions de Paix Sociale (Unions of Social Peace) for the purpose of teaching local populations the "six conditions of social health," a program whose emphasis on labor peace, family stability, and the virtue of thrift clearly reflected the political views of liberal elites.[3]

During Le Play's lifetime, the conflicts between the two main priorities, social research and social reform, did not disrupt the functioning of his group. In the long run, however, these conflicts not only led to serious disagreements among Le Play's followers after his death but also compromised the monographic method and figured importantly in the eventual eclipse of Le Play's contribution.

Not surprisingly, the conflicts between the Society's competing interests led to a split shortly after Le Play's death. One group, headed by de Tourville and Demolins, dedicated themselves to studying and improving Le Play's method. They suspected that Le Play's commitment to reform had led him to draw premature conclusions, and they resolved to disassociate the method from ideological biases. The Society's journal, *La Réforme Sociale,* promoted the views of the more traditional faction, emphasizing reform, which represented the majority of the group. In 1886 they demanded Demolins's resignation as editor of *La Réforme Sociale.* De Tourville and Demolins created their own review, *La Science sociale d'après la méthode de Le Play* (The Science of Society Based on Le Play's Method).[4] The two groups evolved separately until 1926, when dwindling memberships and an erosion of their differences in orientation brought them together again. Only de Tourville's group made a significant attempt to improve Le Play's ideas and methods.[5]

Most of the members of *La Science sociale* came from either the landed gentry or the "haute bourgeoisie," and the donations of wealthy followers from these classes paid for the library and free courses which the group offered, and also for the field research which the group conducted. Their journal's thirty-seven contributors included eight businessmen, seven teachers, five clergymen, five "men of letters," three lawyers, and two doctors.[6] More than half of these men had attended either law school or the Ecole Libre des Sciences Politiques, which trained students for high administrative positions, and only two went to engineering schools.

The backgrounds of de Tourville and Demolins, the group's leaders, are fairly typical. De Tourville (1842–1903)[7] was called "l'abbé" by his disciples because he had studied theology at the Grand Seminaire and was an ordained priest. He came from an aristocratic, landowning family from Normandy. His father was a lawyer at one of the most prestigious French courts, la cour de cassation and a member of the Conseil d'état. In addition to his seminary studies, de Tourville studied law and went to the Ecole des Chartres, an institute which specialized in ancient history. When he met Le Play, he was curate of the church of St. Augustine in Paris. When the Society split in 1886, de Tourville retired from his duties as a priest in order to devote all of his time to improving Le Play's method. He became the intellectual and moral leader of *La Science sociale* and also gave it significant financial support.

De Tourville's colleague Demolins (1852–1907)[8] was born in Marseilles and grew up in a family which had owned land in Provence for a long time. His father was a doctor and the rest of his family engaged in business. He was expected to go into business, but instead he became a historian after receiving his secondary education in a Jesuit school. Like de Tourville, he went to the Ecole des Chartres, where he wrote several essays on social history. After cofounding *La Science sociale* with de Tourville, he directed it for the rest of his life. De Tourville and Demolins, who were considered the group's theoreticians, never conducted field research. Instead, they based their analyses on historical information, classical texts, and on regional monographs done by younger followers.

The backgrounds of members of *La Science sociale* reveal important reasons for the group's isolation from the mainstream of French academic life and for the near disappearance in France of Le Play's tradition, despite the well-developed organizational structure of Le Play's groups. First, his followers never established themselves in the nation's most prestigious universities. Several taught at state provincial universities and abroad, in private universities and business institutes, but none ever reached the Sorbonne and only two –Melin and Gérin– taught courses dealing directly with social science. Several taught only part-time, devoting most of their energy to their business careers.[9] Second, the businessmen in *La Science sociale* carried out Le Play's conception of an "applied" social science by trying to modernize France through private enterprise and initiative. This practical approach was scarcely designed to meet the requirements of a French academic career. Third, the extensive involvement of Le Play's followers in business and finance tended to commit them to the defense of vested interests, a posture incompatible with French academic tradition. Finally, the religious orientation of some members of *La Science sociale* led many to dismiss their approach as unscientific. Because of these features, Le Play's followers provide a sharp contrast to Durkheim's followers, who came to dominate French academic sociology.[10]

The main achievements of *La Science sociale* were de Tourville's creation of a new tool of investigation—the *nomenclature*[11]—and the development of a "particularist" theory of society. De Tourville and his followers believed they were upholding Le Play's most important methodological principles, particularly his emphasis on direct observation and the use of classificatory devices. But along with their general belief that Le Play's own a priori ideas had ruined some of his conclusions, they also criticized the monographic method on two specific points. First, they believed that Le Play's family budgets had overemphasized the economic aspects of family life at the expense of social, educational, and psychological factors. Consequently, they rejected Le Play's claim that his budgets provided an exhaustive account of family life. More important, they believed that family monographs, which did not allow for a systematic study of institutions outside the family, did not provide a basis for conclusions about society as a whole. To broaden the scope of Le Play's method, de Tourville resolved to study how all social groups are formed and maintained.[12] To systematize this research he developed his nomenclature, a complex classificatory scheme which enabled him to study every social group, from the smallest (the family) to the largest (the state). In rejecting family monographs as an adequate unit of analysis, de Tourville blithely discarded some of Le Play's most challenging contributions, including his typologies of workers and societies and his theories of social mobility. Consequently, *La Science sociale* made little effort to evaluate or elaborate Le Play's empirical findings.

Edmond Demolins described the nomenclature as "an extraordinarily accurate and convenient instrument of social dissection. It provides a kind of sieve which permits us to sift all elements of a social type and to classify them, according to their qualities, within a series of twenty-five divisions."[13] Sorokin saw the nomenclature as "a most innovative instrument of research, which combines all relevant factors which affect social life and organization and combines them in a logical, systematic, and causal way."[14] Within each of the twenty-five categories, de Tourville distinguished 365 subcategories. As table 6 shows, the first nine categories incorporate the contributions of Le Play's family monographs, but the other sixteen provide a more exhaustive classification of wider social groups. De Tourville believed he had created an instrument that, unlike Le Play's classifications in the family monograph, was more than a descriptive classificatory scheme and that the items of his nomenclature reflected a causal chain which began with geographical factors.

La Science sociale developed this theory further. In 1903 Demolins put the nomenclature to good use in his book *Comment la route crée le type social* (How the Route Creates Social Types), whose main thesis was that the migratory routes of the nomads of the Asian steppes had determined the development of new types of families and societies. His argument was a refinement of Le Play's rudimentary attempt to establish general connections between environment and his three "ages of work," although Demolins makes no reference to this part of Le Play's work. Demolins's study of the people of the steppes also borrowed Le Play's concepts of the patriarchal family and the communal society, as well as his conclusion that these structures inhibited individual initiative and social mobility. Le Play, however, had never made a systematic effort to weigh the relative importance of different environmental factors. Demolins, with the aid of the nomenclature, offered a series of clearly defined causal links:

> The steppes determine the pastoral art practiced by its inhabitants, which determines community of labor, which determines the patriarchal family, which determines the limited character of manufacturing and commerce, which determines the character of the arts, public worship, public authorities, and so on.[15]

Using the nomenclature to analyze the geographical environments that the Asian nomads encountered during their migrations, Demolins developed his account of particularist families and societies—two types of social organization which appear in

TABLE SIX
The Main Divisions of the Nomenclature

1. Means of existence		I.	Place of the family (geography and ecology)
		II.	Work of the family
		III.	Property of the family
		IV.	Movable property
		V.	Salary and wages
		VI.	Savings
2. Continuity of the race		VII.	Type of family
3. Material needs		VIII.	Standard of living and material existence of the family
		IX.	Phases of family existence
		X.	Patronage
		XI.	Commerce
4. Moral and intellectual needs		XII.	Intellectual culture
		XIII.	Religion
5. General social facts	a. Private sphere	XIV.	Neighborhood
		XV.	Corporations
		XVI.	County
	b. Public sphere (local	XVII.	Groups of counties
		XVIII.	The city
	national)	XIX.	Provincial divisions
		XX.	The provinces
		XXI.	The state
		XXII.	The expansion of the race
	c. Foreign relations	XXIII.	Foreign countries
6. History of the race		XXIV.	History of the race
7. Conclusion		XXV.	Rank of the race

Taken from P. Descamps, *La Sociologie expérimentale* (1933), p. 34.

none of Le Play's categories. He concentrated on one group that settled in the western part of Scandinavia. The character of the fjords and the scarcity of fertile land in the new environment forced them to fish for a living. Such nomadic fishing required small boats, which could not carry all the members of an extended patriarchal family. Consequently, these big groups were broken up into smaller units which consisted of couples and their young children. Later in the life cycle grown children had to leave the home and settle elsewhere because their parents rarely had enough land to share. This type of family is somewhat similar to Le Play's "unstable" family type, another nuclear family unit, with the difference, however, that the particularist family shaped a new type of man characterized by initiative, self-reliance, and independence.[16] These initial changes were followed by changes in the boundaries between "public" and "private" life caused by the erosion of the communal values which had dominated patriarchal societies. The private life of the family took on greater meaning, and work relations based on contracts replaced the old nonvoluntary work relationships. This, in turn, led to the election of leaders and to self-government, which are the key characteristics of the particularist society.

De Tourville went on to expand Demolins's analysis of patriarchal and particularist societies into a broad interpretation of history in his book *Les Origines des grands peuples actuels* (The Growth of Modern Nations) in 1892. According to de Tourville, Scandinavian societies spread their independent way of life through migrations to other parts of Europe—especially England, where particularist principles took deepest root. Much later, Englishmen established particularist societies in America, Australia, and New Zealand. De Tourville saw all of history as a struggle between particularist and patriarchal modes of organization. For example, he thought that Mediterranean societies became patriarchal after the Roman conquest of the peoples of Europe and he believed that particularist forces regained the upper hand with the advent of feudalism.

When Le Play's followers developed the particularist theory, they were not simply repeating his ideas, as they were in much of their other work. In fact, they replaced those of Le Play's ideas—the stem family, for example, and his concept of patronage—whose function seemed to them more prescriptive than descriptive.[17] Ironically, however, de Tourville's theory of history led to similarly crude ideological applications, including reform programs. For the members of *La Science sociale* the particularist society's economic achievements, made possible by private initiative and political liberties, clearly demonstrated that system's superiority to a patriarchy.

The theory implied that a modern society should strive to become particularist. Demolins spoke for the group when he argued that England's successful efforts to spread particularist principles to India, Burma, Egypt, and other nations clearly demonstrated "Anglo-Saxon superiority." Some societies, he believed, were particularist to begin with, but any society could become particularist if the right principles were put forth and taught to the children in school and in the family. Demolins was convinced that France could not hope to become a particularist society unless its schools applied British educational theories. In 1899 he created a school on the British model—L'Ecole des Roches—which became one of the main activities of *La Science sociale*. Thus, Le Play's scientific and ideological commitments, which had become entangled toward the end of his life, had run afoul of each other again in the work of *La Science sociale,* in spite of all the group's efforts to keep the two priorities separate.

After de Tourville's death in 1904, *La Science sociale* made another effort to get away from ideological questions, this time concentrating on a methodological critique of the nomenclature. Some questioned the existence of causal links between the items in the nomenclature's categories—particularly the concept of geographic determinism. Gérin devised a method based on what he called "analytical keys," whose purpose was to study social groups more closely than the nomenclature had done.[18] Others devised a "questionnaire for social investigation" in order to make the nomenclature a more precise technique for research,[19] and still others created new tools and proposed new guidelines for research.[20] Some of the studies undertaken during this period—particularly de Rousiers's monographs of industries in England and the United States[21] and the regional monographs of Butel and

Pinot—represent *La Science sociale*'s best field research.[22] However, no member emerged to provide the intellectual leadership which de Tourville had provided.

It is certainly true that Le Play's followers discarded and obscured his methodological and theoretical contributions. At the same time, we must keep in mind the criticism raised by Bureau, a member of *La Science sociale*, after de Tourville's death. Bureau questioned the validity of sociological theories whose proponents assumed that the "maintenance, perpetuation, and development of social harmony is a good and desirable thing."[23] He supported his contention that this assumption reflected the point of view of a specific social group, and pointed out how few contemporary scientists or philosophers accepted *La Science sociale*'s theories or methods. This assumption is no corruption of Le Play's vision perpetuated by his followers; it closely resembles one of the "axioms" in Le Play's own account of his science of society. The repeated failure of the followers to keep their reformist and ideological preoccupations in check reflects the special mixture of social activism and scientific method which Le Play had originally proposed.

Le Play's school exerted its strongest influence in Anglo-Saxon countries.[24] In England, Patrick Geddes (a Scottish biologist, 1854-1932), Victor Branford (the railway engineer, 1864-1930), and A. J. Herbertson (professor of geography at Oxford University) continued the tradition of regional surveys and used the Le Play formula of geographical determinism—"place-work-folk"—as an important focus in their research and planning. To promote regional surveys, they created the Sociological Society of London and the Le Play House in Westminster. Despite their close contacts with Demolins and their own conviction that they were Le Playists, there is little evidence that Geddes and Branford ever read Le Play's work. Furthermore, they seem to have been embarrassed by Le Play's polemical reputation. Consequently, they promoted the ideas of his followers and published several of their books, at the expense of Le Play's original work.[25] Le Play's influence on Charles Booth and on workers' budgets compiled by Britain's Department of Labour was acknowledged in 1893 at a meeting where Booth commented on Le

Play's monographic method and saw his family budgets as an important innovation.[26]

In America, the work of Le Play received somewhat more recognition due in part to de Rousiers's several trips to the United States. At the end of one of his stays he was asked to describe the activities of the group publishing *La Science sociale*. In 1894 the report was published by the American Academy of Political and Social Sciences, which was critical of Le Play's work.[27] Later, as I have mentioned, the sociologists Sorokin, Zimmerman, and Frampton tried to disseminate Le Play's ideas, emphasizing his contribution as a rural sociologist and a theorist of social change.[28] Le Play's influence in Canada was spread through the work of his disciple Leon Gérin, who has been described as the father of Canadian sociology. Finally, it should be noted that Le Play's ideas had a great impact in Spain, Turkey, and Portugal between the wars,[29] and were taught in Hungary by Alexander Szalai.

The impact of Le Playist ideas seems to have been greatest among nonsociologists. In France, social geographers such as Vidal de la Blache, Jean Brunhes, and Henri Mendras acknowledged Le Play's influence on their work;[30] and in England Patrick Geddes and Victor Branford—city planners—undertook several surveys using Le Play's ideas about "place-work-folk."[31] Economists have used Le Play's ideas on family budgets,[32] and some anthropologists—Conrad Arensberg, for example—have acknowledged their debt to the Le Playists' regional surveys and their particularist theory, but they rarely mention Le Play or his disciples.[33] The Le Playist influence seems to have been most fruitful in Philippe Ariès's studies on the history of French populations and his social history of family life.[34]

10

CONCLUSION

The analysis of Le Play's life and work enables us now to see more clearly the misperceptions which have obscured his contribution to sociology. Anyone whose works anticipate as many later developments as Le Play's do clearly belongs beside Saint-Simon and Auguste Comte as one of the founders of sociology. In this volume I have shown that Le Play initiated a number of later methodological developments such as scaling, index construction, the combined use of quantitative and qualitative indicators, typologies, categorization, deviant case analysis, budget analysis based on consumption patterns, and detailed guides for field research and comparative analysis.[1] Le Play used concepts that have become central to modern sociological thinking, including those of aspiration, mobility, socialization, social system, and social constraint. He also operationalized concepts such as authority, community, solidarity, and status. Le Play was the first to analyze empirically the relationships between mobility and family structure, to scrutinize the intersection between family and work, to point to the links between morality and economic success. Modern researchers, studying issues similar to those Le Play studied, have developed empirical generalizations and proposed middle-range theories about social happiness, consumption patterns, family life, social mobility, and social change which in many ways resemble Le Play's formulations. Le Play proposed a new research paradigm in which the researcher himself defined the issues to be studied and collected his own data. Finally, Le Play introduced the practice of team research and created the first private research bureau in France.

Introduction

In spite of all of Le Play's achievements, Comtean positivism soon eclipsed his particular brand of sociology. Later sociologists—particularly that most eminent product of the positivist tradition, Emile Durkheim—disdained Le Play's ideas. Despite this repudiation, there are important similarities between the ideas of the two men.[2] I will try to show how Le Play's ideas are connected to the mainstream of sociological thought by pointing out these similarities. The differences between Le Play and Durkheim also deserve attention because they indicate important discontinuities in the development of the social sciences. The discussion of Le Play's theory and methodology will throw light on why some sociological approaches and paradigms prosper while others are set aside.[3] The obstacles faced by Le Playists in diffusing their ideas and methods may help us further understand the development of sociology and the lack of institutionalization of applied social research in France.[4]

Le Play and Durkheim both believed that social facts should be analyzed in terms of observable characteristics, and the study of "morality" was at the center of their sociological concerns. Both men paid a great deal of attention to the role of the family in society. Both rejected utilitarian as well as idealistic conceptions of society but combined elements of those traditions in their analysis of society. Both proposed an institutional approach and both men believed that their research could be used to improve society. Finally, Le Play's *Les Ouvriers européens* and Durkheim's *De la division du travail social* proposed strikingly similar theories of social change.

Le Play and Durkheim explained the transition from traditional society to modern society as a result of changes in the bases of social solidarity. For both the key issue was understanding the changes in the social content of a society's collective beliefs and the changes in the social structure. Durkheim called these collective beliefs *la conscience collective,* believing that this *conscience* was strong in traditional societies and weak in modern ones. Le Play, as mentioned above, spoke of a "collective spirit" or "mentality" and distinguished between a "spirit of tradition" and a "spirit of innovation." For both, collective beliefs or ethos exist independently of the individuals making up society and control and regulate individual behavior through customs, mores, institutions, laws, and oral traditions.[5] Unlike other early sociologists who studied social change, they did not concentrate solely on the contrasts between traditional and modern societies. Le Play's analysis of social trends and Durkheim's analysis of changes in the bases of social solidarity emphasized continuities.[6] Le Play and Durkheim saw the same general pattern in the transition from traditional to modern society: changes in the moral content of collective beliefs, the decline of the collective conscience, the decrease of the power of the group over the individual, and the growth of what Durkheim called "moral individualism" or what Le Play called "individual morality."[7]

These striking similarities do not reduce the real differences between Le Play and Durkheim. For Durkheim, the shift from mechanical to organic solidarity was due to an increase in the division of labor which led societies to become more differentiated and individuals to become more dependent on each other. Le Play also emphasized the emergence in modern society of new links of solidarity to replace the old ones, but he believed that these links resulted not from an increased division of labor but from increased social mobility. He believed that social mobility—made possible by the acquisition of property—creates new duties toward those who rank below and those who rank above, duties which define the individual's social position. In modern society, social rights and obligations were no longer determined by customs, mores, laws, or any other form of external control, but by internal pressures. Therefore, Le Play argued, religion is becoming increasingly important in modern society with the disappearance of traditional forms of social control. According to Le Play, people who lacked religious faith had to acquire a sense of duty in other ways. Unlike Durkheim, Le Play saw the emergence of a new morality as the result of lessons learned through hard work and suffering, and through a long process of socialization in the home, the school, and the community.

Both Le Play and Durkheim emphasized the role of professional organizations and voluntary associations in the creation of new links of solidarity. However, while Durkheim stressed the role of the public sphere and perceived the state as an important intermediary between the individual and society, Le Play emphasized the private sphere, criticizing state intervention as a sign of imperfection or decadence. These divergent emphases reflect not only differences between two basic visions of society but also between the historical periods in which the two men wrote. Le Play envisioned a society made up of small and self-sufficient shopkeepers, businessmen, and farmers striving to achieve economic security and a sense of pride through property ownership, protected from bureaucratic interference and the fluctuations of the market.[8] Durkheim, on the other hand, saw modern society as a set of highly differentiated but interrelated institutions with strong organic links, supported by the action of the state and professional associations.[9] For Le Play, private life—especially family life—was becoming increasingly important, both for the socialization of the young and as a sanctuary from the encroachments of public bureaucracies and market forces.[10] Durkheim thought that the family should cooperate with the state to help promote organic solidarity.

Le Play's discussion of "free will" resembles eighteenth-century treatments of that concept and has led many to dismiss him as antiscientific or prepositivist.[11] For Le Play, "free will" referred to the individual's or society's capacity to choose between "good" and "evil." By "good," he meant a situation that satisfied the conditions for social happiness; an "evil" state of affairs was one that promoted social antagonisms and social crisis. The science of society, by demonstrating how social harmony could be attained, could help individuals and societies in this choice. Like Durkheim, he saw the science of society as a normative science. Unlike Durkheim, however, he stressed volition and the internalization of norms in the family and the workshop—what he called primary education and social training—in the fulfillment of societal needs which were defined as eminently moral and universal.[12]

Le Play's attempt to combine the study of voluntaristic action—that is, an analysis of social behavior in terms of goals and means—with the study of institutions made him a forerunner of such early American sociologists as Charles Horton Cooley and W. I. Thomas. These sociologists adopted an approach quite similar to Le Play's. Like him, they had a pragmatic outlook and rejected a priori, idealistic, or materialistic approaches. Like Le Play, they studied informal, face-to-face relationships, and concentrated on the relationship between individual behavior and the social structure, thereby bringing together micro- and macro-sociological concerns. Finally, they used empirical research to test ideas about the organization and functioning of society and paid particular attention to methodological issues, particularly the quality of empirical research. Janowitz's summary of their approach could apply equally well to Le Play:

> The theoretical empirical tasks of sociology which use the social control orientation have been and continue to be to identify and, whenever possible, to quantify, the magnitude of the variables which serve to facilitate or hinder the group's pursuit or attainment of "higher" collective and moral goals.[13]

Although Le Play did not mention social control, he used very similar concepts, particularly that of *contrainte sociale* (social constraint).

The sophistication of Le Play's analysis of the transition from traditional to modern society contrasts with the naiveté of his conclusions. Unlike Durkheim's analysis in *De la division du travail social*, Le Play's picture of the role of social mobility in promoting greater solidarity is not the result of general principles of social organization; instead, it represents a desired state of affairs. Unlike Durkheim, the great systematic analyst among early sociologists, Le Play failed to sustain a consistent level of analysis which accounted for both the family and society in a systematic way. Finally, unlike Durkheim, Le Play was convinced that the use of the monographic method could bring about needed social change on its own.

The similarities between Le Play and Durkheim are important in showing a continuity of concerns in French sociological tradition. However, the differences are just as important because they call attention to a kind of sociological analysis which has existed alongside the dominant French positivistic orientation but which has gone unrecognized, despite its striking similarities to later developments in the Anglo-Saxon tradition of applied and policy-oriented sociological research.

The comparison between Durkheim and Le Play also shows some of the historical roots of modern functionalism that can be found in Le Play's work. Le Play looked at society as a system of hierarchical layers linked together in a structure, although unlike Comte and Spencer, he never compared society to an organism. Le Play based his analysis of society on the following propositions: all societies have the same basic needs; all societies strive to achieve a state of social happiness—what functionalists would call a state of "equilibrium"; and such a state can only be achieved when society's two basic needs—the equivalent of functional prerequisites—have been fulfilled. Le Play evaluated social institutions according to how effectively they functioned to promote social happiness. When these institutions fail to fulfill society's two basic needs, a state of crisis and social antagonism ensues and such institutions tend to disappear; such a state of affairs, however, does not last. It stimulates mechanisms and institutions by which social harmony can be reinstated. Finally, the state of social harmony is not static but constantly adapts—like the functionalists' "moving equilibrium"—to the requirements of greater and greater personal freedom.[14]

Le Play's approach has these obvious similarities with modern functional analysis but it also differs from that analysis in important ways. As mentioned above, Le Play clearly defined the state of "equilibrium" in explicitly moral terms. Furthermore, his system is not entirely based on self-adjusting and self-balancing mechanisms. These mechanisms do figure in Le Play's theory of change, but they coexist with individual effort and purposive action to restore a state of social harmony. His state of equilibrium is the result of an ongoing struggle between the antisocial tendencies of individuals resulting from their evil nature and the regulatory forces of social institutions. Le Play acknowledged the existence of societal forces beyond individual action but seems to have played them down in order to give greater weight to the role of individual volition. His concern for social reform, meliorism, and social activism led him to emphasize the functions of institutions—instead of their dysfunctions—in order to demonstrate the ways in which social happiness can be achieved. He believed that the analysis of positive deviant cases would provide models for people to imitate. Finally, unlike modern functionalists, he believed that social change also resulted from such exogenous factors as new techniques and inventions, new systems of ideas, and new laws.

The similarities between Le Play's ideas and the main current of positivist thought makes his obscurity all the more puzzling. Evidently, even these strong links have been buried by a number of factors which have already been outlined. First, his detailed studies of the daily lives of families, and of social structures, had little appeal for most of his contemporaries, who preferred abstract and encompassing theories of society. Second, many commentators have misunderstood the specific social realities that Le Play faced and have therefore misunderstood some of his analyses. As mentioned above, many commentators have condemned Le Play's endorsement of the institution of patronage without realizing that patronage was a viable (if short-lived) set of economic and social arrangements which emerged to counteract the forces of the market economy. The purely negative connotations of "paternalism" as an ideology did not emerge until the end of the nineteenth century, when patronage as an institution was disappearing.[15] Similarly, Le Play's preoccupation with teaching leadership responsibilities to the new political and economic elites was no mere ideological obsession; rather, it reflected an important social reality. Until the revolution of 1848, French elites ignored the plight of the working classes. This neglect was particularly serious because the links between political and economic elites were stronger in France than in any other European country.[16] Le Play always stressed the success of England's traditional elites in adapting to the demands of an emerging social and economic system and in directing their nation's modernization. Their leadership, Le Play thought, could be presented as a model to the new elites coming from the ranks of the middle class. French traditional elites, according to Le Play, had failed to adapt to these changes and had abandoned or forgotten their traditional role so that the new elites had no model to imitate in defining their obligations to the working classes. Le Play's monographic method was not intended to serve merely as an instrument of ruling-class power but to compensate for the discontinuity between traditional and modern elites by teaching French leaders their new responsibilities.[17] Understanding these specific social realities will help us grasp Le Play's social purpose and the nature of his science of society.

A third reason for Le Play's obscurity is the failure of the Le Playist groups to sustain the vision of their charismatic leaders, Le Play and de Tourville. The latent anti-intellectualism of Le Play's followers, who were mostly businessmen and civil servants, guaranteed the exclusion of his ideas from the universities. In addition, his followers ignored many of Le Play's valuable contributions, developing instead a theory of geographic determinism that drew the scorn of Durkheim and his followers. Furthermore, academics believed the research of Le Play's followers was biased because it was privately funded, a practice which ran counter to the French tradition of state-sponsored research. Finally, the reactionary views of many of his followers, who sided with the anti-Dreyfusards and supported protofascist groups and Petain's Vichy government, have not helped Le Play's reputation. Maurice Barrès, a right-wing writer, and Charles Maurras, the founder of the ultrarightest organization L'Action Française, viewed Le Play as their intellectual ancestor. Outside France, reactionary and fascist regimes—notably Mussolini's and Salazar's—have adopted some of Le Play's ideas. Thus, Le Playists became an embarrassment to social scientists, who rejected the contribution of the school as a whole.

A fourth reason for Le Play's neglect, even more formidable than those already mentioned, stems from Le Play's own conception of the science of society. Although he saw important similarities between research procedures in the science of society and the natural sciences (especially metallurgy), he rejected the ideas of the Enlightenment, which form the basis of modern science, and believed that the social sciences were based on different sets of assumptions from those of the natural sciences. We can say that Le Play did not use the same paradigm that the scientific community of his time used.[18] Unlike Comte and Spencer, he did not believe that the goal of the science of society was to discover general laws of societal development, and he denied that the science of society furnished a synthesizing and holistic approach to the history of humanity. Furthermore, he never conceived of that science as an academic discipline cut off from the problems and challenges of everyday life. Because he believed that the science of society should be lived and experienced, he did not conceive of social scientists as professionals and experts.[19]

At a time when sociology was emerging as an intellectual discipline and stressing its autonomy from philosophy and political economy, Le Play spoke of a science immersed in all manifestations of social life and stressed social activism and commitment to social reform. He saw the science of society not as a source of new knowledge but as a tool to help persons assess their own positions in society and to learn their duties and obligations to those below and above them in the social hierarchy.[20] Unlike Comte, Le Play did not conceive of the sociologist as the high priest of a new religion of humanity. In Le Play's scheme, the true masters of social science are not sociologists but social authorities—that is, the moral and natural leaders of communities. True, Le Play also believed that he could serve as an expert consultant to political elites and that his findings should be used to introduce social reforms. Nevertheless, these goals were only secondary in importance to the goal of getting people to change their way of life by using the monographic method. Le Play's vision of a new society was based on the successful introduction of the following changes:

> The diffusion of habits of tolerance through free speech; the establishment of public bureaucracies based on the principle of responsibility; and the creation of a series of systematic social surveys to determine the boundaries between the public and the private spheres.[21]

Because Le Play shared some of the basic views of his positivist contemporaries and rejected others, his science of society seems to present a series of paradoxes. Like the positivists, he was deeply committed to using a rigorous scientific method to study society; however, he did not liken his science of society to one of the natural sciences, whose goal is simply to discover the truth. Instead, his first priority was to help achieve social happiness. Thus, his work is at once scientific and moralistic, theoretical and practical, objective and committed.[22] Le Play's approach and ideas are important because they show that, even in its incipient stages, sociology offered a genuine alternative to Comtean positivism.

FRÉDÉRIC LE PLAY
ON FAMILY, WORK, AND SOCIAL CHANGE

I. THE APPRENTICESHIP OF A SOCIAL SCIENTIST

1

DISCOVERING THE SCIENCE OF SOCIETY: FROM ENGINEERING TO SOCIAL SCIENCE

France has had ten governments since 1789. Each has been ushered in and subsequently overthrown by violence. This state of instability and suffering is unprecedented. Thousands of statesmen and writers have searched in vain for a remedy. I myself, although a stranger to politics and literature, was moved to find the secret of a government which would not begin and end in bloodshed.

In 1830 a serious wound left me suspended between life and death for eighteen months. This prolonged physical and mental torture wrought a transformation in my soul which an entire lifetime of happiness could not have produced. When I saw the blood spilt by the July revolution, I dedicated my life to the restoration of social harmony in my country. I have never forgotten that vow, and I offer the public the result of the studies I began in the plains of Saxony and the Harz Mountains exactly a quarter-century ago.

In order to discover the secret of a government which would allow men to enjoy happiness based on peace, I applied the same principles I had applied to the study of plants and minerals to the observation of human societies. I created a scientific approach; in other words, I formulated a method which permitted me to become personally acquainted with all the nuances of peace and discord, of prosperity and suffering, which exist in contemporary

From *Les Ouvriers européens* (Tours: Mame, 1879), vol. 1, pp. vii–viii, and vol. 3, pp. 147–52.

European societies. The object of the present volume is to describe and explain this method.

In July of 1830, at a time when revolutionary passions and socialist utopias were exploding on the scene in Paris, the author of this book—then a student in the School of Mines—had been bedridden for six months following a serious injury received in the chemistry laboratory. Several colleagues who were trying to distract me from my illness were filled with Saint-Simonian ideas. I was powerless in demonstrating through reasoning the danger and error of this fad and realized that in the science of societies, as in the other sciences of observation, only empirical evidence could establish the truth.

A study trip I had made the previous year with my colleague and friend Jean Reynaud had already allowed me to glimpse the true conditions of social order. I had traveled on foot through the part of Germany located between the Moselle, the North Sea, and the Baltic. In accordance with the program set up by my professors, I had concentrated my studies on the exploitation of the forests and mineral deposits of the Harz Mountains. The zeal I brought to this study won me the friendship of one of those social authorities who, at any time and any place, are able to preserve in the midst of social aberrations the traditions of truth. Mr. Alberts, general director of the Harz mines, was kind enough to complete the education of the Parisian student. He taught me that the technical operations of the mines, crushing-mills, foundries, and forests were only a small part of the industrial organization of the mountains he governed. Encouraged by my interest, he explained how the supervision of these operations was only a secondary aspect of the functions which had been entrusted to him by the government, and that his primary duty was to provide for the well-being of the population. In order for me to have a clear and concise appreciation of this fact, he advised me to visit private homes in the mountains and the plains, particularly in Luneberg.

The results of these observations were not at first completely fruitful; but their memory filled the long nights of insomnia and suffering which followed days filled with the talk of my colleagues' rash hopes. Feeling in my sickbed the additional blow of the passions and hatreds being unleashed in the streets, I sought a diversion from my own acute suffering and the nation's ills by recalling the charming memories of the scenes of social harmony I had observed in the Harz Mountains and in Luneberg. The contrast between the day's conversations and the night's memories was devastating; and in this state of mind, which was prolonged by another year of illness, I promised myself that if I ever regained my health, I would devote my life to clarifying the misconceptions which were exposing France to such harsh trials.

Finally cured in September of 1831, I began my new life by a trip to Brittany. By comparing my childhood memories with what I observed during my walks through the countryside, I began to realize that the well-being of yesterday's France had been based on moral habits which were similar in many ways to those of Hanover. In April of 1833, having recovered my health completely, I undertook a long journey through Spain, which was followed by a new study trip each year. At the same time that I was fulfilling my professional obligations as an engineer, I was observing, whenever the occasion presented itself, the social organization of working-class families, the relationships of workers with their employers, and the ideas and feelings of people in all parts of Europe.

Thanks to the evidence revealed by the facts, I was gradually able to shed the prejudices on which the prevailing ideas in France were based. The truth became clear to me through the advice of social authorities and the example of prosperous nations; my conclusions were based on extensive travel—I visited Great Britain seven times, Russia three times, and traveled to most of the other nations of the Continent as well. In the winter I taught metallurgy at the School of Mines in Paris, and during the six summer months, I traveled.

The revolution of February 24, 1848, broke out just when I was going to begin my seventeenth annual study trip. During those terrible days between February and June, two opposing trends emerged in the men who had taken charge of public affairs. Some, the authors of socialist systems, felt they could resolve the social question by forcing the state to intervene between workers and employers to regulate the conditions of work. Others, justifiably concerned over the passions unleashed by these innovations, sought a solution to the difficult situation created by the national workshops. On the invitation of my friend Jean Reynaud, undersecretary of state for public education, I had several conversations with my former professor, Mr. François Arago, who was not comfortable with the two rival schools whose preconceived ideas were competing in the Luxembourg Palace. Nevertheless, the facts that I observed proved—contrary to Mr. Louis Blanc—that among the peaceful peasants of Luneberg, the government does not have to intervene between employer and worker; and that the government can even dispense itself from interfering with the social organization of the community in any way. The monograph on the Harz established, moreover—contrary to Mr. Wolowski, the spokesman of the economists—that the rigid theory of "laissez faire" is in strict opposition to the traditional practices of Hanover's admirable policies; and that if peace reigns in the countryside of Luneberg in the total absence of governmental intervention, it is because all those involved, workers and employers alike, are custom-bound by reciprocal rights and duties. The facts further show that, if peace is based on state intervention in the Harz, it is only because the government there acts as a simple *patron,* in conformity with the traditions concomitant with ownership of the foundries and forests; and lastly, that if the government seems to favor certain local residents who have formed stock companies, by conceding the ownership of the mineral veins to them, it has also transmitted the duty of fulfilling the traditional obligations of the owner toward the mine workers.

The demonstration of the effectiveness of the method of observation was given in 1848, in front of the Luxembourg commissions, in the midst of the fears and hopes excited by the spirit of violence which was then weighing on Paris and which, shortly thereafter, brought about the terrible days of June. The time for methodical discussions had not yet come for the two rival schools, brought face to face in vain in the Luxembourg conferences; they understood that the question could not then be resolved by reason and would be decided by force. Of all the facts presented in the present monograph, each side accepted only those which seemed to support its own biases. In fact, without my knowledge, the chairman of the conference inserted a report of my speech on the social institutions of Hanover in the March 24, 1848, issue of the *Moniteur Universel;* and he mentioned only those facts which seemed to advocate state intervention in the mutual relationships of workers and employers.

Nevertheless, the first steps made in March, April, and May of 1849 to ease the anxiety of the government leaders were not completely without useful results. I was encouraged in my work by the fact that the monograph on the Harz workers had clearly convinced Mr. Arago of the effectiveness of the method of observation in the study of social facts. Mr. Arago conveyed this belief to several of his colleagues in the provisional government of 1848 and in the Academy of Sciences of Paris. Then, together with the academy, he urged me to coordinate all my studies in a work which would be published by the National Printing Office and approved by the academy. Starting in 1848, I began a new consideration of Europe, with the help of the friends whose names figure along with my own at the beginning of the monograph. I rechecked and completed the facts gathered since 1829. Lastly, I tirelessly perfected the original outline improvised in 1848 for the Harz miner; I used a process as painstaking as that used to gather the facts to achieve this goal, rewriting the manuscript of the monographs twenty times until, after three years of work, I was sure that the new facts fell into their natural place within the framework of the earlier edition.

2

SOCIAL ILLS AND THE SCIENCE OF SOCIETY

In a way, history is an everlasting and recurrent picture of the contradiction which reigns between man's aspirations and his most outstanding actions. In effect, societies constantly seek happiness; but even though they can only enjoy happiness in a state of peace, they always revert to a state of war, which is one of the greatest sources of suffering. In our times, this paradox results primarily from the errors which developed in the European mentality during the eighteenth century. One of these errors was the exaggerated predominance accorded to the spirit of innovation over the spirit of tradition. It is clear that contemporary innovations have often ameliorated our physical lives; but they have nearly always disorganized the moral basis of our lives. Thus people today suffer no less than their forefathers, who were guided by tradition.

Another error, linked to the preceding one, is the belief that a basic law of humanity, "the development of the human spirit," necessarily results in a gradual lessening of the intensity of suffering. In view of our contemporary struggles and catastrophes, these doctrines offer no assurances concerning the fate of Europe or the welfare of my own country. Modern history gives me no cause for optimism. I would even suspect that the wars which have been waged over the past four centuries under the pretext of protecting religious beliefs or other important social

From *Les Ouvriers européens* (Tours: Mame, 1879), vol. 1, pp. 3–11.

interests have wreaked just as much harm as the historic barbarian invasions which were motivated by a desire for plunder. What is more, there are widespread and permanent causes of discord at work today under our very eyes which were only localized and temporary phenomena in the past.

The evil which is shaking European societies to their very foundations today is only one aspect of that eternal threat to humanity—discord—but it is one of the most dangerous aspects. This evil differs from anything known in the past, in both its sources and its proportions; thus history may rightly call it "the scourge of the nineteenth century." For, in the past, periods of crisis and bloodshed were separated by periods of true peace. The elements of social harmony were strongly established in private life. Self-interest, ennobled by a sense of duty, led every individual to respect others: children obeyed the father in the house; workers obeyed the master in the workshop; and in every locality, fathers and masters respectfully obeyed the "social authority" which judiciously maintained the link between emotional ties and vested interests....

The present state of suffering began half a century ago. It continues to worsen in the manufacturing regions; and private life has become characterized by internecine strife. The societies which are setting this pattern for all of Europe are rapidly marching toward ruin. The dangers they are courting are pointed out in this study, as they are in the Holy Scriptures. Luckily, these societies are not yet at the brink; they have a few years of respite before then. They are succeeding in stamping out the disturbances which are the forerunners of catastrophe; and to this end they are extending the repressive action of the "public powers" to the most remote areas. Nevertheless, neither the courts nor the police nor armed force will be able to quell this social antagonism; indeed, by falling back on these powers, the government simply emphasizes the presence of the existing dangers. The role of public power is reduced to peacefully organizing the manifestations of the ills which afflict us. But distressing struggles are hidden beneath a facade of harmony. At home and at work, discord can be seen in the silent allegiance of employees with their masters' enemies or competitors, in the habits of infidelity which corrupt the character of the workers, and especially in the instability of the reciprocal work agreements which form the very foundation of the system of work and domestic life. At first glance, the ripples caused by these minor conflicts seem less serious than the violent upheaval of civil strife; but those small conflicts actually trouble the happiness of working-class families more deeply because of their unremitting influence on daily life. These personal sufferings become a constant preoccupation of the parties involved; and the energies which are applied to private and national interests in prosperous nations are thus paralyzed to a surprising degree. If these sufferings are studied in detail according to the method set forth in this work, their pernicious character can be seen immediately. It is astonishing to learn that a special vocabulary to express these details of the daily life in the workshops and in the home is being developed today and is used openly—although we see no trace of it in times of social harmony. Moreover, it would be inexcusable for the rich and for those in power in Western societies to abandon themselves any longer to the illusions fostered by a deceptive calm. The events of 1830, 1848, and 1871 have shown that all of their social structures already have difficulty resisting the force of outside pressures. Everything indicates that these fearful warnings will be repeated more and more frequently if the work of rebuilding does not begin soon....

It becomes more and more clear to me that the principal obstacles to curing these social ills are the false diagnoses of the necessary cure which have been conceived by two groups of concerned men: traditionalists and innovators.

Traditionalists are often narrow-minded and act without caution. They are thus unaware of how much the political instability since 1789 has shaken them and, because of this, they occasionally fall into error. They are no longer truly familiar with the old customs that assured social harmony in the great ages of prosperity; and they remain attached to the past more on principle than as a result of a reasoned conviction. They have neglected the study of those prosperous ages. First of all, such study would enlighten them; second, it would counteract the prejudices which are perpetuated by the unpleasant memories of the decadence of the Old Regime. Finally, the traditionalists have not sufficiently studied the great empires which have achieved the dominant positions formerly held by Spain and France which at the same time have preserved the traditional European institutions. They do not even try to show us how today's prospering countries reconcile submission to the old principles with acceptance of the useful changes which have occurred in the last hundred years with regard to the land, living conditions, organization of work, and the means of existence. In short, traditionalists are confident of the excellence of their principles, and they voice only sterile reaffirmations of them in the daily political debates. They advise a foundering nation to return to eternal truths through its own efforts, even though it is beseiged by a great number of talented and creative men.

The innovators are often at the head of this struggle. They are no less adamant nor more open-minded than their rivals. When they are not completely mistaken, they are still farther from the truth than the traditionalists, but their propaganda is more skillful and ardent. The innovators who have been influential for more than a century are not only incapable of preserving the truths necessary for social harmony; they actually distort ideas, customs, and institutions by exalting the precepts of the Social Contract and the triple credo of the Revolution. As the foundations of private life crumble and the old ways fade in the home, workshops, and entire regions, the innovators meet less resistance and become more ambitious. The useful changes which occur every day in our physical life thanks to a rapid succession of ingenious inventions have made a deep impression on them and they are carried away by a false analogy. They become persuaded that similar transformations must occur on a moral level in certain immutable elements of human nature. They might as well claim that a change in the style of clothing implies a modification in the form or operation of the stomach. It is true that the French surpass other Europeans in the movement called "progress," which stems in part from the disastrous influence of fashion; but at the same time, the French are corrupting the others by their example, and are teaching errors which are a prelude to national ruin. Every day the innovators tell us that man's genius will not be limited to the creation of the physical sciences, which so easily multiply the number of families living in any given place by increasing the means of existence tenfold. Human genius will be even more successful with regard to the other elements contributing to social happiness. Everyone should therefore contribute to the invention of "social science," which would allow man to achieve every kind of good in this life—including peace and stability. It is no longer possible to restrain people who are bent on this line of reasoning; they are likely to dare anything. It would be useless to try to counteract this dangerous inclination by appealing to the works of the sages, contemporary facts, or universal experience: these people will not read, see, or listen. They reject these arguments because they are nearly all blinded by preconceived ideas. They are all more or less motivated by scorn, hatred, and distrust; for they conceive of their opponents, the traditionalists, as men of routine mentality whose motives and intentions are devious and perfidious. The innovators who move from theory to action are not discouraged by the persistent failure of their efforts. On the contrary, each new failure feeds their taste for violence and makes them even more hostile to the ideas adopted by prosperous nations. Thus the indolence of the traditionalists and the zeal of the innovators spread the reign of suffering in Western societies every day.

Like the sincere innovators, I was saddened by the spectacle of this suffering and I wished to cure it; but once in action, my path immediately diverged from theirs. As I undertook my long journey, I used the information I had gathered from the beginning as my daily guide. Thus I was able to draw near to my goal, while my critics were waylaid by preconceived ideas. In the works which make up the Library of Social Science, I set forth the preventive practices and remedies offered to France by her remaining national traditions and by the customs of the prospering peoples whom I observed. Nonetheless, I have been careful to indicate to the reader where he can verify these remedies, or find them himself in the same sources into which I delved.

In all honesty, I cannot hope that many men in a country divided by discord and ravaged by eleven revolutions will be immediately disposed to accept evidence based on facts which are contrary to their political or religious beliefs. Nevertheless, I have confidence in the scientific method that bases true science on the observation of social facts....

II. THE NATURE AND SCOPE OF THE SCIENCE OF SOCIETY

3

THE USE OF DIRECT OBSERVATION

The reforms necessitated by the present condition of the workers must be based on a knowledge of the facts which concern them.

All pressing social needs prompt crowds of men to action. For many years, and particularly in our own times, a multitude of general systems have been formulated whose object is the betterment of the lot of the suffering classes and the reorganization of society. One does not need to enter into an examination of these systems to see that none of them has sufficiently withstood the test of experience. The men directly involved in government and those whose great authority in some way directs public opinion agree that, notwithstanding the diversity of their political and administrative leanings, the general theories which have been expounded thus far are incompatible with the facts and could not be usefully applied. It is true that the writers whose self-interest lies in spreading these theories sometimes explain their lack of success by the egotism of the governing classes of society. But a closer observation of Europe belies this accusation: there is no government with the desire, much less the power, to reject an improvement called for by public opinion. On the contrary, what the statesmen charged with initiating reforms lack is the support of the kind of unanimous opinion which is a sure indication of the direction society should take. Today, as in the past, ignorance

From *Les Ouvriers européens* (Paris: Imprimerie Impériale, 1855), pp. 10–11.

and prejudice are the principal obstacles to progress. But in our times more than ever before, humanity, obeying an irresistible need for improvements, is ready to accept any truth which carries the seal of evidence.

But if Western societies have been unable to rely on general theories to remedy the disorders which have developed in their midst, they have not remained inactive. Partial reforms of proven efficacy are being adopted every day, and it is important to point out that the most successful and generally approved attempts at social reform are the ones based on the actual practice of other societies. Reforms which have already been successful thus seem to determine the nature of those that we can look for in the future. It is probable that social reforms will continue to be made by means of a series of specific solutions indicated by experience, and that they will not be devised by a single thinker. In order to realize this goal, it is imperative to enter more deeply and more methodically into the practice of observation. Social science will thus follow the same progressive stages of development as astronomy, physics, chemistry, natural history, and, in general, all knowledge based on the observation of facts.

During the early history of these sciences, however, description and classification were only of secondary importance: they were, moreover, subordinated to ideas conceived a priori and to theories based on a striking but incomplete observation. But in their more recent history, as fertile as the other was sterile, totally different methods have been followed. As far as the limitations of the human mind allowed, the yoke of preconceived notions was gradually thrown off; close scrutiny was taken as the fundamental process in the evaluation of facts, and these facts were not considered sufficiently known until their exact weight, measure, or description could be specified; only then could a theory be presented. Under the influence of this method, our most valuable forces, those which seek after the truth, are no longer exhausted in endless speculation. Scientific controversies in the future will be brought into check by observations of the same facts, and the dispute will be resolved by the strength of the evidence.

Social science, on the contrary, has remained in the state of weakness that characterized the early stages of the natural sciences; it is made up for the most part of theories and countertheories proposed by mutually antagonistic authors. It can truly be said that the most ardent enemies of this science are its own proponents. The debates concerning the organization of labor, property, and exchange are nearly as thorny as those in recent centuries which dealt with the transmutation of metals, the universal panacea, phlogiston, etc.; like those classic controversies, these modern details will be settled once and for all by the influence of the experimental method.

Even though the principles which should guide the development of social science and the physical sciences are similar, this similarity in no way mitigates against the profound differences which must be maintained in the evaluation of essentially different kinds of phenomena. Neither must this similarity mislead us in the selection of a method for the observation of social phenomena. By their very nature, these phenomena are more readily available to the observer than those which, in detail or in general, pertain to the physical world. Sufficient knowledge of them can be acquired without recourse to methods of extreme precision such as, for example, those which apply to the study of physics, chemistry, and astronomy. It is true that some special difficulties are created when observers draw inferences of a moral nature from social facts, but this obstacle can be more easily overcome than many others over which the human spirit has triumphed in other realms of inquiry.

In order to preclude all controversy over the standards of morality and justice used in the evaluation of the facts, it is proper to set aside secondary considerations in favor of the basic principles adopted by civilized nations. Thus, insofar as the structure of industry and the direction which must be given to the governing of the laboring classes are concerned, we will not allow ourselves to resolve these issues according to preconceived ideas touching on the freedom of transactions, the setting of salaries, the intervention of the state, the organization of workers, or any other principle of social organization; but we will not hesitate to state that, of two social systems set up in analogous conditions, the one to be preferred is the one which best guarantees the morality and well-being of workers' families, as well as the mutual liking of workers and masters. In order to eliminate all vagueness from these evaluations, we will take as a measure of morality and well-being selected facts whose importance are universally recognized. We shall affirm, for example, that the conditions of family life are good when the head of the family is moderate in his tastes, just and affectionate toward his dependents, and when he finds an assured means of subsistence in regular work; when the woman of the house, faithful to her duties as wife and mother, sees that order and cleanliness prevail in both the household and clothing; when the children respect their parents; and when, finally, all bestow on the aged, the infirm, and the ill, the respect, affection, and care which they deserve. Any new system of organization which would compromise the security of the family, or which would tend to weaken these established virtues, would be considered defective, even though it might otherwise conform to the general tendencies of Western civilization.

These are the principles followed in the present work in ascertaining the living conditions of European workers; this is the moral standard according to which the facts were evaluated. We must now indicate what considerations determined the choice of the direct methods of observation.

STATISTICS VERSUS DIRECT OBSERVATION

The most successful methods of investigation used thus far in both governmental and private studies of social questions can be divided into two main categories. A discussion of their differences will be useful at this point.

The first method of investigation is statistical. Until recently, it has been based primarily on numerical documents provided by the public authorities in such areas as the financial and judicial systems, national defense, and so on. This method is used most widely in countries with a highly centralized administration. With the help of its agents, the governments of these states perform functions which are carried out by private individuals in other countries. Even when it does not intervene directly, the central government supervises the main branches of national activity. The findings gathered by the government are genuine observations whose official origins lend them particular authority. When these results can be expressed in numbers, the job of coordinating them falls to the statisticians. Using these figures, they have devised fairly precise methods of comparing the relative powers of various nations.

Nevertheless, these comparisons are not always as accurate or extensive as could be desired. Statisticians do not make firsthand observations, and they must rely on observations which were not scientifically made. Their comparisons cannot deal with the most

From *Les Ouvriers européens* (Paris: Imprimerie Impériale, 1855), pp. 11–12.

essential aspects of social activity, for these areas always lie in the private realm, even in those nations where governmental activity is the most extensive. The attempt to fill these gaps by appealing to the good will of the individuals or companies involved has usually been in vain, along with attempts to demand that the agents of public authority directly collect the information which the routine exercise of their official functions does not collect. These studies have rarely led to reliable results, either because the agents employed lacked good will or aptitude or because they did not have the necessary authority to overcome the difficulties occasioned by the studies.

The statisticians have been even less successful in studying the more private aspects of human behavior, analyzing social conditions, comparing moral and intellectual qualities, and, in general, in evaluating those elements essential to understanding the situation of the laboring classes. The reasons for this failure are obvious. Nationwide official findings concentrate on the facts which most interest the government and gloss over all other considerations. They cannot take into account either the special nature of individuals or the kind of environment in which they live. The official findings thus neglect the very facts that should be considered in a scientific evaluation of the lives of individuals or of social groups. Suppose, for example, we measure criminal offenses in two countries of equal size by comparing court records from those nations, and use this data to study the relative morality of the respective populations. Our conclusions would be quite unreliable. Evaluations of this kind, based on a simple comparison of figures, inevitably lead to errors. The extent of this error becomes clear through direct observation. This method would reveal the differences between the institutions and customs of the two countries in such areas as the effectiveness of methods of repression, the corruptness of judges, the influx of criminal elements from abroad, etc.

Of course, ingenious scholars working with statistical data have sometimes overcome the difficulties inherent in insufficient or imprecise official reports. They have supplemented conclusions based on simple numerical comparisons with moral evaluations or distinctions based on specific observations. However, this combination of methods is not as rigorous as the pure method. Whoever uses this technique must possess a rare combination of qualities: impeccable judgment, complete impartiality, and a thorough knowledge of the subject. When these qualities are lacking, the use of combined methods can lead to very unreliable conclusions. As has often been correctly noted, arranging numbers is an art which can be used to prove anything.

In summary, the statistical method does not involve direct observation of the facts; it is a more or less plausible compilation and interpretation of facts gathered from various—and for the most part unscientific—sources. Although they seem universally applicable and seductively consistent, statistical documents have made only a minor contribution to the progress of social science. Statesmen have occasionally found statistics useful to justify their positions, but people with experience in government rarely use them as a basis for their programs or decision-making.

A second method of investigation is widely used. It differs from the statistical method on several essential points. No general framework is set up to encompass all social questions. Instead, each question is defined as narrowly as possible and is studied separately. This allows a more thorough treatment and produces more practical and useful conclusions. Instead of considering the entire country in terms of each question, one studies in detail particular cases or special areas. Observation is no longer carried out by a great number of agents, each performing a certain task or methodically verifying a single fact. Instead, a few specialists who are well acquainted with the subject make the observations. These men never divorce the actual facts from the moral considerations that make them important. With this system, knowledge of the facts no longer depends on more or less secondhand inductions. The facts are verified directly at the source of the observations. Every day, large commercial and industrial operations use this direct method with great success; it has been even more successful in the governing of some nations. In England, for example, when the need arises to change either the general administration of the country, private interests, or the condition of certain social classes, the Parliament orders an investigation to determine the actual conditions and the probable outcome of the proposed change. The government chooses a small number of persons qualified by their previous experience to conduct these investigations. They are granted extensive powers which enable them to carry out their mission: they have the right to call any subject of Great Britain to testify before them if they believe that person can provide useful information; they question witnesses under oath; they can fine witnesses for refusing to testify or for obviously concealing the truth. Among these valuable investigations are the ones which since 1830 have dealt with municipal corporations and particularly with workers employed in agriculture, mining, and industry. The results of these investigations have brought about a change in the most deep-rooted economic opinions. The memorable reforms which they provoked inaugurated a new era in England and probably saved that country from the disturbances which have struck many Western nations since then. This period of parliamentary commissions in Great Britain has focused attention on the practical use that social science can make of the method of direct observation. Moreover, the parliamentary investigations are not rigidly structured. Experience has shown that it is useful to allow great freedom to both the persons who direct these investigations and those who analyze the results. The advantages offered by the flexible structure of the investigations have often been demonstrated. Occasionally a respondent's spontaneous and unexpected statement has given an entirely new direction to the research and exercised a major influence on the overall shape of the proposed reforms. It would be desirable, however, if the English investigations had been conducted with more rigor, while maintaining all their flexibility. The studies would be just as useful with this improvement, and what is more, they would often produce more valuable results for social science.

5

THE COMPARATIVE STUDY OF EUROPEAN WORKERS

During the course of the studies which led to the present work, it became clear that the method of direct observation was extremely useful. The original materials were collected before it was realized that they might be published independently. Nevertheless, a comparison of some partial findings gathered under this system indicated that far-reaching conclusions could be derived from more extensive studies. This development became especially intriguing after the discovery of the many differences between the metalworkers of France and Germany and the workers observed in factories of Northern and Eastern Europe.

In spite of its small area, the manufacturing zone of Western Europe wields a considerable influence over the rest of the world. The Western worker's time is usually devoted to a single kind of work: his family's existence depends nearly exclusively on his wages, i.e., remuneration proportional to the labor accomplished by the worker. With few exceptions, occupation, income, and expenditures are constant all year round. A family's existence can therefore often be summarized by its weekly budget. This is not the case in the rest of Europe, or even in the agricultural areas interspersed in the manufacturing districts. In addition to their wages, workers in those areas commonly receive a great number of commodities, foodstuffs, and services. Included in these services are usufructs on land property and the right to use property

From *Les Ouvriers européens* (Paris: Imprimerie Impériale, 1855), p. 12.

adjacent to their dwellings. The allocation of these goods and services varies according to the region, climate, local occupation, and social status. Unlike wages, these goods do not simply reimburse the worker in proportion to the work accomplished. Rather, they tend to assure him of a means of existence proportional to the needs of his family in any eventuality. These methods of payment cause extreme variations in family income and expenditures. Moreover, they allow each member of the family to engage in numerous odd jobs whose profits, added to the principal income, help to complicate the budget even further. Indeed, there are few families who do not supplement the income of the head of the family by engaging in local occupations which range from raising domestic animals, weaving cloth in the home, hunting, fishing, picking wild fruits and plants, and gathering wood, to investing in family businesses or in various commercial enterprises or transportation systems.

In addition, custom and social institutions often combine to guarantee the workers' possession of the working tools used in both their principal occupation and their odd jobs. Thus the workers supplement the various resources which have just been mentioned with revenue resembling the revenue the upper classes of society receive from their capital or real estate. The European worker today is therefore far from a simple wage earner; he nearly always acts as a landowner or proprietor as well. The complex nature of European workers results in great variety in their lives. This variety has been all but overlooked in the few sketchy observations which have been made in the manufacturing regions of the West.

Moreover, this complexity and variety are not immediately apparent to the observer. In order to distinguish the nuances described in the monographs which make up this work, it was necessary to come into close contact with the populations to be studied. Staying with the families in their homes was essential to the accuracy of these descriptions. Over an extended period the author gradually became familiar with all the facets of the families' lives: their language, habits, needs, and feelings; their passions and their prejudices. He guarded against inaccurate or biased responses; he took pains to overcome the hesitation or suspicions of people who did not initially understand the goal or significance of the investigations. He was not satisfied with merely checking the findings against one another but pursued the study of each type until the findings were as accurate as possible.

Curiosity and scientific interest are not the only reasons for conducting a comparative study of the condition of European workers. These studies will furnish statesmen with a solid basis for resolving the social questions discussed at the beginning of this introduction. They will be of special help in accomplishing the reforms which are necessary to improve the living conditions of several categories of Western workers. It is hoped that the facts revealed in this study will work toward this end. However, only a few pertinent considerations can be included within the limits of this introduction.

In many respects, the present living conditions of laborers in Northern, Eastern, and Central Europe are comparable to those of laborers of regions of Europe in the not-so-distant past. A general study of Europe is therefore useful even to those persons who are only interested in the East, since an understanding of tradition is often indispensable to an accurate evaluation of the present. Such investigations can be especially useful in France, where social and political revolutions have sharply modified old ways of thinking. The most popular authors today are committed to the new social order. In a reaction against the abuses of the old economic system, they have naturally tended to overlook the advantages which it offered. But these abuses are gone forever, and it seems that the time has come to take a less jaundiced look at the past. In order to gain insight, readers need not wait for a talented historian to recreate the spirit of the past for them. In many cases we have only to observe the facts which are still before our eyes. In fact, many of the old economic institutions have been preserved here and there on our very own territory.

The dominant institutions of northern and eastern countries still retain a social organization analogous to these old forms. These too can provide us with valuable information. Thus, through direct observation we can get a clear idea of facts which have been distorted by prejudice or ignorance.

If we want to recapture the mentality of the past and thereby gain a comprehensive understanding of the present situation of the working classes in the West, the best way to proceed is to study conditions in the countries where the agricultural and industrial techniques, the organization of labor, and the mutual relations of the various social classes remain like those which existed in France in past centuries. A summary of such observations is offered in the first fourteen monographs of the Atlas,* dealing with Russia, the Scandinavian countries, Turkey, Hungary, and the other countries of Central Europe. These studies offer some very useful preliminary findings. They show that although the old institutions were less favorable to the growth of industry and the rapid advancement of gifted individuals than the institutions recently established in the West, they did offer security to all social classes. A lack of security is keenly felt today, especially among lower-class persons and the improvident classes. A methodical comparison of these two social systems—one designed for stability and the other for progress—will provide a wealth of information; the lessons of experience will teach us how to reconcile these two equally compelling social needs.

The present work consists of descriptions of thirty-six types of workers. These descriptions were chosen from hundreds of observations made on numerous field trips. The selection was guided by the considerations mentioned above. It is hoped that the study of these monographs will help answer the general questions which arise in the attempt to better the lot of the working classes. Most important, it is hoped that this study will serve to illustrate the method of observation which must be followed if we are to become better informed on all social questions. Rather than proceed by one of those general theories which have been so abused in the social sciences, the author has laid out the facts, and the reader is left to draw his own conclusions.

*The Atlas was a section of the first edition of *European Workers* (1855)–Ed.

6

THE SUBJECT MATTER OF THE SCIENCE OF SOCIETY

We have transcended partisan hatreds, and we can ask true social science for solutions which politics alone cannot give us. We study the institutions of the past not to restore their abuses but to find in them the unfettered aspirations of our national genius and thus to comprehend the trends of the future. The patterns of our secular traditions are still apparent in our countryside and in our thoughts; we seek in these traditions the bases of a new order which our fathers vainly tried to establish on pure abstractions. We are friends of progress but fear disorder and sterile agitation. We call to the field of experience, sown with the seed of study and discussion, all men who want to make our country free, great, and prosperous....

Despite our differences of opinion, we are all truly convinced that only the observation of the facts can restore harmony to a nation divided by social antagonism, as France is today.

Each monograph is a collection of questions answered by observation. It is a living picture of a family, in which we see in action the principles leading toward progress or decadence. The more our work advances, the more we recognize that this kind of study is superior to those whose sole basis is a search for natural rights and justice. Such studies rely too absolutely on their guiding principle, their conclusions are construed too rigidly, they are too easily blinded by the arrogance of pure reason, and too quick

From *Instruction sur la méthode d'observation* (Paris: Société des études pratiques d'économie social, 1862), pp. 5–12.

to pose the problems and solve them. They usually produce a fruitless confrontation of conflicting opinions. The method of the Society of Social Economics leads to more reliable results. It takes into account the social situation and era, relies on experience, and tries to establish a clear picture of the results before searching for causes. It guards more effectively against the seduction of preconceived opinions. Moreover, when natural rights and justice are really predominant factors in certain social interests, our method will always make this fact clear. Those great principles would in no way be diminished if they were accepted as the end product of the experience of the human race. By stating the lessons of this experience, we will distinguish good principles from bad ones by examining their own consequences. We will point out those principles which are sanctioned by time and those which hinder the progress of mores and ideas. Finally, we will assuage the hatred born from the strength of beliefs without falling into indifference or skepticism.

In short, our doubts and debates have usually centered around five groups of questions:

1. What influence should religion have in social reform?

2. On what principles should the organization of the family be based? How can paternal authority be reconciled with the aspirations toward liberty which form one of the principal characteristics of modern civilization? Is a high birthrate in marriages desirable or dangerous? And is a low birthrate a source of prosperity and well-being?

3. Are the benefits of property better assured by a system of obligatory division of inheritances than by a system of free testamentary distribution? Should large- or small-scale farming be encouraged? Can the advantages of both systems be combined?

4. Can the present organization of industry be reconciled with moral progress? What emphasis should be given in the future to large and small industries, to private and collective interests?

5. Can a great nation maintain its position without increasing its population and founding colonies with the aid of a vast system of emigration? What boundaries should be established in a perfected civilization between the domains of the state, corporate bodies [*corps constitués*], voluntary associations, the family, and the

individual? Should the state intervene directly in agriculture, industry, and commerce, systems of aid, the diffusion of the arts and sciences, the education of the young, and, in general, in all social interests which are not directly concerned with the general welfare? . . .

As our work develops, it continues to shed light on a fact which I have already pointed out. Despite its scientific nature, our method is as comprehensible to people of limited intelligence as it is to those with the most developed minds. Familiarity with literature or philosophical and historical speculation is less important for success than close contact with the people to be studied and sound judgment formed by practicing a useful profession or simply by fulfilling social duties.

7

DEFINING "WORKERS," "ASSOCIATIONS," AND "SOCIAL SYSTEMS"

The first problem in a methodical study of European workers is to specify exactly which persons can be included in this category. The more familiar we are with the subject, the more we see that it is very difficult to make an absolute distinction between those persons designated in French by the generic term "workers" and those who are members of other social classes. The term "workers" has no exact equivalent in every language. It is particularly ambiguous to Eastern European languages because the persons to whom it applies live under different conditions than workers in France and other Western nations. Within all countries, moreover, the boundaries which separate true "workers" from people of other social classes are so slight that it is hard to distinguish them. In many respects, people at the bottom of the social class whose role is manual labor in agriculture and industry blend into the class generically labeled "domestic servants," whose work is limited exclusively to personal service. Conversely, members of the upper ranks of the same class have much in common with landowners and proprietors; that is, the persons who own land property or are in charge of agricultural or industrial enterprises. Similar difficulties arise in choosing terms to define the main categories of workers, the social institutions which govern them, their relationship to other social classes, and so on. It was therefore necessary to establish precise definitions of the terms which applied to the facts to be studied....

From *Les Ouvriers européens* (Paris: Imprimerie Impériale, 1855), p. 17.

"Workers," "Associations," and "Social Systems"

The social class dealt with in this study comprises those people described by the French word "worker" as it is ordinarily used in the common language. To be included within the limits of this class, a worker's duties must not be confined essentially to personal service; neither may his additional income from property ownership or management be more important than the remuneration he receives for manual labor. In short, we have observed and included in the present study under the generic term "worker" only those persons who perform manual labor (aside from the personal service of a master), whose principal means of existence is remuneration received for this labor, but who may also own or manage some property.

Within these limits, workers fall naturally into seven main categories which are frequently distinguished in this study. They are: (1) domestic workers; (2) day laborers; (3) job workers; (4) farm tenants; (5) master artisans or (6) owners; and (7) proprietors who are primarily self-employed.

In general, workers cannot provide themselves with the means of existence unaided. They must either join with "masters" who provide the means of production and a consumer market for their products, or join various kinds of *associations*. These work agreements are usually determined by "obligations" which correspond to the nature of the social structure.

There are two main types of associations: *cooperatives* and *corporations*. The word "cooperative" has many meanings. It is used here to mean groups of workers who share a piece of real property, a commercial enterprise, or a consumer market. The groups may be based on a system of more or less common interests or a system of joint individual interests. The work "corporation" is also used here in a limited sense. It is applied to all groups of workers whose members are bound by common interests other than those of communities, these interests being, however, of a more specific nature than the general relationships existing among inhabitants of the same country, sharing the same religion or government.

The persons or institutions included in each of these definitions vary widely in European societies. Too strict an application of these terms would lead to serious errors in a comparison of those societies. For the sake of accuracy, it is necessary to modify these meanings according to the nature of the social structure. In all societies there are certain basic conditions whose influence is preponderant. Any change in these conditions implies a radical modification in the physical and moral condition of both individuals and social classes. Among the most important of these basic conditions are the fixed or mobile nature of dwellings, the nature and duration of the work relationships which bind workers to masters, the relative proportion of cultivated and uncultivated land, etc. There are four main systems of social structure in Europe. The first includes all the nomadic peoples who are important only in the easternmost part of Europe; the other three consist of sedentary populations. The first of these is characterized by obligatory work agreements which are binding on both workers and masters; the second, by long-term work agreements entered into freely by both parties, and the third, by temporary work agreements or by the absence of any reciprocal agreement.

III. THE MONOGRAPHIC METHOD

8

THE STUDY OF WORKING-CLASS FAMILIES

The considerations we have just mentioned prove sufficiently that, in order to get a true picture of the physical and moral condition of a working class family, it is necessary first to establish both the nature of the work obligation under which the family procures the means of labor, and the level occupied by the family in the series of worker types we have just defined.

As for the description of this condition, it must consist essentially of a complete analysis of the family's resources and the means by which the necessities of life are provided. In order to coordinate the elements of such a description, it is necessary to establish (1) the nature of the work performed by each member of the family and the remuneration for that work; and (2) all expenditures and consumption occasioned by the physical and moral needs of the family, in accordance with local custom. In other words, it is necessary to methodically compare the family's income and expenditures.

These observations are very complex. They must include innumerable circumstances; for the most insignificant details of family life take on real importance because of their repetition and far-reaching consequences.

These details are numerous enough when we study a single family. If we compare one family with another, or one region with another, we seem to be confronted with an almost infinite diversity of nuances, stemming from individual character and emo-

From *Les Ouvriers européens* (Paris: Imprimerie Impériale, 1855), pt. 1, sec. 10, pp. 21–22.

tions, the varied and uneven pressure of government and laws, and the even more varied influence of the soil, climate, agriculture, industry, and commerce.

If, as has been established previously, the examination of these questions is an obligation toward the suffering classes and an indispensable means of reform for the peoples of the West, one cannot abandon this study because of the difficulties which it presents; but the forces used must be proportional to the obstacles to be conquered. The statesmen of the Continent, following the example of those in Great Britain, must see to it at all costs that the facts are established: this is the only way to correct the evils which exist at the present time, to ward off the perils the future may hold, to mend the social fabric, and to satisfy all interests within the limits traced by reason and justice.

Nevertheless, the difficulties of observation which we have just pointed out are less serious than they first appear. They would be more of a problem in a study of the bourgeoisie or the tiny social class of the very wealthy, because families in these classes, aided by the resources at their disposal, are able to escape the influence of their immediate milieu....

The worker's means of existence are thus essentially subordinated to the combined influences of the soil and climate. These influences, together with the modifications introduced by human industry, are usually constant over large areas inhabited by the same race and subject to the same natural conditions. Thus the fundamental elements of workers' lives in these regions are remarkably uniform. Their habits, formed by the nature of the environment, are generalized even further by many factors: tradition and custom, which exercise so much power over human actions; or a concerted effort on the part of the government, religious authorities, or landowners and proprietors. Together with similar occupations and pleasures, these different influences inhibit or neutralize the growth of individual propensities among workers of the same district, race, and profession. These effects extend to the fundamental details of their existence, in the same way that biologists reports consistency and regularity among the individuals of the same species.

In this way, the laboring classes lend themselves to methodical observation. The observer is able to apply facts established for a small number of families to entire populations or, at least, to entire categories of workers. This same principle promises truly scientific results when a suitable method of observation is chosen.

Moreover, observation is the best method in all matters of this kind. If one studies the living conditions of a certain number of families of average family size and age, who live in the same area and are employed in the same occupation, one will generally arrive at identical results. Secondary types or noteworthy exceptions are rarely encountered, except in the manufacturing districts and large cities of the West, where workers abandoned to the whims of individual choice are constantly tempted to adopt the habits of other social classes.

Like all detailed studies, this method is composed of stages which differ widely in terms of the number and importance of the difficulties which a serious observer must overcome. When observations are first begun, the facts seem to multiply indefinitely; the subject seems to grow more complicated than had been anticipated, and every new effort creates new obstacles. The observer, alarmed by his apparent incompetence, is soon tempted to give up his project. Nevertheless, if he persists, he finally reaches a stage where the facts seem to sort themselves out in a uniform framework and where simplicity and clarity replace complication and obscurity.

During the course of the special studies which gave birth to this work, for example, many details which at first seemed accidental and whose description did not seem to lead to any useful results, contributed in the long run to the isolation of laws which were evidently essential to the preservation of societies. After greater reflection, facts which at first seemed only bizarre exceptions proved striking confirmation of these laws. The discovery of the principal laws which govern the lives of the working classes permitted a considerable reduction in the scope of studies of all the types of workers who make up those classes. Moreover, it was also possible to include in each special inquiry the specific factors concerning the labor and domestic life of the workers which were of interest to economists and statesmen.

What is more, another equally important result was achieved.

Simplicity in summarization of the facts was added to ease of observation. It was possible to classify results concerning the most diverse conditions and the most disparate civilizations in such a uniform framework that all the complex details observed in the various areas of agriculture and industry could be taken in at a single glance. The method which we are now presenting to the public did not truly take its final form until the day this result was obtained.

THE RULES OF SOCIAL INVESTIGATION

The numerous details that are listed in the following chapters and that figure in all the monographs can only be gathered by a long and painstaking investigation. In order to succeed, the observer must inspect all parts of the dwelling; he must inventory the furniture, utensils, linen, and clothing; estimate the amount of available cash reserves, the value of the furniture, domestic animals, special materials for labors and industries, and, in general, all the family's property. He must estimate stocks of food; weigh the foodstuffs which make up the various meals, according to the season; and, finally, he must closely examine the labors of each of the members of the family—outside the home, as well as within. The study of domestic chores can sometimes appear infinitely complex to the observer; this is precisely the case for the most simple races, which cultivate the raw materials for textiles, make their own clothing, and even produce the soap used to wash these clothes. Other areas of investigation are even more delicate: these include inquiries on the family's moral and intellectual life, religion, education, and recreation; or sentiments of family relationships and friendships, the relationships between workers and masters, or employers, associates, domestic servants, and apprentices; and, finally, all the peculiarities of a family history. Nevertheless, this last task is easier to accomplish than might first be expected, for the workers generally enjoy talking about their childhood or their "old folks"; they like to describe local tradi-

From *Les Ouvriers européens* (Tours: Mame, 1879), vol. 1, pp. 220–27.

tions and they will elaborate on these subjects voluntarily, without waiting for questions from their interlocutor. Moreover, the local social elites can fill in any gaps in this information, either from their own observations of the present or from the daybooks which their predecessors often kept in the past. At first one might well have feared that such inquiries would seem like an intolerable inquisition for the persons being questioned.

In addition, when an observer is placed in a world which is completely foreign to him, he is at first unable to understand the purpose of objects, the sequence of labors, the true meaning of ideas, and the precise expression of sentiments. He must therefore address numerous questions to the family being observed, thus causing that family to lose a considerable amount of time. The difficulty frequently becomes even greater when the observer must make his inquiries in a foreign language modified by local dialects. It is thus easily foreseeable that extensive questioning can result in extreme mental fatigue for persons who are not accustomed to reflection and whose ability to coordinate their ideas is limited....

Even without an explanation, any intelligent observer would understand why the following proceedings must be followed in order to win the goodwill of the families. Do not make an investigation any more abrupt than it may unfortunately seem, since the families may be unwilling to be questioned. You may, however, shorten the preliminary steps by putting yourself under the recommendation of a carefully selected local elite. Win the family's confidence and sympathy by informing them of your concern for them and goal of helpfulness and service to the public. Sustain the attention of the participants by stories which might interest them. Compensate them with pecuniary indemnities for any time lost because of the investigation. Discreetly praise the men's wisdom, the women's grace, and the children's manners, and judiciously distribute small gifts to all.

All of these rules for a successful investigation will be ineffective or even harmful if they are not guided by the fundamental virtue of the observer: a respect for science. In the hands of a false scholar the method of observation can become a means of corruption, as logic can for the sophist. Yet in the realm of social science, observation of permanent facts offers guarantees of accuracy which do not exist in the realm of pure reasoning, when applied to the understanding of the changing factors of private life or politics. A badly observed population retains all the elements necessary for a decisive counter-inquiry; the error propagated by ignorance or bad faith can always be refuted by a monograph based on the investigation of a true scholar.

In this kind of work, as in all other scientific work, there is no substitute for that devotion to the truth in which the scholar's probity resides. Nevertheless, insofar as possible, guarantees of accuracy should be built into the method itself. The method of family monographs satisfies this requirement. The surest method by which a foreign observer can familiarize himself with the moral and physical life of a family is very similar to the technique which chemists use to discover the composition of minerals. A mineral is identified when the analysis has isolated each of the elements which enter into its composition, and when it has been verified that the weight of all these elements is exactly equal to the weight of the original sample. The same kind of numerical verification is always available to scholars who methodically analyze the social unit we call the family....

In fact, study of the monographs published in *European Workers*, makes it clear that sooner or later all of the actions which together constitute the life of a working-class family can be expressed in the form of a receipt or an expenditure. It therefore follows that a family's receipts, evaluated in money, should exactly equal the combined total of expenditures and savings. Thus, an observer can be said to be in complete possession of all the information pertaining to a family when, having analyzed all the elements contained in the two parts of the domestic budget, he arrives at an exact correspondence between the two totals.

At first glance, this principle seems to reduce social science to the study of the physical aspects of human life. In reality, however, it is the shortest path to the opposite goal: a study of man's moral values. A comparison of domestic budgets often dramatically highlights this fact, for in these matters a single figure is often more eloquent than a long speech. Thus, for example, there can be no doubt of the degradation of a stevedore of the Paris suburbs when examination of his budget reveals that he spends 185 francs (or 12 percent of his income) annually to inebriate himself in cabarets while he does not spend a single centime on the moral education of his five children ranging in age from four to fourteen years.

In order to reach the end of his study with confidence, the observer can rely on two infallible guidelines. He will succeed if he has observed all the details of the family's situation with respect to their knowledge of moral law and the acquisition of their daily bread. It can always be demonstrated that families suffer or prosper in proportion to the absence or the presence of these two conditions which contribute directly to happiness or unhappiness. The figures which constitute the most important part of the monographs, that is, the domestic budget, clearly indicate these elements. Nevertheless, this information must be developed in all necessary detail in all the parts of the text which are appended to the budget.

10

THE MONOGRAPHIC METHOD

In scientific matters, only direct observation of facts can lead to rigorous conclusions and to their acceptance. This principle is acknowledged today in the physical sciences, but it is still unrecognized in social science. The practitioners of social science are generally inspired by preconceived ideas which perpetuate antagonisms and which cannot serve as a basis for systematic action. People imbued with such biases tend to disdain the facts and the conclusions which can be induced from them. Social science thus remains in a situation comparable to that of the physical sciences when they were based on the conceptions of astrology and alchemy; social science will not be established until it is founded on observation.

But the field of observation in social matters is vast, and whoever ventures there without a guide will inevitably flounder. The method described in the present *instruction* provides a guideline; it directs observers through the labyrinth of facts. This method gives them a standard measure of accuracy and directs them toward conclusions which will be accepted as general laws once they are sufficiently verified by observation.

This method consists: (1) in basing the study of populations on that of a few, carefully chosen laboring families; and (2) in describing these families according to a determined and uniform framework. The family being the true social unit, we proceed like

From *Instruction sur la méthode d'observation* (Paris: Société des études pratiques d'économie social, 1862), pp. 13–25.

the zoologist who applies the investigative techniques of anatomy and physiology to a few individuals in order to describe an entire species. This method uses the simplest cases to discover the laws of social science and can then consider the influences which modify these laws in more complex cases....

Treating social questions from an exclusive point of view is a common error today. In contrast, the method of monographs provides a comprehensive view of a family's life in its entirety. What is more, the observer is guided by rules determined with rigorous precision and by a complete question-book applicable to all families, whatever latitude and whatever civilization they belong to. This uniform framework facilitates the comparisons on which true social laws should be founded.

The need to make social studies precise and complete complicates the monographs somewhat. Nevertheless, the use of this method is not limited to very cultivated minds; it has often been applied successfully by men who have little education but are guided by good sense. Any judicious and attentive observer will succeed in this kind of work if he will first study the models already published in the first three volumes of *Workers of the World* and obey the following instructions.

The method of monographs does not require the observer to limit himself to a particular area, class, or family. The main advantage of this method is that it allows a rapid assessment of the mores of any given country. Not only is a lengthy stay in that country unnecessary, but it is possible to study a country at a distance, if a native-born family who lived there for many years is available for study.

Moreover, any agricultural or industrial class of an area can be observed. Nevertheless, in a region which has not been previously described, it is preferable to focus on the peasants, that is, the small agricultural proprietors who spend all of their time working with their families on their property and are not obliged to work elsewhere as salaried employees. This class always forms the base of a civilization. Thanks to the nature of its labors and habits, which result from the ownership of land, it preserves better than the others the imprint of local genius.

In any given social class, it is important to select a family native to the area and of nearly average conditions, that is, neither superior nor inferior to the others in respect to its material situation or its morality. Wherever possible, a complete household should be described, for such studies are usually more valuable than those of childless households, not to mention those of single persons. Finally, it is necessary to use a family which demonstrates its willingness to be observed by complying with the request of the observer or influential persons of the locality.

Once the families for the monograph have been chosen, the desired results will be obtained from this study if two conditions are met. The first is a sincere love for science, which leads one to seek the truth and record the facts with scrupulous accuracy. It is not, however, necessary that the observer be completely impartial or imbued with true social principles at the outset of the study; observers often begin work intending to use the facts to demonstrate an erroneous principle in which they believe. But by using this method, the truth can always be distinguished from the falsehood. The passion which leads so many good men today to defend error will be the principal force which will lead to the truth; thus social science will follow the pattern set by the physical sciences. Moreover, we need not fear that this partiality will result in deliberate dissimulation or alteration of the facts. This kind of dishonesty is rare, and the method offers complete protection against it, thanks to the controls which it includes.

A second condition necessary for an accurate evaluation of the facts contained in these monographs is to gain the confidence of the family under study. At times, not even the promise of a reward will convince a family to admit an observer, often a stranger, into the secrets of their personal lives for a week or ten days. On the contrary, however, many families will submit to a minute inquiry and prolonged questioning if the observer convinces them that he is only investigating the conditions of the working classes in order to use these facts to establish the principles which will make possible an improvement in their lives.

The elements of a monograph can be collected by the simultaneous use of three methods. These are by no means equally important. The first consists in observing the facts, the second in questioning the laboring man on those matters which cannot be directly observed, and the third in collecting information from persons of the area who have known the family for many years or who affect it through relationships of patronage.

Direct observation must include even those details which first seem useless, but whose necessity soon becomes apparent. In general, it is necessary to gather the facts without immediately drawing conclusions. It is only after the study of the family is completed and the observations have been classified in the framework adopted for the monographs that one can try to draw general conclusions from them based on induction.

Questioning should be conducted in the order indicated by the method. Nevertheless, this order must not be followed too rigorously. The workingman will naturally tend to elaborate on certain subjects: he will enjoy relating memories of his youth and telling his family history. It is important not to interrupt him, so that useful information will not be lost. Too many questions will tire him—if they do not bore him or make him suspicious—and they will be a constant reminder that he is being questioned. It is much better to listen than to ask questions, especially, as is often the case, when differences in dialect or native language make understanding questions and answers difficult for both parties.

Extreme caution should be observed in questioning the directing classes of the locality, who often know less than one would think about the social system to which they belong. Moreover, their statements should always be checked against directly observed facts or facts revealed in statements from the family.

All monographs are supplemented by a double-entry budget of receipts and expenditures, which is preceded by preliminary observations and followed by notes.

The preliminary observations will allow the observer to gain the confidence of the subjects. They will gradually prepare the worker to answer the numerous questions of the budget and even to understand why it is necessary. Finally, they will give the observer a body of preliminary ideas about the mores and life of the family, the place where it lives, and the population to which it belongs.

It is not necessary to complete the preliminary observations at once. One need not, for example, insist that the workingman being questioned return to a detail which was omitted in an earlier paragraph. Only the budgets will give precision to the information received; they will allow the verification of its accuracy and they will suggest questions which might have been overlooked at first.

In questioning the workingman, and even in a first draft of the budgets, one should make all evaluations of quantities and values with local measures and currencies. For the final draft, the author will convert local units into metric units, and, if necessary, he will indicate the conversion rates in a special note.

Information pertaining to quantities and prices of objects bought, sold, produced, or consumed will always be based on a year of average prosperity for agriculture, industry, and commerce in general, and for the particular household under consideration.

It will often be impossible for the workingman to give the figures for the two budgets and the attached accounts for an entire year, although he can easily indicate them for a week or a day. In general, the observer should use every means possible to spare the members of the family any unaccustomed intellectual effort which they are not used to and which might alter the accuracy of their statements.

The notes include important facts concerning the social system, noteworthy exceptions, and general observations and conclusions which the author draws from his studies as a whole. The material for these notes will be furnished by the family and the area that are the object of the monograph. It will also be provided by persons who have lived in the area for many years and who are familiar with the customs and habits of the population. But these statements must always be checked against observed facts.

11

MONOGRAPH ON THE MINER OF THE UPPER HARZ MINING CORPORATION

Miners of the Corporations of the Silver and Lead Mines of the Upper Harz Mountains (Hanover)

Piece-worker and worker-owner in a system of long-term voluntary work agreements.

According to the documents gathered in person in 1829 and 1845 by Messrs. A. de Saint-Leger and F. Le Play, with the gracious help of Mme. Alberts and the collaboration of M. Degenhardt of the town of Clausthal.

PRELIMINARY OBSERVATIONS DEFINING THE CONDITIONS OF THE VARIOUS MEMBERS OF THE FAMILY. DEFINITION OF THE ENVIRONMENT, WORK ORGANIZATION, AND FAMILY STRUCTURE.

Section 1: Nature of the Soil, Populations, and Work Organization

...The worker of the upper Harz Mountains with whom this monograph is primarily concerned lives in the town of Clausthal, near the silver and lead mines located 700 meters above sea level. Dominated by the Broken, this group of mountains is located near the common border of the Hanover and Brunswick plains, the duchies of Anhalt, Brandenberg and Mansfield, and Stolberg. The

From *Les Ouvriers européens* (Tours: Mame, 1879), vol. 8, pp. 99–129.

land consists primarily of transitional clay schist, richly veined with mineral deposits which have been exploited for nine centuries. Because of the latitude (58°48′) and the considerable elevation above sea level, the climate is very harsh and ill suited for the cultivation of grains, fruit, potatoes, and most vegetables; kitchen gardens produce little besides cabbage and a few salad greens or herbs. In contrast, however, the Harz Mountains are ideally suited for the production of resinous wood....

These mines are owned by private companies of shareholders, but the same vein is often sectioned among several companies by means of divisions perpendicular to the general direction of the deposit. All these individual enterprises are coordinated under the direction of mining officers named by the government. The forests and foundries are state property; the wood needed to support the underground excavations is furnished to the mining companies free of change. The minerals are purchased by the domanial foundries. The prices are determined in conformity with current values and according to the grade of ore of the useful metals.

The entire population is either directly or indirectly involved in the mining industry. In keeping with tradition, the administration does not allow the number of merchants and artisans to increase beyond the limits set by the true needs of the population. Through direct and indirect measures it prevents outsiders from taking advantage of the vices of the workers, and it forestalls the danger of usurious loans.... The population is mainly composed of workers whose entire life is spent in tasks associated with the mines, crushing mills, and foundries. The rest of the population is divided into three main groups: woodsmen, charcoal-burners, and forest guards, whose dwellings are scattered throughout the forests; independent haulers *(Fuhrherrn),* who own farmland in the valleys and lower slopes of the mountains, particularly meadows where they raise from two to six horses; and, finally, the domestic workers employed by the Fuhrherrn. Often, as in Carinthia, forest work and charcoal making is performed by these latter. The workers who are directly employed by the administration of the mines and factories work for it on a long-term basis, under a system of corporations of which the Harz region can be considered one of the most outstanding examples today.

In the upper Harz there is a tendency for the population to increase beyond the limits imposed by the industrial organization and warranted by the natural resources; up to now, however, the general administration has not failed in its duties of patronage. Thus it has recently created two new sources of work: it employs the children, particularly the young girls, in plantings which regenerate the forests more efficiently than natural reseeding; and it employs the adults in the construction of a great number of roads through the forests and in various other works beneficial to the mining industry. In summary, this interesting region has preserved the customs of patronage common to all the old social systems in all their purity and at the same time has managed to avoid the drawbacks of commercial competition. It must be noted that this success is achieved by a group of industries based on the exploitation of mines, waterways, and forests, where competition is strictly limited as a result of the nature of the raw materials. It could not be hoped, then, that the same organization could be applied to the various branches of the manufacturing industry whose means of production are unlimited. Nevertheless, the mines of the Harz Mountains—located today at a mere thirty-six hours from Paris—can at least serve as a basis of comparison and as an example of the old European tradition; and they can provide valuable information to the statesmen who must deal with the pressing social questions which face Western Europe today.

Section 2: Civil Status of the Family

The family consists of the husband, wife, and their three children.

	Age
1. Karl M——, head of the family, born in Clausthal, married for fifteen years	40
2. Anna R——, his wife, born in Andreasberg	35
3. Franz M——, their eldest son	14
4. Gretchen M——, their eldest daughter	11
5. Wilhelm M——, their second son	8

Section 3: Religion and Moral Habits

The family is Lutheran; the members of the family attend church services regularly on Sundays and holidays. These good habits are not due to religious feelings alone; they also stem from the entire body of customs which encourage hard work and temperance among the workers. Nonetheless, one must note the unfortunate influence which is exercised on the young people by the regulations which forbid workers in the mining corporations of the upper Harz to marry before the age of twenty-five. As in many German states, these regulations are designed to limit the growth of the population. In fact, however, they often have only one result: to weaken the sense of moral order in the populace.

Section 4: Hygiene and Health Services

Although the climate is harsh, it is salubrious. Occasionally insufficient food and the nature of the work, which exposes the worker to the influence of humidity and sudden chills, result in illness. These circumstances may even lead to premature death or incurable infirmity. Medical services are well organized, either in the home or in hospitals. This service is paid for by an emergency fund supported by deductions taken from the workers' wages and various donations.

Section 5: The Rank of the Family

The worker belongs to the category of piece-worker and worker-owner because he is paid according to the quantity of work he performs. Nevertheless, as frequently happens in this kind of work (excavating rock in the mines), payment according to quantity differs little in fact from payment by the day. The work to be done varies widely, depending on the kind of rock to be excavated; and the administration sets the price so that the workers' wages vary only slightly—from 8.68 francs to 9.52 francs a week. If the salary drops below the lower limit, the difference is made up to the worker; when it goes above the upper limit, the price rate is lowered. In short, the worker is paid according to the number of hours he works rather than according to the quantity produced. The worker owns property under conditions described in Section 6.

Section 6: Means of Existence of the Family
Property (Household Goods and Clothing Excluded)

Real property: the worker nominally owns two properties—a house worth 2,300 F and a kitchen-garden worth 40 F.

This property belongs to the worker under very unusual conditions which constitute a kind of possession midway between ownership and subsidy. The workers of Clausthal and Zellerfield nominally own their homes and the adjoining garden; and they acquire them under special conditions. When a worker dies and a house is put up for sale, another worker has the right to acquire it; offers being equal, his bid is given preference over those of any investors, merchants, or local officials who might also desire the property. The worker is favored even if he cannot pay the slightest fraction of the purchase price. The necessary money is loaned to him at 4 percent interest by the general administration of the mines, which takes a mortgage on the building as a pledge for the loan. In reality, then, the worker is simply a tenant of the general administration. The acquisition of the building is reduced, as it were, to a kind of rental contract: interest paid on the mortgage becomes a kind of rent. Nevertheless, the important moral effects of this arrangement cannot be denied: besides being best suited for the demands of human dignity, it has all the advantages of the Russian system of subsidy; it defends the worker against his own lack of foresight and against the avidity of usurers; and finally, it raises the worker, at least nominally, in the social hierarchy and introduces him to a sense of ownership within the limits of his moral and intellectual capacities.

Since the capital indicated above is balanced by an equal debt, there is nothing to include in this category in the family's possessions.

Domestic Animals............0.00 F

The climate, which does not permit the cultivation of grain, fruit, or starchy vegetables, is also incompatible to the raising of fowl. Ordinary workers never become the owners of meadows and thus cannot raise a milk cow. In general, only master-workers and merchants raise milk cows.

Special materials for professional work and other labors ....12.00 F
1. For gardening—various tools, 5.00 F
2. For excavating rock and hauling firewood: one hatchet and one wheelbarrow, 7.00 F.

Rights to allocations of several mutual aid funds which provide a pension to aged or infirm workers and to their widows and orphans..................42.00 F

Rights to allocation of a mutual aid fund which guarantees the worker a decent burial ....8.40 F

Rights to the allocations of various mutual aid funds which provide medical and surgical aid and cash subsidies to the ill...............................0.00 F

   TOTAL VALUE OF PROPERTY 62.40 F

Section 7: Subsidies

The principle of patronage, which has been preserved intact in the Harz mining corporations, can be seen in the many subsidies which are provided. As has been indicated above, the dwelling and adjoining garden constitute, in some regards, a permanent subsidy. The worker has the right to gather firewood free of charge in the domanial forests and to buy whatever firewood he does not have the time to gather personally at a price below market value. Since the worker's wages are more or less fixed, the administration tries to prevent any eventuality which would provoke an increase in expenses; thus wheat is sold to workers at a fixed price which is always below market value. The insurance funds which furnish all sorts of aid to sick or infirm workers, widows, and orphans are supported much more by the subsidies of the general administration than by the deductions taken from workers' wages. Finally, the expenses of the boys' schools are completely absorbed by the administration.

Section 8: Work and Other Tasks Carried Out by Family Members

The nature of the work: The worker's primary job is to excavate metal-bearing or sterile rock; in other words, the fundamental work of mining. Each week the worker works six shifts consisting of eight hours' actual work. But each shift is really eleven hours long if the time needed to descend into the mine and to come back to daylight is included. The worker sometimes works additional hours by prolonging certain shifts beyond their normal duration.

The worker's secondary labors include gathering firewood for the household, cultivating the garden, keeping up the house.

The wife's work: The wife's principal work is the care of the household. Among her secondary jobs, the most important is transporting baskets of foodstuffs. Twice a week the wife goes to the towns of Goslar or Osterode, located on the Hanover plains, to buy wheat, potatoes, etc., which she then takes back to Clausthal, a distance of ten kilometers over a climb of 400 meters. Part of the goods transported in this way are for household consumption; part is delivered at a set fee to the town's wealthier residents; the rest is sold at the market at a profit representing the costs of transportation.

Her other jobs include tending the garden, carrying hay for the owners of the meadows on the outskirts of Clausthal and Zellerfield, and, finally, making cotton and linen clothes for the family.

The eldest son's work: The eldest son, age fourteen, performs whatever work is given to him in the workshops where the ore is prepared mechanically (the raw ore is enriched and prepared for smelting); he receives a fixed salary for each day of work.... The family rents parts of the house to another (nonrelated) family.

THE FAMILY'S WAY OF LIFE

Section 9: Food and Meals

The basic foods are rye bread, pork, sausage, butter, potatoes, and cabbage. Bread is prepared in each household; it is baked for a small fee by the same bakers who make the bread for the wealthier segment of the population. Meat is generally boiled; potatoes are cooked in salted water; cabbage is generally eaten raw. The household makes as much cabbage into sauerkraut as it has fat to use in the seasoning.

Section 10: The Dwelling, Household Goods, and Clothing

The house, which the worker possesses under the conditions described above, consists of a ground floor and one upper floor. The owner and his family occupy one heated room and two smaller rooms on the first floor, as well as a small room on the second floor used as an attic and storage room. He rents the remaining two rooms on the second floor to another family of workers; but these tenants have no use of the vegetable garden.

The household goods include:
Furniture: clean and well-kept ....260.00 F
1. Beds: three beds with bedclothes for the parents, male children, and the daughter, 180.00 F.
2. Other furniture: two tables, six chairs, one dresser, one chest, 80.00 F. The cast-iron stove used for heating belongs to the house and is included in its value.
Utensils: reduced to the absolute necessary ....33.70 F
1. For food preparation and service: kitchenware, glassware, spoons, knives, and forks, total 25.00 F.
2. For various uses: one mine lamp (which lasts the miner's lifetime), 3.70 F; two baskets for the wife's various transports, 5.00 F.
Total: 8.70 F.
Clothing ....200.00 F

Following one of those ancient customs which are unfortunately fading in the rest of Europe, the Harz miners and young boys wear a traditional costume which gives a remarkable quality of dignity to the entire worker population. This costume is very well suited to the worker's tasks and to the climate. It consists of a loose-fitting jacket with a large, turned-down collar *(Kittel),* trousers of the same black cloth as the Kittel, a black leather apron *(Arschleder)* which covers the bottom of the torso and thighs and is fastened around the loins and the bottom of the Kittel with a buckled belt, a plumed shako, boots, a cane with a decorative head in the form of a hammer, etc. (See below in the table of expenditures, other clothing.) The tendency to abandon this local costume is already very pronounced in the Harz. The miner wears his costume only on official occasions or when he must see his superiors. He prefers nowadays to wear a frock coat and a cap to go to church—a less distinguished outfit—rather than his local costume.

The worker's clothing: 104.00 F.

1. Traditional costume: one Kittel and one pair of trousers of black cloth; one plumed hat; one Arschleder and one buckled belt; 18.00 F.

2. Sunday clothes: one frock coat; one vest and one pair of cloth trousers; one pair of boots; one cap: 41.00 F.

3. Work clothes: two black linen smocks; one cloth jacket; three pairs of linen trousers; two ties; four linen shirts; six pairs of woolen socks; two pairs of shoes; one pair of suspenders; one work cap; one Arschleder: 45.00 F.

Wife's clothing, Sunday and work clothing: 50.00 F.

Children's clothing, Sunday and work clothing: 46.00 F.

TOTAL VALUE OF HOUSEHOLD GOODS
AND CLOTHING ....493.70 F

Section 11: Recreations

Smoking tobacco is the major source of pleasure of the Harz workers. The criticism which is often addressed to wealthier persons who habitually smoke could not be made to such workers, who by means of an annual expenditure of 10 francs avail themselves of a nearly constant source of pleasure which, in their frugal existence, could not be replaced by anything else. These workers rarely go to the tavern. They drink a little brandy, generally in small portions consumed in the home after the main meal. Family reunions in the evening and the severe Lutheran services, along with these modest joys, are the miners' only diversions from their difficult and assiduous labors.

FAMILY HISTORY

Section 12: Major Phases of the Family's Life

The children attend school until the age of fourteen. At this age the boys begin to work in the workshops where the raw ores are sorted, crushed, and washed. They perform these duties, which are well suited for adolescence, and they continue some of their studies until the development of their physical forces allows them to take up work in the mines and foundries.

When the girls leave school they begin to help their mother in all her work, within their ability, particularly in the housework and carrying foodstuffs.

Following the principles adopted by several German states, the administration of the Harz mines tries to limit the growth of the population by retarding the age of marriage as much as possible. Here, in general, workers may not marry until the age of twenty-five. The only result of this policy is to create illicit unions and undermine public morality. Most of the time, moreover, children born in these unions are legitimized by marriage as soon as the parents reach the required age.

The family, once it is formed, lives in the physical and moral conditions described in the present monograph. Although they work hard and lead a frugal existence in a harsh and somber climate, the family is nevertheless satisfied with its life and happy in its native land. In recent years, the Harz miners have resisted the temptation of higher wages and all kinds of other inducements which have drawn the workers of northern Germany to work in the railroads and which have so deeply disturbed the old relationships of patronage. Perhaps no other example can better indicate the natural tendency of the working-class populations and demonstrate that, even in the face of attractive innovations, workers will still prefer a harsh but secure existence based on affectionate patronage and sound subsidies.

Section 13: Customs and Institutions Which Guarantee the Physical and Moral Well-Being of the Family

Each member of the family is protected throughout his life by a complete system of social institutions which has often been imitated by other mining corporations and which seems to have originated with the Harz mining corporations. Government-supported schools provide the boys with moral and religious training as well as a basic education. Tradition obliges the government to provide work for the adults, even when the exploitation of the mines is not profitable. Mutual insurance funds provide medical, surgical, and pharmaceutical aid to the sick, as well as cash payments. They provide temporary assistance or permanent aid to the aged, infirm, widows, and orphans. Finally, at the worker's death they provide a decent burial. The insurance funds which play an important role in the life of the working-class population of the Harz Mountains are supported by various means, in part by deductions taken from workers' wages and largely by subsidies from the general administration.

In summary, as a member of the mining corporation the Harz worker possesses a kind of legal mortgage on the mineral and forest resources of this area which protects him and his family from any unforeseen misfortunes. In this respect his condition is very similar to that of mine workers in Russia and Sweden.

A comparison of the forests and mines of these two regions with those of the Harz is a subject of study ideally suited to highlight the true principles of social organization. This comparison demonstrates the danger of preconceived ideas, in whose name some contemporary men of letters would base new social systems on "unconditional freedom and equality." In reality, these systems invariably lead to social antagonism and instability, while stability and social harmony are preserved in these three regions: in Russia, despite the reciprocal dependence of masters and workers; in Sweden, despite the feudal system of property ownership; and in the Harz, despite certain incursions of the state into the system of work relationships.

The social organization described in the present monograph reduces to an absolute minimum the material satisfactions of the workers; but at the same time it protects them from any unforeseen misfortune which might befall the family or society. The satisfaction of the working families provides a useful lesson, for it proves that the security of one's daily bread is the primary condition of well-being. This happy state of affairs is not unique to the Harz Mountains; it is found all through Hanover and even throughout the Saxon plains....

Section 14: Budget of Annual Receipts

A. Sources of Receipts	Approximate Value of the Sources of Receipts
Section I: Family Property	(Value of Property)
Article 1: Real Property	
Lodging: House	2,380.00 F
Rural property: Garden	40.00 F
Article 2: Personal Property	
Special material for work and other labor:	
for gardening	5.00 F
for cutting and transporting firewood	8.00 F
Article 3: Rights to allocations of Mutual Aid Funds	
Funds which accumulate the family's contributions:	
Pension benefits for aged or crippled workers, widows, and orphans under working age	42.00 F
Burial fund, providing a decent burial for workers	8.40 F
Funds which immediately reimburse the family's contribution:	
Medical and surgical care, plus cash subsidies in case of illness	0.00 F
TOTAL VALUE OF PROPERTY (excluding debts)	2,402.40 F
Section II: Family Subsidies	
Article 1: Property received as usufructs (The family receives no property as usufructs.)	
Article 2: Rights of Usage on Domanial Property	
Rights to a section of firewood	
Article 3: Allocation of goods and services	
For food	
For lodging	
For the education of the children	
For health care	
For professional work	
For debts	
For insurance	

Section III: Work Performed by the Family
Description of Work and Time Allocation

	Amount of Work (Workdays)		
	Father	Mother	Eldest son
Worker's principal labor, performed as piecework for the mine administration:			
Excavating rock in the mines: forty-nine weeks of six eight-hour shifts	294		
Excavating rock in the mines: extra shifts	24		
Wife's principal labor, performed for family:			
housework, food preparation, laundering and mending of clothing and linens		110	
Son's principal labor, performed as day-work for the mine administration: work in the crushing-mill or ore washeries			312
Secondary labors:			
Gathering 2,000 kilos of wood in the domanial forests	2		
Transporting 3,900 kilos of wood a distance of 8 kilometers	18		
Back-packing foodstuffs from the valley to the mountain, for family consumption		59	
Gardening	3	8	
Back-packing hay for owners of meadows on harvest days		8	
Various work in private homes (laundry, etc.)		69	
Back-packing foodstuffs for others or for sale in the market		43	
Upkeep of the house	6		
Sewing new clothing (cotton and linen) for the family		30	
TOTAL WORKDAYS (all family members)	347	327	312

Section IV: Work Performed by the Family (for its own benefit)
Substitution of piece-work for day-work
Work undertaken for the benefit of the family:
  Gardening
  Rental of part of the house

B. Receipts	Sum Total	
Section I: Income from Property	Value of Goods Rec'd in Kind	Cash Receipts
Article 1: Income from Real Property		
Interest (4%) on value of the house	61.33 F	39.67 F
Interest (4%) on value of the garden	1.60 F	
Article 2: Income from Personal Property		
Interest on value of this material	0.25 F	
Article 3: Allocations of the Mutual Aid Funds (no current revenue)		
The value of the allocation is assumed equal to the family's annual contribution, 4.80 F. This sum, which is simply the reimbursement of the equivalent sum paid into the fund, is omitted here, as is the expenditure which balances it.		
TOTAL INCOME FROM PROPERTY	63.53 F	39.67 F
Section II: Income from Subsidies		
Article 1: Income from property received as usufructs. (The family has no income of this kind.)		
Article 2: Income from rights of usage		
Wood (2,000 kilos) with an estimated value of 16.00 F	6.21 F	
Article 3: Goods and Services Allotted		
Reduction (0.065 F per kilo) on the market value of 729 kilos of rye purchased at the domanial stores	47.38 F	
Reduction of interest (1%) on the sum of 2,300.00 F lent by the administration for acquisition of the house	15.34 F	7.66 F
Reduction (0.30 F per 100 kilos) on the market value of 1,900 kilos of wood purchased at the domanial stores	5.70 F	
Expenditure made by the administration for the boys' school: per worker family	9.00 F	
Contribution of the administration to the funds which allocate medical care and cash subsidies to the ill: per worker family	74.20 F	6.75 F
Reduction of interest (1%) on the sum of 40.00 F lent by the administration for acquisition of the garden	0.40 F	
Reduction of interest on a sum of 2,340.00 F due to the administration for acquisition of the house and garden (see above)		
Annual contribution of the administration to the fund which allocates pensions to aged or infirm workers, widows, and orphans below working age: per worker family	13.20 F	
TOTAL INCOME FROM SUBSIDIES	101.43 F	14.41 F

Section III: Wages (excluding the portion of income described in Section IV)

Daily Wages				Sum Total of Receipts	
Father	Mother	Oldest Son		Value of Goods Rec'd in Kind	Cash Receipts
			Salary that a day-worker would receive for this work (no wage can be assigned for this work)		
1.48 F					435.12 F
1.48 F					35.53 F
		0.233 F	Total wages rec'd for this work		69.57 F
0.62 F			Total wages rec'd for this work (or equivalent cost to the administration)	1.24 F	
0.62 F				11.16 F	
	0.62 F		Total wages rec'd for this work	36.58 F	
	0.62 F				26.66 F
0.62 F	0.31 F			4.34 F	
	0.06 F				16.48 F
	0.37 F		Food, estimated value	25.53 F	
	0.31 F		Cash		21.39 F
0.62 F				2.48 F	1.24 F
	0.31 F			9.30 F	
			TOTAL FAMILY WAGES	90.63 F	605.98 F

Section IV: Profits from Additional Work (including the portion of wages considered as profit from the investments of the day-worker; see Section III).

	Wages by Day or by Shift	Value of Goods Rec'd in Kind	Cash Receipts
NOTE: A day-worker performing the same kind of work would receive	1.48 F		22.26 F
Wage increase resulting from this substitution	0.07 F		
Total average wage, by shift	1.55 F	4.91 F	9.43 F
TOTAL PROFITS ACCRUING FROM THIS LABOR		4.91 F	31.69 F

NOTE: In addition to the above-mentioned receipts, the professional work provides a receipt of 1.50 F which is reapplied to the same occupations; this receipt and the expenditure which balances it have been omitted from the respective budgets.

TOTAL ANNUAL RECEIPTS (Balancing expenditures) ....943.25 F   260.50 F   682.75 F

Section 15: Budget of Annual Expenditures

Section I: Expenditures for Food	Price and Weight of Foodstuffs		Sum Total of Expenditures	
			Value of Consumed Goods in Kind	Cash Expenditure
	Quantity Consumed	Price Per K		
Food consumed by the household (by the worker for 365 days; his wife for 296 days; and three children aged 14, 11, and 8 for 365 days):				
Grains: Rye, consumed as bread (16.00 F)	889.0 K	0.728 F	70.32 F	176.66 F
Fats: Butter, lard	18.3 K	1.430 F		26.17 F
Beef or mutton fat	8.1 K	1.230 F		8.05 F
Total Weight & Average Price	24.4 K	1.402 F		
Dairy Products & Eggs				
Cow's milk	114.0 K	0.140 F		15.96 F
Chicken eggs	4.5 K	0.700 F		3.15 F
Total Weight & Average Price	118.5 K	0.161 F		
Meat & Fish				
Pork: meat—49 K at 0.77 F, 37.73 F; sausage, blood sausage, etc., 36.5 K at 0.88 F, 32.12 F	85.5 K	0.817 F		69.85 F
Fish: (family consumes none)				
Total Weight & Average Price	85.5 K	0.817 F		
Fruits & Vegetables				
Tubers: potatoes, purchase price at Goslar, 0.075 F per K; transportation from Goslar to Clausthal, 0.020 F	338.0 K	0.095 F	6.76 F	25.35 F
Dried legumes: lentils, purchase price at Goslar, per kilo, 0.115 F; transportation from Goslar to Clausthal, 0.20 F	10.0 K	0.170 F	0.20 F	1.50 F

Section I: Expenditures for Food	Price and Weight		Sum Total of Expenditures	
	Quantity Consumed	Price Per K	Value of Consumed Goods	Cash Expenditures
Green veg. for cooking: cabbage, beans, etc.				
Root veg.: carrots				
Seasoning veg.: onions, parsley, sorrel				
Cucurbitaceous plants: cucumbers				
In all 310 K purchased in Goslar (including transportation), 200 K provided by garden	510.0 K	0.072 F	17.83 F	19.00 F
Fruits with seeds and pits: apples (purchased at Goslar—purchase and transportation)	15.0 K	0.110 F	0.35 F	1.30 F
Total Weight & Average Price	873.0 K	0.083 F		
Condiments & Stimulants				
Salt	36.0 K	0.120 F		4.32 F
Sweets: molasses	4.7 K	1.420 F		6.67 F
Aromatic beverages: coffee	2.8 K	1.330 F		3.72 F
Total Weight & Average Price	43.5 K	0.338 F		
Fermented Beverages				
Brandy (consumed in small quantities before meals)	25.0 K	0.540 F		13.50 F
Beer (diluted with three parts water)	148.0 K	0.100 F		14.80 F
Total Weight & Average Price	173.0 K	0.164 F		
Food prepared and consumed outside the home.				
Various foods: the wife's food for 69 workdays in private homes (14, Sec. III), estimated value 0.37 F				25.53 F
TOTAL EXPENDITURES FOR FOOD			120.99 F	390.20 F

	Sum Total of Expenditures	
Section II: Living Expenses	Value of Consumed Goods in Kind	Cash Expenditures
Lodging: Rental for the part of the house occupied by the family, 76.67 F; upkeep of the house, 3.72 F	79.15 F	1.24 F
Furnishings: Upkeep of bed linen, utensils, furniture		7.29 F
Heat: wood, 3,900 K @ 0.676 F	24.66 F	1.71 F
Light: oil, 12.2 K @ 1.22 F;		
candles, 4 K @ 1.34 F & 5.36 F		20.24 F
TOTAL LIVING EXPENSES	103.81 F	30.39 F
Section III: Expenditures on Clothing		
Clothing:		
Worker's: purchased & homemade	4.65 F	67.24 F
Wife's: " "	2.32 F	33.62 F
Children's: " "	2.33 F	33.62 F
Laundry: Soap, 11.2 K @ 1.10 F & 12.32 F		
Starch, 1.00 F		13.32 F
TOTAL CLOTHING EXPENSES	9.30 F	147.80 F
Section IV: Expenditures pertaining to moral needs, amusements, and health services		
Religion: contribution for the support of the clergy and church		1.96 F
Education of the children: boys' school fees paid by the administration, 9.00 F; girls' school paid by the family	9.00 F	5.12 F
Contributions and charity: (there are no indigents in the area since the infirm, aged, widows, and orphans are subsidized by the administration.)		
Amusements and ceremonies: smoking tobacco, 8.6 K @ 1.13 F		9.72 F
Health Services: Medical and surgical care, medicines, bandages, etc.: costs paid by a mutual insurance fund	4.20 F	1.80 F
TOTAL EXPENSES PERTAINING TO MORAL NEEDS, AMUSEMENTS AND HEALTH SERVICES	13.20 F	18.60 F

	Sum Total of Expenditures	
Section V: Expenditures pertaining to professional work, debts, taxes, and insurance	Value of Consumed Goods in Kind	Cash Expenditures
NOTE: The sum total of expenditures pertaining to the work exercised for benefit of the family amounts to 47.66 F. This sum is balanced by the receipts provided by these same occupations, to wit:		
Cash and goods used for household consumption and included in this category in the budget ... 46.16 F		
Cash and goods reapplied to the professional work as floating capital which cannot therefore be included in the household's expenses .... 1.50 F		
Interest on Debts: Interest on the money owed the general administration (2,340.00 F) following acquisition of the house and garden: 4% interest		93.60 F
Taxes: (the family pays no direct taxes)		
Insurance of the family's moral and physical well-being: annual contribution to several mutual aid funds providing a pension for aged or infirm workers, widows, and orphans below working age, and a decent burial for workers:		
Contribution withheld from the worker's wages: portion of the total withheld (6.96 F) which is applicable to this insurance, 2.16 F; contribution of the administration, 13.20 F	13.20 F	2.16 F
Annual contribution to various mutual aid funds providing medical and surgical care, with cash subsidies for sick workers:		
Contribution withheld from the worker's wages: portion of the total withheld (6.96 F) which is applicable to this insurance, 4.80 F. This sum merely passes through the Society's coffers and returns to the family in the form of medical care and cash subsidies: thus this sum has been omitted here, as has the receipt which balances it.		
Annual contribution of the administration. This sum is partly spent by the worker (4.20 F) in the form of medical and surgical care, and is included in this category above (Sec. IV); in part it is transmitted through the fund as cash (6.75 F) to the worker who spends it for various household needs; as such, this portion is already included in preceding articles.		
TOTAL EXPENDITURES FOR PROFESSIONAL WORK, DEBTS, TAXES, AND INSURANCE	13.20 F	95.76 F
Annual Savings		
Since the workers are protected against any unforeseen eventualities by the corporation's social welfare institutions, and they dispose of only a fixed salary which is just sufficient for their needs, they save money only in exceptional circumstances.		
TOTAL ANNUAL EXPENDITURES (Balanced by Receipts) 943.25	260.50 F	682.75 F

VARIOUS ELEMENTS OF THE SOCIAL ORGANIZATION
Important Facts of Social Organization; Noteworthy Details; General Observations; Conclusions

Section 17: The Mining Corporation of the Upper Harz Mountains

Most of the mineral veins on which the industry of the upper Harz Mountains is based are granted to companies of shareholders whose members generally live outside the district. For several centuries, management of the operations has been confined to an administration placed under the control of the country's rulers. The engineers in charge of the works must think more in terms of future interests than present benefits, and aim less at producing immediate profits than at spreading profits evenly over an extended period....

The state owns the forests which provide wood for the support of the underground excavations and firewood for the foundries and the workers' homes....

The sale of the metals produced and the purchase of materials needed for operation of the mines and foundries and for the support of the population are done by commercial administrations organized through the state.

The profits realized in the various branches of activity do not revert immediately either to the shareholders or the state. Substantial reserves are withheld to insure a calm weathering of the critical periods caused by natural disasters, wars, and political revolutions....

Compared with more prosperous centers of the mining industry, the mines of the upper Harz are poor in metals. The climate is harsh; the soil, covered with forests, is not suitable for the cultivation of grains or the production of other foodstuffs, with the exception of milk and cabbage. The population must thus seek all essential foods in the nearby plains. The people are patient and docile but lack initiative and energy. They are more disposed to be satisfied with their moderate degree of well-being than to try to achieve a better life.

It is in these difficult conditions that the corporations of miners, founders, and woodsmen of the Harz Mountains have developed and been preserved since the eleventh century.

Wages and income are just sufficient to allow each member a modest existence, in harmony with his position in the social hierarchy; but the permanence of this existence is guaranteed by the reserves which have already been mentioned and by the system of institutions which guarantees the perpetuation of the mining companies. Tradition guarantees the corporations a kind of right to work in the metal deposits and related industries, under the authority of the government. Their members have a veritable legal mortgage on the products which are extracted, which cannot be superseded either by the right of the owners or of a third party. A complete system of social institutions, listed below, provides for all immediate or eventual needs which may arise from birth to death.

Thus the general administration sells wheat to the workers of each corporation at a fixed price, which is lowered in bumper years.... The administration provides 36.21 kilos of wheat a month at this rate for each unmarried workman and twice this amount for each married man. The sizeable expense occasioned by these sales at reduced rates is shared: half is covered by the state, a third by the stock companies, and a sixth by a fund called the *Bergbaukasse* which is fed by the tithe levied on mine production.

In case of illness or injury the worker receives his full salary for two weeks; if he is away from work longer, he is paid 3.71 F a week regardless of the length of his illness. All medical, surgical, and pharmaceutical aid, moreover, is provided free of charge.

When injuries, premature infirmity, or old age result in permanent disability, the worker receives a pension of 3.71 F a week, half of which is payable to his widow; in addition he receives a weekly subsidy of 0.46 F for each child under the age of fourteen. Three special funds provide for this pension aid and subsidies.... The organization of these funds is closely related to local customs and the basic structure of local industry. One cannot recommend too strongly that they be studied by administrators concerned by the state of neglect and isolation of the lower segments of the population in the "systems of liberty" which are better suited for a more moral and intelligent population....

The Harz system also includes institutions no less varied or effective which organize primary education, support the church, and assure the workers of a decent burial. The arrangement by which workers can become the owners of their own homes is one of the most useful of this system of subsidies. Home ownership is, in effect, the most necessary condition of well-being for all families. The problem of restoring this well-being to the improvident families of the cities ranks first among the problems connected with reform in the West. The elements of the solution can clearly be seen in the Harz system.

In summary, the climate, the relative poverty of the mineral deposits, and the nature of the work impose a harsh and toilsome life on the population; but social institutions guarantee that no unforeseen circumstances can trouble the calm of this life. The Harz corporation was formed with a single and exclusive objective: its sole purpose is the deeply felt necessity of providing the workers a means of livelihood which cannot be compromised by public calamities, commercial fluctuations, or individual moral imperfection. This goal has been achieved by preserving intact the principles of industrial hierarchy and patronage; and elsewhere, among populations whose moral and intellectual development is still not perfected, abandonment of these principles has compromised the real elements of the race's well-being.

IV. THEORY OF SOCIAL MOBILITY

12

CONSTRUCTING A SOCIAL HIERARCHY

Workers can be recognized by certain common traits which were indicated in the definition given earlier; these traits distinguish them from society's other classes. At the same time, workers are far from being equal among themselves. In Europe, more than on the other continents, they can be distinguished from each other by three principal circumstances: their occupation, their rank in the hierarchy of workers in that occupation, the terms of their relationship with the men at the top of that hierarchy.

In my description of the population's livelihoods, I compared the "social value" of the different groups of familiar trades. As a criterion of social value, I chose the relative aptitudes of each of these trades to maintain moral order among the families who work at them. It is thus sufficient to mention a worker's occupation at the head of the monograph's main title in order to give the reader a preliminary method of assigning a family's true rank in a systematic classification of the race.

Rarely do all the workers in a single occupation attain the same rank. Raising themselves bit by bit from the lowest position to the one which reflects affluence and virtue in the most advanced degree, they can occupy six stations which are generally ranked in an order which I will indicate. The special nuances of each echelon vary in Europe's different regions: I will describe the echelons which are most common in Western Europe.

From *Les Ouvriers européens* (Tours: Mame, 1879), vol. 1, pp. 229–36.

Domestic workers rarely have their own household: they are unmarried and attached to their employer's household. They work exclusively for this employer. They are compensated in different ways: in part by a salary, in larger part by subsidies in kind to provide for their basic needs. In societies with simple mores, the domestic worker's position is modest but secure and in harmony with his inner feelings; sometimes his situation can become permanent, with the aid of marriage and certain allocations which give the domestic worker the characteristics of a tenant.

In complicated Western societies, the domestic worker, though he earns a somewhat larger salary, is rarely satisfied with his situation and is clearly inclined to change it.

Day-laborers are heads of households; and in simple eastern and northern societies they invariably own their own dwellings. In the West, they are reduced more and more often to that abnormal condition which is one of the principal causes of social antagonism and instability in this region: they must content themselves with dwellings provided by landowners who extract a living from renting out their property. Day-laborers work entirely for other people, either for a single patron or for several employers. They are compensated in part by subsidies which are distributed according to the needs of their families, in larger part by a cash salary, whose size depends on the number of workdays the worker has provided.

Job-workers are heads of households and work exclusively for other people, just as day-laborers do. But two important characteristics set them a cut above day-laborers. With the employer, they negotiate a contract that is advantageous to both parties: they promise faithfully to accomplish a given amount of work in exchange for an agreed price. By physical exertion and by constant application, they reduce the employer's expenses and increase the income from their daily labor. In addition, they acquire legitimate independence by becoming free to budget their time according to their own needs. Thus they take an important step toward the independent status of the master craftsman who works for himself.

Worker-tenants are still another step closer to independence.

They exploit, for their own profit, a piece of property provided in exchange for rent by an owner who belongs to a different social class. The leasing of this property is invariably the basis for a lucrative exploitation. It brings two families together in a natural association. The first family is relatively rich. On the property, it owns more equipment than it can exploit by itself. Often families in this position completely renounce exploitation of their property to live off the income from rents: they seek the honor which among strong races is assured to those large proprietors who fulfill their traditional function of patronage on behalf of the tenant and who serve the public interest without financial compensation. The second family lacks the necessary capital for a successful exploitation, but it does have the moral virtues which, along with the proprietor's patronage, are sufficient to assure success. Leasing property to tenants is a fruitful arrangement when each family fulfills the duties which its social condition requires. It has none of the unwholesome characteristics to be found in the renting of dwellings, a practice which occurs when proprietors have lost touch with the spirit of patronage, and when the lessee possesses none of those qualities which, as I just indicated, are essential to good tenants. Unlike the workers previously mentioned, tenants cannot be classified as a group of similarly situated families; tenants occupy a whole series of social positions, ranging from the bottom of the working class to the top, including the domestic worker who has the right to own one of the farm animals in his employer's herd and the master craftsman who pays rent for the use of a piece of property which will provide enough work for him and every member of his family. All of the day-laborers and job-workers in this category at least "hold" their dwellings. In towns, the dwelling is accompanied by a workshop or a little store; in the country, by stables and various rural outbuildings. These tenants are specially called urban *bordiers* and rural *bordiers*.

Worker-proprietors occupy all the positions which worker-tenants occupy, but they differ in that they are full owners of their property. This difference, even between those who occupy equally important property, implies the social superiority of the proprietor over the tenant. Monographs comparing the two classes demonstrate this superiority in material wealth, intellectual development, and moral values. The proprietor doesn't have to deduct the cost of rent from the yield of his exploitation. He is too discerning to make mistakes in judgment that would jeopardize his success; and to avoid these perils, he does not have to resort to the patronage of a proprietor the way a tenant does. Finally, he resists the vices which arise from the sensual appetites and the traps set by moneylenders. The contrast which I have just presented shows that a group of tenants cannot be immediately transformed into independent proprietors. Evidence for this truth can be found in the results of the imprudent laws which have been passed since 1848 to emancipate the feudal tenants of Russia, Hungary, and Austria. Certain tenants who lived happily under the authority of their traditional masters have begun to fall under the harsh sway of saloon-keepers and usurers.

Master craftsmen, whether they are tenants or proprietors, are a class above the rest. They can be recognized by one characteristic which leaves a strong imprint on all their activities: they work exclusively for themselves. This is the situation of the nail-maker and the rope-maker who have settled in workshops; this is also the case for the blacksmith, the mason, the carpenter, and other workers in the building trades who have, in addition to their own workshop or their own dwelling, a clientele for their trade in their vicinity. They have reached the limit which separates workers from masters at the point when, still working with their own hands but completely losing the characteristics of day-laborers and job-workers, they rely on the assistance of members of their families and, when necessary, of domestic workers. Worker-masters have two special names in the West's most common trades: they are called *peasants* in agriculture and *artisans* in the manufacturing industries in towns and in the country.

The particular features which distinguish these six categories of workers form a complex combination of ideas. This complexity would hinder simplicity and the clarity of the monographs if it were necessary to reproduce for each monograph the peculiarities of every worker described. It was therefore useful to summarize these distinguishing features in six words, and briefly to convey the worker's situation by mentioning one of these words in the title.

A worker's status is not completely accounted for by the financial terms of his relationship with his employer. The most important feature to bring out is not the salary which the employer pays to the domestic worker, the day-laborer, or the job-worker, nor is it the amount of rent that the tenant pays the proprietor: most important is the nature and duration of the arrangement which links the two parties. Generally, this information applies not only to the description of a particular worker; it characterizes the entire society to which the worker belongs. Often it enables us to tell in advance whether peace or dissension is a society's primary characteristic.

13

INTRAGENERATIONAL MOBILITY

Trades which are pursued for the profit of the family vary widely in importance, depending on a country's social organization and on a worker's place in the hierarchy he belongs to. Even more pronounced differences can be observed in the way the roles which a worker and the members of his family play in a family trade can vary from one place to another. The framework of the budget has been designed in such a way that the budget can reflect these distinctions in the most detailed way.

In general, for a given social organization, the number and importance of family trades increase in proportion as the worker climbs the rungs of the ladder which separates the simple domestic worker from the worker-proprietor.

In the West, the domestic worker is often obliged to remain unmarried and cannot devote himself to work which is not directly connected to his service to his employer. However, as we have previously indicated, this rule has exceptions which are linked to the distinguishing features of each society. These exceptions can be found mainly in countries where a domestic worker's station is essentially temporary, a stage during which the worker does his apprenticeship for his main occupation and acquires, through savings, the means to become in his turn head of a household and to advance to a higher social station.

Day-laborers often obtain substantial revenue by exploiting domestic animals, by cultivating fruits and vegetables, by pre-

From *Les Ouvriers européens* (Tours: Mame, 1878), vol. 1, pp. 282–85.

paring textile fabrics, and generally by pursuing trades which require little capital and simple materials. Some day-laborers are even beginning to find ways to make extra money while doing their main job for an employer. Thus, for example, instead of receiving tools from the boss, as a majority of salaried workers do, they furnish these tools themselves. This arrangement provides a supplement to their salary which is ordinarily rather considerable in comparison with the cost of providing the tools. The portion of this supplement which exceeds the expenditure of the capital required to buy the tool and the interest on the loan required to obtain that capital is a genuine business profit and must be entered in the fourth section of the budget. This type of profit is common among day-laborers who use their own scythes to harvest hay or grain, or who use their own pickaxes to prepare earthworks.

Job-workers are more capable than day-laborers of expanding the range of trades which are pursued entirely for the profit of their families. They owe this superiority to three principal causes: they are more active and intelligent; they have more extensive resources at their disposal; they are freer to budget their time according to their personal needs. In addition, they develop the various agricultural and manufacturing trades on a larger scale than day-laborers do, and they are more ambitious entrepreneurs. They specialize in arranging the time they spend on their main job in a multitude of ingenious ways. They are thus able to accomplish more work than the average worker under the same conditions, and consequently they receive greater compensation. The portion of this salary which exceeds that of the simple day-laborer for the same amount of time worked must be considered a profit of the job-worker's own trade. This kind of trade has three advantages over that of the day-laborer: it guarantees that time will be better spent; it spawns faster and more perfect work techniques; it protects the boss against losses of finished products by making the job-worker responsible for all the losses which the events of human life make possible. The job-worker often undertakes at his own expense to provide not only tools but also industrial equipment, workshops, and raw materials. Using a system which provides bonuses for good manufactured products and penalties for bad ones, the job-worker sometimes commits himself to guaranteeing good products, or at least assuming responsibility for defective products. Finally, drawing even closer to the status of master craftsmen, certain job-workers hire assistants—particularly apprentices—at their own expense. In the highly complex investment which this arrangement involves, the job-worker ordinarily clears a certain profit, after he has seen to the costs of supporting the apprentice and buying materials for this more or less inexperienced helper to work with.

It has been necessary to distinguish between two kinds of compensation which day-workers and job-workers receive. With respect to work accomplished, I have entered in the third section of the receipts budget that portion of a worker's compensation which is not a return on an investment or a trade of his own; I am referring to the salary which the day-laborer who can only offer his time would receive for doing the same work that a job-worker does. In view of the considerations which have just been discussed, I have assigned the second portion of a worker's compensation to the fourth and last section of the budget, which deals with the various trades which a family pursues for its own profit. However, since these distinctions are rarely observed in practice, I have taken care in each budget, after computing both portions of the job-worker's daily income, to add them together.

Workers who in various degrees possess the characteristics of tenants, proprietors, and master craftsmen specialize in pursuing (either for their own profit or in a joint venture with the proprietor) one of the major trades. This trade will be pursued in concert with some auxiliary trades, which will be conducted either by the worker himself or by his wife and children. These cases are exactly analogous to those which have just been examined. The principal differences which should be pointed out are that business profits here take on more importance than salaries and that the calculation of these profits involves larger quantities and a wider variety of elements.

14

COMPARING OCCUPATIONAL STYLES

Most of the working-class population of large Russian cities is composed of itinerant workers; but such workers are a relatively small minority in Paris today. There are two main classes of itinerant workers. The first are *short-term, seasonal workers:* masons, for example, who work in Paris during the summer and return to their native province each winter, to a small agricultural property acquired through the savings of the head of the family as well as by inheritance. The second category of itinerant workers includes *long-term itinerants,* such as water-carriers, stove and chimney repairmen, stevedores, fuel vendors, junk dealers, etc. With the help of their relatives at home, these workers use their savings to acquire and enlarge a small property in the native province, to which they retire in their old age. Most workers in the first category inhabit France's Massif Central, especially the Marche and Limousin areas, that is, the edge of the Massif Central closest to Paris. Members of the second category can travel greater distances from home without difficulty. Many of them come from the mountains of the Rouergue and Auvergne regions; others emigrate from Savoy and even from the high valleys of the Piedmont region; and thus for more than two centuries the stove and chimney repairmen of Paris have been recruited exclusively from the valley of Domo d'Ossola, north of Lake Maggiore.

From *Les Ouvriers européens* (Tours: Mame, 1879), vol. 6, pp. 287–301.

Masons have more settled ways than most other itinerant workers. They usually come from families of small owner-farmers in rural communities which share communal pastureland; each family usually owns at least one milk cow. The children begin their toilsome career at about the age of six by taking the domestic animals out to pasture—either their family's or those entrusted to their care by neighboring farmers or landowners. At about sixteen years of age, the boys select their future occupation. The most intelligent and ablest boys are taken on as apprentices by the principal rural artisans of the area. Those with the least physical strength or intellectual ability take positions as shepherds or domestic servants with local farmers or landowners or simply become day-laborers, and the others become helpers to either their father, a relative, or some friend of the family who has been an itinerant mason for some time; they go to Paris under his care to complete their apprenticeship in the trade.

The young workers are introduced to the tasks and modest habits of the occupation by their master, who traditionally wields firm authority over them. A young man is paid two francs a day for his first season and can send his family savings amounting to seventy francs each year. Toward the fourth season, the salary is raised to 2.5 francs a day, and the savings amount to 110 francs; finally, at about the ninth season, the salary is raised to 3.5 francs daily and the annual savings amount to 200 francs. At the age of twenty-five or twenty-six, the mason marries in his native province, never in Paris: the comparison he is able to make of the habits of the laboring classes in the two localities easily convince him that it would be difficult to find a Parisian woman with the simplicity, thrift, aptitude for outdoor labor, and strong determination which are necessary to help him acquire a small property.

During his stay in Paris the mason lives with all the economic restrictions appropriate to his bachelor status. His food consists of meat or vegetable soup, bread, boiled beef, vegetables, salad, cheese, and a moderate amount of wine and brandy. It costs him about 38 francs a month. The price of lodging, including the evening soup, costs only about 8 francs a month. Usually, ten workers of the same profession are lodged together in the same room, where they sleep two to a bed. The room is unheated, and it is lit by an inexpensive tallow candle which each roommate provides in turn. The roommates usually pass the hours between the end of their day's work and bedtime in the kitchen where the landlady is preparing their supper. Their clothing consists of a smock, a pair of trousers, a coarse linen shirt, a vest, a tie, a cap, and shoes. This costs 7 or 8 francs a month, and laundry costs 1.5 francs. Expenses for tools amount to only a few francs each season. A mason can limit his monthly expenses to 60 francs if he abstains from frequenting taverns—a dangerous reef for many—and if he limits himself to the use of smoking tobacco, the cheapest of all amusements. Under such conditions he can accumulate the annual savings previously mentioned, notwithstanding the occasional slack periods which may occur. It is worth mentioning that this sizeable sum is saved on a salary which is much lower than that of many sedentary workers who, on the contrary, always spend more than they earn or, at the very least, never fail to incur as many debts as their creditors will allow.

At the age of forty-five, masons who have continued to make this kind of seasonal migration usually own a house, a vegetable garden, one or two hectares of arable land and meadow, a cow, and several domestic animals. The total value of this property ranges from 6,000 to 10,000 francs. Henceforward the head of the family remains at home, tilling his own property and working for nearby farmers or landowners in his spare time. He then begins to enjoy the ease and consideration which he has achieved through hard work and foresight.

These mores provide a striking contrast with those of the sedentary population. Nevertheless, it is clear that in the last years they have been changing due to the influence of events which have disrupted former work habits and affected everyone's thinking. Thus, during their stay in Paris young masons seem more likely than before to form illicit relationships, to spend money on clothing, and to frequent meeting-places and pleasure halls. At the same time that their chances of rising to the status of owner are diminishing, young masons are becoming more prone to feelings of jealousy which are developing against the upper classes of society. This depravement occurs far from the influence of the family in men who have retained their natural roughness and in whom the love of material gain has developed without the counterbalance of religious sentiment; it sometimes takes on a tone of vulgarity which is never found in sedentary Parisian workers, even in much less comfortable circumstances. These tendencies are still only nascent; if they were to develop, the system of seasonal migration would no longer maintain a happy state of equilibrium as it has in the past and would be a constant source of disturbances in French society.

The sedentary workers of Paris hold numerous jobs in industrial organizations, ranging from large mechanized factories owned by rich manufacturers to small home workshops which are classified with communal workshops [*fabriques collectives*]. Despite this diversity, there is one common characteristic which generally distinguishes these workers from itinerant workers: the absence of any propensity for thrift. In fact, should a worker possess this characteristic, he quickly rises to the status of master artisan or small businessman. The general ease of entering the ranks of the bourgeoisie, for an intelligent worker, makes the provident worker relatively more common in our society than in less advanced civilizations, where social estates are rigidly fixed; the provident worker can thus be considered only as a transitional type.

We can say that that most common types of Parisian worker are best described through their expenditures, particularly those which deal with clothing and amusements. They can be divided into two main groups according to the nature of these expenditures.

The habits of workers in the first group are completely different from those of the bourgeoisie. They dress in smocks, jackets, or overcoats; their main amusement is relaxing outside the city limits in the numerous cabarets and taverns near the toll-gate wall or in the villages of Suresne, Belleville, Charonne, Bagnolet, Romainville, Chentilly, Montrouge, Vaugirard, etc.—places frequented only by their equals. They rarely read newspapers and, in general, they are not interested in politics except when events concern them directly. They are not jealous of their employer's influence, but rather of his leisure, and would like to be less burdened by their work and free to indulge in their weekly debauches for more than a single day. The liaisons which they establish in places of amusement are usually short-lived. This kind of life continues until their old age if they are not influenced by an orderly and laborious woman to adopt, with the state of matrimony, a more regular life.

Workers in the second group, due to the nature of their occupation, and the influence of a certain intellectual milieu stemming from the work setting, are constantly incited to copy furnishings, clothing, and amusements of the lower middle class. Like workers in the previous group, they have little propensity for marriage; but their relationships are more stable and they often demand the same consideration for their mistress as for a legitimate wife. They frequent the theaters, small cafés, and public dance halls of the inner city of Paris, where they mingle with young people of a higher social position: members of the lower middle class and shopkeepers.

Their homes are rarely well-kept; furnishings are nearly always neglected. Clothing represents at least two-thirds of the total assets, and articles whose value can most easily be converted into cash are regularly deposited at pawn shops [*monts-de-piété*] to serve as collateral for loans.

In view of the slack periods which occur regularly in many occupations, it is unusual for the Parisian worker to be employed more than 280 days a year. But regardless of industry's needs, Mondays are always used not for rest but for enjoyment. At least half of the household's income is spent on food, and the other half, in nearly equal portions, goes for lodging, clothing, and leisure.

In general, these workers have no feeling for religion, not even the women. They never go to church and observe no religious rituals. Often, neither member of these illicit relationships remains faithful to the other. The woman is authorized to conduct the household affairs, and she sometimes uses her authority to introduce a little order in the way the money is used. But this influence does not extend to the selection of amusements, and the woman is often prohibited from even participating in them. On the contrary, however, married women in the same class have a more dignified and influential position, and adultery is very infrequent among married couples.

Discussions pertaining to wages and especially time stipulations on the completion of work are a permanent source of irritation and distrust between workers and employers. This antagonism exerts a harmful influence on the character of both worker and employer. It is particularly detrimental to the qualities of the worker, who would be more loyal and open-minded under better conditions. Slack periods and destructive competition aggravate the disadvantages inherent in their system of labor, in addition to the problems caused by the workers' own improvidence. Thus, throughout their lives workers are exposed to alternating periods of misery and demoralizing amusements, always followed by a wretched old age.

Recently, the antagonisms engendered by this social organization have been stirred up by interest groups hoping to profit from such disturbances or by political parties seeking support in them. These influences have led the Parisian worker to take a greater part in political debates than his natural inclination and intellectual capacity would normally warrant. The largest class of workers to whom most of the above-mentioned characteristics apply are the tailors, and this group is one of those among whom the taste for politics has most developed over the past three years. This type of worker avidly seeks literature which accepts the present antagonism between workers and employers and suggests the possibility of a social order in which workers, without ceasing to be improvident, would nevertheless be in a position of greater importance. The workers, however, are not eager to pursue the development of social systems proposed to attain this goal; indeed, most workers showed little interest in the meetings which were held in 1848 to discuss such systems methodically; the majority of workers merely sympathize with writers who advocate the creation of such a new order.

The favorite reading material of the tailor is histories of the Revolution of 1789. He approves of authors who develop the idea that this revolution was desirable and that it ameliorated the condition of the laboring classes. He is exalted by the dramatic presentation of men and events which he finds in the works of so many famous authors; and he is empassioned by narratives which describe in glowing terms all the personages whose talents, energy, and passions most contributed to the destruction of the "Ancien Régime." He does not realize that the principal cause of his own social inferiority is in himself, but likes to think that men like these will strike new blows for progress and save him from the many calamities which still beset him. These popular heroes are a frequent topic of conversation in the workshops: the workers who best expound on their actions and manage to recite a few snatches of their speeches to the Revolutionary Assembly easily win the admiration of their comrades. Young workers from the provinces, where so little learning exists, are particularly impressed by this knowledge of history.

Moreover, the Parisian worker in general, and the tailor in particular, are not simply concerned with their own interests in this vague aspiration for political and social revolutions. On the contrary, they hope that by encouraging new upheavals they will contribute to general social progress and national grandeur.

These aspirations played an important role in the creation of the many worker groups which aroused great public interest in the wake of the events of 1848. These associations grew out of a spirit of antagonism toward employers, particularly the small entrepreneurs who had risen from the working class and often acted as middle men between worker-producers and merchants in the Parisian system of group production. These associations were also founded in the hope that work undertaken on a group basis would assure the workers, in addition to their former wages, of the profits which presently accrue to intermediaries and merchants. Moreover, the promoters of these associations were inspired by noble intentions and were convinced that they would gradually attract the entire working-class population. They wanted to guarantee equal advantages to all the members, regardless of their skills or when they joined the organization. At first this enthusiasm and confidence resulted in praiseworthy efforts in many groups. In order to build up a social fund, the members submitted to much greater privations than those they had suffered in the normal economic system. Unusually gifted administrators managed the groups' business and accepted only the wages of a simple worker for their labor. But although these initial achievements are certainly worthy of admiration, these enterprises did not go on to produce the results which had been expected. Good manners, hard work, and thrift, which the members accepted as points of honor, resulted in real advantages, as they would in any social system; but the functioning of these organizations did not offer any particular practical advantage. The most skilled workers and the most intelligent merchants soon realized that they had greater independence and easier access to social advancement in the regular system. With few exceptions, most of the worker-groups created in the excitement of the 1848 movement quickly failed. The only portion of the working-class population that they successfully attached was the limited number of workers whose elevated virtues enabled them to fulfill the demands of group endeavor but who lacked the initiative and energy necessary for success in a free-market system. The history of these endeavors—even as it is found in the works of their supporters—substantiates the other facts stated in this study: it shows how difficult it is to implement the principle of community in spite of the general trends of modern civilization.

The Parisian worker's failings are often paired with remarkable qualities. He is able to feel the noblest sentiments: compassion, selflessness, enthusiasm. But in the difficult situation in which he often finds himself as a result of his improvidence, these qualities rarely come into play and remain, as it were, in a latent state. Thus an unfettered desire for pleasure leads to unending penury, and although the worker would like to help his aged and destitute parents, his weekly debauchery constantly deprives him of the means.

The substitution of antagonism for loyalty in worker-employer relations is detrimental to the morals of the improvident worker because it deprives him of the opportunity to demonstrate his natural virtues in the only way which is accessible to him. A worker can best manifest his virtue of self-sacrifice by his desire to act well, by his concern for his employer's interests, and by the sacrifice of tastes and passions that are incompatible with regular work. This is easier for the worker compared to the kind of self-sacrifice that consists of helping his relatives by means of a sum of money. A sense of duty created through relationships based on solidarity teaches habits which will eventually raise the morality of even the most common people, while the seeds of more noble sentiments often remain sterile and cannot come to fruition when they are scattered in a void among the workers. The kind of virtue which is manifested in sustained help and protection is the special attribute of the upper classes; it can be seen in workers in sudden flashes of brief duration, but the virtue which is most within their means is manifested by fulfilling their duty to their employer.

The kind of solidarity which has been destroyed today in many Parisian workshops and in much of French society has survived in northern and eastern countries—not because the two classes of society there are inspired by any more noble sentiments concerning their reciprocal duties, but because traditions are supported by positive legislation to preclude the detrimental consequences of individual moral imperfections. The most prosperous and stable societies have been able to reconcile the preservation of social harmony with the suppression of those bonds which hamper individual action; but they have not been able to achieve this goal without the tutelary intervention of religion. It is for this reason in particular that England has thus far been spared the trials which France has suffered and which have spread to other nations of the Continent with the progress of civil liberty and the flood of skepticism. Moreover, comparative studies do not indicate any inferiority in the working classes of France and Germany, and thus the main responsibility for the temporary decadence in those countries lies with the upper classes of society. In the course of this work, we have often had occasion to point out the harmful consequences of the weakening of religious sentiment and the growing taste for luxury among employers in Parisian manufactures. In large measure, these new habits are responsible for the gradual fading of the sentiments of solidarity, patronage, and, as it were, the strong family loyalty that characterized Parisian manufactures at the beginning of this century. The scope of this study does not permit us to develop this point, even though it would provide many valuable lessons. We will merely indicate its importance and state that all the elements necessary for a methodical comparison of the old and the new systems of organization in Parisian workshops can still be found today.

Any discussion of the principal categories of Parisian workers must include the sculptors, designers, chiselers, engravers, etc., who play such an important role in the production of tasteful and costly objets d'art and luxury items which are famous throughout the world. It is an important question whether or not residence in a great city develops the artistic aptitudes and noble qualities in the masses which would occur spontaneously in an isolated pastoral life as a result of meditation and contemplation, or would develop in the pastimes of less developed civilizations.... Nevertheless, it cannot be denied that the workers' taste and manual dexterity provide ample means for the execution of artistic conceptions, that is to say, they are the principal cause of the success of Parisian manufactures. It is worth noting that although these workers earn higher salaries because of their skill, they are precisely the ones who manifest the least propensity for thrift and foresight, and they best represent the prevailing type of worker whose main characteristics have just been described.

The image we have drawn of the habits of the working-class population of Paris in no way describes the sizeable and admirable minority in whom we find good habits as well as improvidence. It is just this noteworthy type which we have tried to describe in the present work. By choosing this type of worker in an occupation at the bottom of the social hierarchy, we give sufficient proof that this type is not just an exception in Paris. The worker with religious feelings nowhere in the world—even in Geneva, which is so unusual in this respect—achieves a higher moral level than in Paris. The reason is clear when one analyzes the influences which affect him daily, and the magnitude of the ordeals which give the measure of his moral superiority. Such workers must often resist the example set by employers imbued with the skeptical mentality of the past century as well as the harmful influences which stem from an organization that deprives him of the most legitimate pastimes. Moral strength is always a rare quality, but on this strength alone the religious worker must withstand the jests of his comrades without irritation or shame, and he must have enough control over his emotions to resist the temptations of places of pleasures or immorality which are so enticing and are placed within the reach of every income or intellect. Without entering more deeply into this question than is possible in a simple note on the details of the workers' life, one can easily understand that these men must cling to their religious sentiment—their only support in the midst of so many trials—with uncommon zeal and nobility.

Many workers are abandoned without protection or counsel to the isolation which the new system creates in the midst of vast metropolises. What is more, the very generosity of their feelings often precludes the calculations and planning necessary for provident behavior. Thus, sometimes on their own, sometimes with the responsibilities and burdens of a large family, they are beset by all the ills caused by uneven wages, slack periods, and illness. One of the most touching type of worker in Paris and London is the group of young girls who live alone in straitened and precarious circumstances, depending on what they earn from poorly paid work which is all too often unavailable. It is only with the greatest energy and sobriety that they can provide the most basic necessities; but strengthened by their religious worship, they demonstrate an almost superhuman virtue in resisting the most contagious examples and the most criminal temptations. The extent of their privations, the elevation and nobility of their sentiments can only be truly appreciated by the priest who aids them with his counsel and the kindly doctor or charitable matron who helps them in their most difficult moments. Although the study of our society's miseries is so often discouraging, we can glimpse the dawn of a better day when these patrons of the poor declare that Paris is one of the cities in Europe where the religious worker has reached the greatest moral heights.

At the beginning of this note, we discussed the many workers who, thanks to steady work and stringent economy, rapidly rise above the station in which they were born. But these men usually add to their distinctive characteristics shortcomings shared with other workers in the same social position.... A constant preoccupation with profit and thrift develops egotism and harshness; and this disposition has a harmful effect on their inferiors and even on their family. It leads to a kind of hatred which has not been unimportant in the social upheavals of recent years; and thus amidst the volatile emotions produced by the events of 1848, the workers of Paris manifested particular animosity towards the small businessmen whose origins were in the working class itself and who generally acted as middlemen between the workers and the merchants in the system of "group production" [*fabrique collective*]. Without considering the consequences, or conscious only of their own inferiority, the masses were incited to destroy precisely that avenue which leads most directly to the advancement of the best workers in the present system of manufacture in Paris.

The moral imperfection of the men who rise from the working class is a result of human nature. Foresight and planning, which alone can raise the worker from the status in which he was born, constantly force him to resist the impulses of his heart. The spontaneous gesture of a man who has always been governed by these traits is to resist the inclination to satisfy either his senses or moral sentiments by spending money. Thus, if such men are not moved by exceptional love for their neighbors, or if they are not constantly reminded of their obligations to their fellow men by the all-important influence of religion, it is clear that they will develop all the shortcomings inherent in exaggerated self-interest.

This is not at all the case with most workers, who nearly always manifest a touching and instinctive generosity which is completely free from calculation. Their improvidence allows them to follow their natural inclinations; they respond equally to the excitement of their senses, leading to abuses of sensual pleasure, and to the call of their hearts, which urges them to help their fellow men. Thus one can say that the absence of religious sentiment is less harmful to the personalities of the poor than to those of the rich. Contrary to the widely accepted opinion, then, we can conclude that the preservation of social harmony depends more upon the fostering of religion among the rich than among the poor.

In England, the social system is firmly maintained under the guidance of the most eminent religious leaders, even though the masses are nearly completely ignorant of religion; but a revolution would soon become imminent if the ruling classes should lose, along with their religion, their sense of obligation toward the lower classes. Careful observation of European societies has always confirmed this truth. In those countries where religious sentiment is only slightly developed, workers avoid the reefs of improvidence only to founder on those of egotism, while employers amass greater wealth only to increase their taste for luxury and stray further from righteousness. Among religious countries, on the contrary, the successful worker often retains a genuine concern for the suffering of others, and the employer, while increasing his fortune, alters neither the simplicity of his life nor his affectionate relationship with his inferiors. It is only in such conditions that the risks of energetic industrial growth can be reconciled—in all classes of society—with the practice of charity.

15

CONDITIONS OF SOCIAL MOBILITY

If one tries to go to the heart of the matter, according to the spirit of the method presented in this work, one soon finds that all these varieties of the working class belong, on the whole, to two main types. The first type, still too rare in the present state of civilization, includes those workers who are sustained by their sense of foresight and who, by saving, are constantly building up first properties and then revenues which augment the resources created by labor. The second type is far more common and includes all the individuals dominated by the opposite propensity; among them consumption is always greater than income and has no limits other than credit, no check besides necessity. As soon as a family's domestic life is analyzed and a budget is established, one or the other of these propensities can be seen, as it were, in every detail of family life. Intermediate cases which could be called a neutral state between these two extremes are only exceptions due to anomalies of situation or character and are hardly observed in a general study.

The political and social laws of each country certainly exercise an influence on the development of the sense of foresight among the laboring classes; nevertheless, they are not at all the major influence on the production of these two types since the most opposing tendencies occur simultaneously in the population of a single nation. On the other hand, one cannot consider these ten-

From *Les Ouvriers européens* (Paris: Imprimerie Impériale, 1855), pp. 20–21.

dencies solely as the result of a natural disposition which, like the intellectual faculties, for example, is distinctive of individuals who have developed in the same social milieu. The causes of this phenomenon are not as general as great political influences; nevertheless its sources are more widespread than influences derived from individual characteristics.

Among the principal causes revealed by observation, the most important include the influence of the family, early education, and marriage; habits communicated by the exercise of an occupation and the system of work agreement, and, finally, the general influence on workers' habits provided by either their community, corporation, or system of patronage, or by the complete and sustained exercise of their individual freedom. Tendencies which result from the climate, the topography of the land, natural resources, and the separation or combination of agricultural and industrial labors must also be included. The result and combined effect of all these factors is to encourage or discourage the growth of foresight among nearly all the families in a given region, community, or occupation. To sum up in a few words the present conditions, one can say that as a result of the social and political direction Europe has taken in the past two centuries, the majority of the laboring classes has reached our times devoid of a sense of foresight and that, as of today, the tendency toward ownership of property through saving exists only among the workers of a few regions, communities, and occupations because of the causes indicated above.

The geographical location of these privileged areas would be among the most valuable information which could be provided for the completion of the studies begun in this work. I had the opportunity of observing a rather large number of these areas during the course of my research. I gathered the material for several interesting monographs in these places, concerning among other types the stevedores and migrating boatmen of central Russia, the Ural grain merchants, the Hunsdruck metal founders, the sharecroppers of Old Castille, the migrant workers of Galicia, the Pen-ty, or agricultural day-laborers of lower Brittany, the migrant harvesters of the Soissons region, the Auvergne miners, the Maine blacksmiths, and lastly the master laundry-men of the

Paris suburbs. In general, the superiority of these types cannot be attributed to local conditions that are more favorable to agriculture or industry than conditions elsewhere; on the contrary, in many of these areas the soil, climate, and geographical location generally oppose serious obstacles to human activity. In order to provide the necessities of life, many of these types must migrate periodically and seek the means of work on more fertile soil, in a softer climate, or in areas closer to the great commercial routes. The distinguished position these workers occupy in the European family cannot even be attributed to intellectual superiority, since their mental aptitudes are usually less developed than those of the working classes raised in the great centers of population and industry.

The reasons for their success thus belong exclusively to the moral order: they stem in particular from a love of work and from temperance. These difficult virtues are in turn developed and sustained, on the one hand, by religious feeling, parental authority, and public opinion which permits marriage only among those young people who have given sufficient guarantees to society; and on the other hand, by the unwavering perseverance with which the workers dream—from the very outset of their careers—of one day enjoying the consideration and well-being which is attached to the dignity of the position of head of the family and property owner in their homeland....

This remarkable set of habits is most prevalent in the mountains of Galicia, Asturia, and Biscay in Spain; in the mountains of the Auvergne, in the Marche and Limousin regions in France; in nearly all of Savoy; in the high valleys of the Piedmont region and Lombardy, the Venetian state, the Tyrol, and nearly the entire Apennine chain in Italy. In a slightly different form, the propensity for saving and ownership can still be found to a great degree among the mule-drivers and wagoners of many Spanish provinces; the laundrymen, market-gardeners, and dairy-men of the Paris suburbs; the mowers of Normandy, Picardy, and the Soissons region; the linen and hemp combers of the Franche-Comté; the stove-makers and smokers of the Domo d'Ossola Valley in Piedmont; the blacksmiths of Lucquois and Bergamo;

Conditions of Social Mobility 233

the migrant foresters of Bohemia, etc. The same qualities and similar habits can also be seen among certain categories of agricultural workers, wagoners, and boatmen of northern Germany and Scandinavia; the fishermen of several Mediterranean shores and the North Sea; the wagoners of southern Russia and Siberia; the farmers and horse-raisers of the Don Valley; the Volga and Kama boatmen; the hunters of the northern forests of Russia, etc.

An observer willing to devote himself to this kind of study would derive great satisfaction at penetrating these cases, which are still all too rare in the midst of European civilization, and at finding—often among uneducated men—the true independence engendered by property acquired through work. Nowhere is this characteristic more marked or more assured by local habits than in France in the districts which have just been mentioned. The author will not attempt to prove that France is superior to the other nations of Europe in this respect; it is possible that some nations which appear, at least, to be less actively engaged on the road to reform—Spain, for example—have succeeded in emancipating a larger proportion of their laboring people under the influence of private property and communal goods. Nonetheless, there is no question that France would rank prominently in the kind of inquiry proposed and outlined in the present work. It is equally certain that the reforms appropriate to France's customs and needs, those which, despite passions and prejudice, would result from such an inquiry, would find ample support among many categories of worker-owners.

Aside from these elite populations, which are one of the glories of European civilization, the defects, vices, and misfortunes which are engendered by lack of foresight, laziness, and immorality are all too common among the inferior types of the working class. Nonetheless, wherever the wisdom of the ruling classes and enlightened governmental action maintain the regular play of social institutions, one can see incontestable progress in the condition of the working-class population.

The gradually ascending order of social conditions starts with the shepherd of the steppes in the eastern region of Europe, freed from the uncertainty and violent habits of nomadic life by the principles of authority, the influence of the Christian religion, and the appeal of several civilized habits. Above this type is the peasant who, although initially reluctant to undertake the labors of agriculture, is beginning to appreciate the security of sedentary life and the joys of the domestic hearth. At a higher level, solidarity between peasant and landowner and between worker and managers is established by a succession of personal relationships and common interests. Still higher on the social scale, when a sense of responsibility begins to develop among the heads of family, the landowners and proprietors soon find it to their advantage to enlarge the arena of the worker's personal freedom, proportionately diminishing their duties of protection and patronage. At these higher levels, the worker has become accustomed to subordinating his actions to the inspiration of religion and moral feelings and can guard against the arousal of his physical appetites or the bad example of inferior types in the population, thanks to the habit of work, the force of public opinion, or the kindly support of his superiors; he finally achieves the state of emancipation which no legislator can provide or disregard: individual independence based on property acquired by work and saving.

Among peoples who lack foresight, and for inferior types in general, progress toward this end is made with the aid of a powerful family structure and under the beneficial influence of the community, corporation, or the patronage system; for superior types, and in particular among populations already initiated in the attitudes and habits of property, progress results mostly through complete personal freedom.

Of course, at any given moment this march upward is not always visible in the entire population or for the workers of the main occupations in a given locality. In one place it may be retarded by ignorance and violent passions; in another, moral disturbances and political revolutions contrary to the true needs of the country cause momentary backsliding. Observers everywhere bemoan the slowness of this progress when they measure it against the duration of a human life: in the physical order, a short lapse of time suffices to develop the products of the earth, while in the moral order the space of at least one generation and often of several centuries is necessary before humanity can be sure of acquiring a virtue or a moral idea that will guard it against the evils engendered by vice or prejudice. Any observer who does not sufficiently consider these anomalies and laws could be led to doubt in this progress or to misconstrue the work of emancipation and the transformation which is being affected every day in European society to the profit of the laboring classes. A more patient and wider study would reveal a thousand signs of this progress, the laborious accomplishment of the supreme task imposed on man's efforts by the Divine Will.

V. THEORY OF SOCIAL CHANGE

16

SOCIAL SYSTEMS AND SOCIAL CHANGE

The opposite ends of Europe offer striking contrasts today: while the peoples of the North and the East are largely satisfied with their fate and live in a state of tranquility which impresses all observers, those of the West, prompted either by necessity or by a kind of vertigo, are constantly agitating to modify their customs and institutions. The studies summarized in this work have provided the opportunity to establish this fact which in many respects dominates the social questions facing our times; the comparative situation of these peoples is made especially clear in the *Atlas,* composed of thirty-six monographs describing a corresponding number of agricultural or industrial workers. These types, observed in all the countries of Europe, shed some light on the specific nature of the civilizations in this part of the world; they furnish particularly precise information on the relative state of well-being of the various European peoples and thus explain the singular contrast which has just been indicated....

In all stages of civilization, the well-being of a laboring family is based on two essential elements: work, which provides the means of existence; foresight, which regulates the use of those means. However, the love of work is often lacking in less advanced societies, and foresight is found even less frequently. Even among those societies which are incontestably in the vanguard of civilization, these virtues are insufficiently developed among the

From *Les Ouvriers européens* (Paris: Imprimerie Impériale, 1855), pp. 9–10.

masses. Societies could not be preserved, therefore, if institutions and custom did not compensate proportionately for individual deficiencies among the members of the improvident classes.

The need for compensation is urgent because the common people become violent whenever this need is left unsatisfied. Indeed, one can say that the means used to compensate for individual deficiencies are the most outstanding features of social organization everywhere. In the same way that childhood, adolescence, and manhood succeed one another during the course of an individual lifetime, Europe's most advanced peoples have passed through three main systems of social organization. These patterns can still be seen today.

The first system, that of nonvoluntary, permanent work agreements, is adopted for those populations whose moral sense is the least developed. This system requires the least intellectual effort from the upper classes and the government. From a practical point of view, it can be considered the simplest and most efficient, for it leaves little opportunity for social freedom on the part of the laborers and imposes the responsibility for their wellbeing on their masters. This relationship is described in the present work by several noteworthy examples. With many variations, it still reigns over half of Europe, particularly in Russia and the Slavic provinces of Turkey and Central Europe. All forms of nonvoluntary, permanent work agreements impose labor on the worker under conditions determined by law and custom. Conversely, the master is obliged to provide for the needs of the worker and his family in all circumstances. The worker is therefore guaranteed a true legal mortgage on the product of his labor. In all systems based on this principle, the mutual obligations of these two groups are equally aggravated or eased when the social order is satisfactorily maintained. Moreover, we would form a very mistaken impression of such societies if we imagined that the inhabitants, who enjoy the security and well-being provided by the system, also suffer because of the state of dependence which is imposed upon them. On the contrary, wherever this social order has not been corrupted by decadent morals and where masters fulfill their obligations honorably, the workers are devoted to the social institutions and are passionately opposed to change. Their blind obstinacy leads to the maintenance of the established regime, and even extends to the preservation of elements which, if modified, would bring about an immediate and beneficial change in their lives. Often, in fact, the masters are powerless to initiate the slightest progress in social habits or methods of labor.

In many northern countries and in Central and Western Europe, the love of work has been developed in the masses by a long history of tutelary influences. Many societies have been able to take advantage of the system of long-term voluntary work agreements without compromising the well-being of laboring families. Such agreements imply a greater development of individual freedom. But although steady progress is being made in this direction, foresight and its concomitant moral values are nowhere so widespread or developed that we can dispense with those protective institutions which foster the transition to a system based on individual freedom, toward which all nations seem to aspire. Such institutions are the fruit of experience and necessity. Wherever they function satisfactorily, they reconcile the liberty required by the most outstanding individuals with the protection essential to those classes ranked lower in terms of morality, intelligence, and energy. These institutions, described in several monographs of the *Atlas,* are largely unknown since they are based on custom and tradition rather than written laws. They are dominant, or at least widespread, in Sweden, Central Europe, and many of the provinces of the South and West; what is more, they can be considered the true foundation of European societies. In systems of long-term voluntary work agreements, the conditions which assure the well-being and security of the populace are not formally imposed by law. Rather, families gladly accept the order handed down by tradition and passed on from generation to generation in harmony with the mores. The concerned interest of the landowners and manufacturers is particularly helpful in perpetuating this order. In this type of system, far more than in the preceding one, the guidance of the upper classes nearly always plays an important role. This system satisfies the noble urges of human individuality better than the previous one. It is the one best suited to the movement toward progress, which has become not only a general concern but also a way of life for all the members of European society. In effect, the gifted individual is no longer completely bound by the old order and can rise to a higher station in life. The example set by the most distinguished families spurs the populace to better itself. Thus the social order maintains an ideal balance between respect for tradition, which assures the well-being of the greatest number, and the spirit of innovation, which fosters the success of a select minority. Social progress is no longer initiated exclusively by the ruling classes, as in the preceding system. The common people obediently accept the general pattern set for them. Nevertheless, they are no longer passive. They take an active role in the attempts at human improvement which are so important to the future of European society.

This system of "patronage" and tradition, which replaced the system of nonvoluntary, permanent work agreements among the majority of European peoples, has itself been modified in many countries. In response to various pressures, it has given way to a system of temporary work agreements and work without agreements. The growth of democratic institutions has sometimes diminished the influence of the upper classes or even destroyed the overall social order. Consequently, the responsibility for providing the necessities of life has passed to the hands of laboring families themselves. The people of Norway and parts of Switzerland and Spain exhibit a special aptitude for this system. Among these races this transformation has been gradual and has not resulted in a national decline. It has even uplifted the moral character of the populace.

This system has been particularly successful in localities where strong municipal institutions provide for the exploitation of an ample supply of community-owned property. A similar transformation of earlier patterns of "patronage" has taken place in many parts of England, France, Belgium, and northwestern Germany, where democratic political tendencies have been combined with dramatic technological innovations.

This change in the social organization has both positive and negative results. They are all the more serious because they have taken society by surprise, occurring under the very nose of the present generation. The most common characteristic of the newly emerging social order is the sudden gathering of large numbers of workers close to the many coal-mining areas in this region of Europe. In these industrial centers, master and worker have become strangers. They are only remotely bound by a short-term contract and remain free of all reciprocal obligations. The worker is no longer tied to the workshop which employs him, the house in which he lives, or the land where he was born; he often rejects the benefits of a sedentary life and the achievements of civilization. In some cases, the worker even reverts to the habits of peoples ranked beneath him on the scale of European civilizations.... All too often, these new nomads fall below their predecessors in terms of morality and well-being, and official inquiries confirm that this regression is accompanied by the most distressing social implications.

At the same time that this new state of affairs seems to be relentlessly pervading all the industrial regions of the West, incontestable progress is being made in all branches of human activity. New social entities, unknown in older societies, are developing in all classes—living testimony to this double movement of progress and decadence. Despite a new outpouring of vital forces, all the elements of the social order are gradually being undermined. These contradictory symptoms are particularly evident in countries which have been shaken by political upheavals. Outstanding individuals are emerging from the lower ranks of society to carry Western civilization to heights unknown in the past. At the same time, however, the masses are left without assistance or guidance to make their own decisions, and they are vulnerable to the dangers of social isolation. They are groping for their basic need—security. In a complete reversal of the tendencies of previous social systems, it is the least enlightened classes which are most eager for innovation. But this need for change is as blind as was the attachment to tradition in the former system. Too often it leaves the masses at the mercy of malevolent exploiters who manipulate popular sentiment for their own purposes. Thus several Western societies are threatened by a catastrophe which could obliterate the work of centuries.

Wherever such miseries have developed and where such elements of social dissolution are fermenting, the government or the classes responsible for public administration are faced with a serious responsibility. It is clear that to remedy the evils which have occurred they must make efforts which were completely uncalled for in less advanced civilizations. All enlightened men are keenly aware that this situation imperatively calls for reforms; reforms have become one of their principal concerns.

17

AN ANALYSIS OF SOCIAL TRENDS

Definition of the four types of social organization in Europe

Nomadic Peoples

I. *The nomadic system includes the three systems of work agreements existing among sedentary populations*

1. Basic living conditions commit members of these societies to a master (family head, tribal chief, etc.); they are organized in communities.

2. Individuals within each community always remain solidly united to one another and to their chiefs.

3. Individuals never leave the group; it is virtually impossible for them to improve their position independently of the other members of the group, unless they become family head, tribal chief, etc.

4. All members of the community enjoy about the same level of well-being.

5. Land is uncultivated and provides natural pasture.

Sedentary Peoples

II. *System of nonvoluntary permanent work agreements*

1. Workingmen committed to a master (landed gentry, landowner, etc.) by law or by custom; also often committed to a community.

From *Les Ouvriers européens* (Paris: Imprimerie Impériale, 1855), pp. 16–17.

2. Work agreements are generally incumbent upon both worker and employer; in a few cases obligations rest on only one of the parties.

3. Outstanding individuals can improve their position while either maintaining or severing their obligations to their employers or to the communities to which they belong. Moreover, these obligations gradually become less stringent in their infringements on individual freedom as individuals rise on a moral and intellectual scale.

4. All individuals enjoy at least a minimal level of well-being.

5. A small portion of the land is cultivated.

III. *System of long-term voluntary work agreements*

1. Workingmen are committed to a master (owner, proprietor, merchant, etc.) by their own choice, guided by custom or obligated by long-term contracts; occasionally committed to a community or corporation.

2. The moral obligation or written stipulation which guarantees the permanence of the work agreement weighs equally on the employer and the worker.

3. A few individuals gifted with the quality of foresight rise to a higher social position, including that of owner, proprietor, and *rentier,* due to the beneficial influence of employers, communities, or corporations.

4. Due to the same influences, individuals lacking foresight are able to enjoy a certain minimum of well-being.

5. A considerable portion of the soil is given over to cultivation.

IV. *System of temporary work agreements and work with no agreements*

1. Workingmen temporarily committed to an employer (owner, proprietor, merchant, etc.) or to a clientele (of owners, proprietors, merchants, consumers, etc.); rarely attached to a community, often member of a corporation.

2. The obligations of the employer and the worker can be abrogated in two different cases:

a. Frequent ruptures caused by unreliability, failures, or incompatibility of the two parties; by discussions pertaining to the fixing of wages; by competition resulting in a scarcity or oversupply of workers, etc.
   b. Interruption occurring with the mutual accord of both parties when the worker is able to rise to a new position in the industrial hierarchy.

3. Many individuals gifted with foresight easily rise to a higher social position. This success is most likely when the worker engages in long-term work agreements in each of the successively higher positions he occupies (until he is able to become self-employed).

4. Individuals lacking foresight, who contract only short-term work agreements without improving their inferior position, usually fall into a moral and physical degradation unknown in the other three social systems.

5. The soil is nearly completely cultivated.

18

THE THREE AGES OF WORK

Stable families have recourse to a variety of means in order to provide "daily bread" to their many "offshoot" families. In general, they begin by tilling the portions of their property which are not rich in spontaneous growth; they then augment productivity by employing certain varieties of agricultural labor. As for the rest, they in no way alter the use assigned to the land by previous generations. They allow the establishment of mining and manufacturing workshops only in very limited areas, and these enterprises create new products without infringing on the former labor organization. Stable families also successfully introduce the working of raw materials and the exploitation of metals beneath absolutely sterile soil; and they create the means of transportation necessary to provide food for the manufacturers and miners. Finally, they repeat these same arrangements on a larger scale and outside the country and in uninhabited areas. At the same time, they organize the means of transportation necessary to bring the emigrants to their place of destination and to operate the exchange of the new products with those that the colonists will continue to receive from the mother country.

Among primitive and simple races, all these innovations gradually develop a degree of complication to which reason and experience assign no limit. They multiply and complicate the methods of labor, the means of transportation, the natural products and the

From *La Constitution essentielle de l'humanité* (Tours: Mame, 1881), pp. 48–78.

tools used in harvests, the physical aids which infinitely reinforce human strength, and finally and most importantly, the intellectual culture which fortifies the human mind, stimulates the skills which foster useful inventions, and increasingly promotes new occupational groups.

The infinite extension of systems of innovation brings about further consequences which have an even more decisive effect on national destinies. In primitive social organizations each family procures the products necessary for its existence by its own activity, and it consumes them at the place of production. Under the system of complex labor systems and distant transportation, an extreme variation gradually develops in the reciprocal relationships among families. The first stage is the joining of efforts under the conditions of equality as a result of simple tasks whose object is the harvesting of spontaneous products. Next come hierarchical organizations appropriate to the modern crafts which require the simultaneous participation of numerous families endowed with very diverse skills and molded by very different upbringings, even though they come from the same locality. Finally, under the most complicated systems, commerce establishes daily contacts among men who come from all over to exchange their products. Amidst these associations, hierarchies, and contacts, parents can no longer insure that their children's upbringing will conform to ancestral custom, even in stable families. Depending upon whether the dominant influences reaffirm or undermine moral law, then the race rapidly marches towards prosperity or ruin.

Among the physical and intellectual innovations which so deeply transform the condition of men and things, there are some whose action has been particularly sudden and powerful. In those places which have witnessed their appearance, special periods have been named "historical epochs." This manner of classifying time has often helped to shed a sharper light on the examination of a long series of events. The classification adopted varies according to the nature of the subject, the number of details, and the historical perspective of the author. For the summary overview which is the object of this book, it has been sufficient for me to distinguish three ages in the history of work.

These three ages do not emerge simultaneously in all the inhabitable parts of the earth. They are not linked to the general history of the globe but rather to the specific histories of localities. The simple systems to the east of Europe that were described by the writers of the Old Testament and the first historians of Greece still persist today, in part, in the same areas. Complex systems which are dominant in the West today have gradually replaced the two preceding systems there. The former, nevertheless, have not completely disappeared under the influx of innovations which I have just enumerated; they remain scattered like oases in a few mountains which have to this day remained outside the commercial mainstream and which still constitute the happy homeland of tradition and simplicity.

When I began the study of societies, one of Europe's outstanding traits was still the existence of a variety of social organizations. As I have said before, primitive organizations still survive here and there. Nevertheless, the invention of the railroad has recently opened a new age. It has already produced a greater change among the races who maintain the organization of the primitive age than all the changes which occurred during the course of the preceding age. Thus, without going far beyond the frontiers of Europe, I have been able to observe and compare the primitive organization of work, the characteristic innovations which were gradually introduced during the second age, and finally, the undreamed of transformations which, since the time of my first voyage, have occurred from the shores of the Atlantic to the frontiers of Asia and which are now spreading throughout the world.

In the following paragraphs I shall give a brief definition of the three ages of work. I shall emphasize the major features of work organization which provide for the daily bread. At the same time, I shall show how occupations linked to the major branches of industry appear successively as a function of the nature of the area and the degree of concentration of the population. After outlining the principles of the essential social organization, I shall indicate how each race, according to the nature of the dominant work, is led to obey or violate moral law.

The First Age of Humanity, or the Primitive Organization of Work

Primitive races employ the most simple methods of work: they provide for their existence by harvesting the spontaneous products of the land and waters. Among these races there have always existed several groups that owe their stability and their well-being to one product in particular. The land they inhabit provides abundant meadows eminently suited for the natural development of animals which furnish elements useful for the nourishment, housing, and clothing of man. These races, aside from minor differences, can be divided into two main categories. The first, living in a nomadic state without any fixed residence, are usually called "savages," like the game which they pursue. The second, half-sedentary for the most part, domesticate the most useful animals and breed them through pasturage. In addition to regular work, the hunters include fishing on the rivers and gathering vegetables; the shepherds include the same activities and hunting.

The most frequent type of work of these two races is that executed by the direct application of physical strength, with the aid of weapons, tools, and machines which, although always simple, are sometimes quite ingenious. Among nomadic races, apprenticeship in the work is completely spontaneous among the youth and is based solely on actual practice. Nevertheless, it always results in an unusual dexterity in the use of the instruments of labor and an extraordinary perspicacity in grasping useful or harmful phenomena associated with the nature of the land, animals, and plants; in short, a considerable development of physical strength and its principal skills. Most important, the spirit of tradition is the quality which distinguished the good hunters and pastoral tribes. This spirit can be recognized by a group of well-defined characteristics: the individual has a sense of happiness. He engages in his work with passion, even in inclement conditions....

In summary, the primitive organization of work was based mainly on the abundance of grass, and the primary means of action was simple, hand-wielded tools. Tradition was conserved by the unanimous will of the race. Innovation appeared only—if it appeared at all—when provoked by too great a concentration of families in the interior of the country, leading to a system of emigration, or when introduced by the overwhelming influence of a foreign power.

The Second Age of Work

Pastoral activity, which placed the production of useful animals under man's direction, introduced an initial deviation in the system of spontaneous production. Tools were often used to assist man in tilling the soil without altering the dominant character of the primitive age. Indeed, the second age was not really begun until the day when man learned to harness a domestic animal to the plow, that is, to bend a discrete and separate instrument to his service instead of limiting himself to the force of his own strength.

Supplied with this instrument of labor, the farming family gradually adopted the ideas, sentiments, and habits from which the chief manifestations of the spirit of innovation would issue. The agricultural population understood the advantages which the transformation of the soil afforded them. It thus escaped from the excessive spirit of tradition which, among hunters and shepherds, is reinforced by the belief that their well-being is necessarily linked to the original condition of the land. Torn from this false conception of his relationship with nature, the farmer was no longer afraid to modify his environment. He reconciled tradition and innovation in his own mind—a fruitful change which was the characteristic trait of the second age....

Nevertheless, the second age manifests itself by innovations which are equally fruitful and by even more extraordinary progress. Intellectual efforts were ardently applied to common industries and toward the invention of methods of work organization and machines to implement these methods; and these efforts developed previously unknown forces in the human spirit. Thus, equally fortified in his mental and physical aptitudes, man sought to understand the basic principles and inner constitution of the forces and materials which he used in the practice of his work. To attain this goal, man created the science of the physical world through the observation of facts, and thus opened to humanity a source of intellectual progress of unlimited richness. The study of the physical world has been cultivated with success since the Renaissance; and, in turn, science has brought unlimited means of progress to the arts.

The happy union of science and art has resulted in another innovation whose effect has already been felt in modern societies. Regardless of their point of departure, men who are well endowed with these two skills rapidly arrive at the position of social ascendance assured by the possession of wealth and leadership ability. They thus provide precious elements in the hierarchical organization of society without which a great nation would be unable to acquire a legitimate position of dominance among its rivals.

These are the facts which highlight the essential contrasts between the systems of labor which characterize the first two ages of humanity. Under stable conditions in the primitive age, each peaceful area soon arrives at a permanent state of equilibrium which must always exist between food production and population growth. If, moreover, each family has achieved stability, it possesses physical well-being based on a regular food supply and intellectual resources fixed by the unchanging use of mental faculties. Under this system, in short, tradition regulates the productivity of the soil and the organization of the home and the place of work in an absolute fashion. In the second age, on the contrary, innovation reigns supreme over all the elements of social activity. It tends to increase food production and concentration of the population. Innovation manifests itself by three main phenomena which are at the same time the direct results of the dominant mentality of the time and the cause of successive changes. The salient features of social change in the second age of work can be summed up briefly: the inventions which facilitate physical labor and develop man's intelligence; those which lower the cost of transportation and favor the rapid circulation of commodities, men, and ideas; and finally, the unceasing expansion of the cities, which are the source of this drive toward progress in physical and intellectual life.

The Third Age of Work

In keeping with the point of view that I adopted in this chapter, that is, taking as the sole aim of my study the drive toward increased food production, concentration of the population, and development of intellectual culture, I find a considerable difference between the present and the past. This difference is especially noticeable in the relative rapidity of the movement of men, things, and ideas toward innovation.

The extraordinary acceleration of this movement is due to a number of inventions which are closely related. The steam engine allowed the infinite growth throughout any territory of the great agricultural, manufacturing, and commercial enterprises whose production had previously remained localized and limited when they depended on animals, wind, and waterways for their motor force. Three major inventions have nearly transformed the system of work by lowering the cost and especially by increasing the speed of transportation. The acceleration of movement has been considerable and has varied according to the nature of the space to be traversed—over land or sea—and especially according to the physical nature of the objects to be transported. On the ocean, for both travelers and valuable merchandise, the old speed was tripled by the steamboat; it was increased tenfold on land by the railroad. Everywhere, on land as well as sea, the speed of ideas has been increased a hundred times over by the electric telegraph. Under these influences, innovation is invading all the areas of social activity in immense proportions and with unheard-of speed. It can be summed up in a few striking traits.

Under the influence of the new spirit which appeared in Europe at the time of the Renaissance, great developments were made in the concentration of the population, the circulation of ideas, and the organization of work; but since the opening of the coal age, half a century has sufficed to render the old state of things unrecognizable in many places.

Nevertheless, in times of stability and peace the gradual growth of innovation has been a characteristic common to all the races which have broken with the absolute spirit of tradition by modifying the spontaneous production of the soil with the plow.

The facts which I have just indicated might not sufficiently demonstrate the existence of a force of change comparable in effect to that which caused the primitive races to enter on the path of the second age. But the birth of the third age is justified by an unprecedented revolution within the bosom of humanity: the powerful influence which the railroad will exercise henceforth on the traditions—good or bad—of primitive races....

The causes for the extraordinary transformation that the railroad is now accomplishing in the social world can be clarified by a few simple facts. Under the old system of transportation, large-scale displacements of men could be effected only over short distances, aside from the undertakings of war. Even on roads equipped with the best horse-drawn vehicles, circulation was impeded as soon as the number of travelers increased slightly....

The railroad, together with the steamboat and the electric telegraph, has resulted in the rapid transformation of the world, for better or worse, by the easy transportation of innovative men to areas where the spirit of tradition had reigned since the beginning of human society. For half a century, these marvelous machines have ushered in a host of advantages which, considered by themselves, are obvious benefits. These benefits are available to the stable families of all races and all peoples, prosperous or suffering, who can made judicious use of the inventions of the third age of work.

VI. FAMILY ORGANIZATION

19

FAMILY TYPES
PATRIARCHAL, STEM, UNSTABLE

The family is an everlasting institution, along with religion and property; and as in the case of these other institutions, the family undergoes in its form considerable modifications. Combined with religion and property, the family provides the salient characteristic of each social organization. From a general point of view, families can be divided into two extreme types: the patriarchal family and the unstable family. The stem family provides an intermediate type.

The first kind of family is common among Eastern nomads, Russian peasants, and the Slavs of Central Europe. In this kind of family all the married sons remain near the father, who exercises extensive authority over them and their children. With the exception of a few household objects, property remains undivided among members of the family group. The father directs the labor and accumulates the products not required for the family's daily needs in the form of savings. Among nomadic shepherds, this community lasts throughout the father's lifetime. Among sedentary farmers, the group divides when the productivity of the ancestral land is no longer proportional to the size of the family and, depending on the availability of free land, the "swarm" which leaves the paternal household either settles nearby or emigrates to another area. When this division takes place, the father—thanks to the economy and labor of all—presides at the creation of the new household or the endowing of the emigrants. It is he,

From *La Réforme sociale* (Tours: Mame, 1872), pp. 352–58.

too, who designates the member of the family who will be charged with exercising the new patriarchal authority. The tendency for new households to desire independence is neutralized among the nomads by the necessities of life, which do not allow them to exist in isolation, and among sedentary farmers by the feudal organization of property. In both groups, independence is checked by traditional moral influences. This frame of mind is based on firm religious beliefs. It insures respect for the established order in the areas of work and social habits rather than developing a spirit of initiative. In this state of physical and moral restraint, the community hinders the development which outstanding individuals in the family might achieve in an independent situation. But, on the other hand, the community allows less diligent, less skilled, and morally delinquent individuals to share in the common well-being.

The second type, the unstable family, prevails today among the working-class populations subject to the new manufacturing system of Western Europe. Moreover, this type of family is multiplying among the wealthier classes in France due to a number of influences, chief among them the forced division of property. The family unit starts with the union of husband and wife. At first it expands as children are born; but the family later shrinks as these children, who are completely devoid of any obligation toward their parents and relatives, leave home as bachelors to support themselves or start a new family. The family is finally dissolved when the parents die or, in the case of their premature death, with the dispersion of the minor children. Each child disposes freely of the dowry he receives when he leaves the paternal household; and in all cases he has complete control over the product of his labor. The precocious use of reason, encouraged by teaching in the schools, parental advice, or the example of the upper classes, leads the new generation to do good or evil according to its moral predisposition. This reliance on reasoning often results in an excessive propensity for innovation rather than a spirit of tradition. In this system, a single or married individual is no longer responsible for the needs of his relatives and rapidly rises to a higher situation if he possesses outstanding aptitudes. But in contrast, if he is unskilled or morally delinquent, he falls even faster to a wretched condition, unable to claim any assistance. Unfortunately, this latter state tends to perpetuate itself once it occurs, either because parents can no longer contribute through savings to the establishment of their children, as they do in the first system, or, above all, because the children are left without supervision and succumb to their evil inclinations or are perverted by bad examples at an early age. Thus we are witness to this peculiar social state—a condition unparalled in the annals of history—which has caused us to coin the term "pauperism."

The third type, the stem family, develops spontaneously among those peoples who, having reaped the benefits of agricultural work and sedentary life, have the good sense to defend their private lives against the domination of lawyers, the inroads of bureaucracy, and the excesses of the modern manufacturing system. In this type of social organization, only one married child remains with the parents. All the others receive a dowry and enjoy an independence which is impossible in the patriarchal family. This system perpetuates work habits, moral influences, and ancestral traditions in the paternal home. The family is a permanent source of protection on which all the members can rely throughout life's trials. This system thus offers individuals a security they could never find in the unstable family. The stem family sometimes arises from the traditional influences of patriarchal life, but it is never truly established without the beneficial influence of individual property. This system satisfies both those who are content in the situation in which they were born and those who boldly wish to rise in the social hierarchy through their own initiative. Lastly, it strikes a just balance between paternal authority and the freedom of the children, between stability and the improvement of social conditions. In order to demonstate the superiority of this system, one need only point out that it comes into being wherever the family is free, and that it maintains itself despite events of serious magnitude which may disturb the established order. Thus, should the heir-associate happen to die prematurely, none of his siblings hesitates to give up a promising future, and all would be honored to return home and fill the sudden void.

In summary, as the peoples of Europe become freer and more

prosperous, they modify the patriarchal family, which relies too heavily on the cult of tradition, while at the same time rejecting the unstable family, which is constantly undermined by the spirit of innovation. Firmly adhering to their religious beliefs and the principle of individual property, they tend more and more to organize in stem families, which satisfy both of these tendencies—tradition and innovation—and reconcile two equally imperious needs: a respect for good traditions and the search for useful changes.

20

FAMILY ORGANIZATION IN THE FOUR SOCIAL SYSTEMS OF EUROPE

When we discuss the four social systems and the seven types of workers previously described in this study, the organization of the family must always be the focus of our observations and our basis for arranging the facts. The family is the center of social organization and individual life among all peoples: customs and laws establish a close relationship among persons descended directly from the same bloodlines. Despite an infinite variety of local customs, relatives are obliged to pool their means of existence. Nevertheless, the nature of this sharing varies according to the different social systems in which it occurs.

Among nomadic peoples, all direct descendents of the same father usually remain grouped together. They live in a communal system under the absolute authority of the head of the family. Herds, provisions, and most of the household goods are considered essentially community property; personal property includes only clothing and weapons. When the size of a family no longer permits all the members to remain together, the head of the family arranges a friendly parting and determines what portion of the community property should be given to the new branch. On the other hand, the family often continues to live together even after the death of the head of the family. In this case, the entire family, including even distant relatives, remains united under the direction of the person who is most able to wield patriarchal authority.

From *Les Ouvriers européens* (Paris: Imprimerie Impériale, 1855), p. 18.

In this system, the organization of work and the very fabric of society are defined nearly exclusively by the family.

The family-based society found among nomadic peoples is also widespread among most of the sedentary populations living under a system of nonvoluntary, permanent work agreements. For example, this is the distinctive social characteristic of the Slavs of Russia, Turkey, Hungary, etc. However, in contrast with nomadic tribes, it is impossible for families in these societies to live together in large numbers. The fixed location and limited dimensions of their dwellings and the convenience of locating workers near their place of work make such large family units impractical. It is unusual for all the children to remain in their father's home after marriage. However, property and work are shared, so long as communal living has not become physically impossible. Moreover, even when they have had to set up separate households, the new heads of households still remain closely associated in many areas of activity. They share the use of pastureland and arable fields, and even work together in certain industries. Consequently, people who live under a system of nonvoluntary, permanent work agreements generally have a greater propensity for communal institutions than those who have lived for many years under the other two systems of work obligations: voluntary, long-term work agreements or temporary work agreements. In these two systems, individual choice generally dominates the work relationships.

In effect, under these two systems, individual well-being is no longer so closely bound to the pooling of resources. As societies progress, developing social freedom and the material benefits of civilization, they gradually approach the extreme limits of family organization set by human and divine law. At this extreme, the family unit is reduced to the husband, wife, dependent children, and possibly dependent elderly parents. These small families are no longer faced with the problem of maintaining solidarity among a large group of people. Once reduced to these essential elements, families possessing the necessary intellectual and moral qualities for achieving social success are able to rise in the social hierarchy. On the other hand, however, families lacking these qualities may be crushed in their isolation by miseries and degradations unknown to less civilized peoples. As a general rule, we can say that the laws do not actively promote these unhappy consequences among civilized peoples. But when a society lacks a strong religious spirit, and its laws are too quick to encourage independence rather than solidarity among the population, the lower classes enter a period of decadence. As several official inquiries have proven, men in such conditions are capable of forgetting all the feelings which preserve the family. In many ways, they sink lower than animals. This decadence becomes an even greater threat to all classes of society when special legislation fosters the tendency toward isolation. For example, the laws may be too aggressive in their opposition to the perpetuation of jointly owned family property. When this occurs, the laws conflict with the innate desire of the people and systematically deprive the members of society of advantages which even nomads enjoy.

This is not to say, however, that family size and influence must diminish indefinitely as individual freedom—the great need of modern times—increases. Of all races, the Anglo-Saxons have best understood the close connection between the growth of individual freedom and the progress of civilization; yet this race also recognizes the need to staunchly maintain the organization of the family under the watchful aegis of paternal authority. The English constitution offers new households numerous routes for improving this social condition. Nevertheless, it preserves paternal control over the transfer of property, a power which was achieved among the nomads. Paternal love is the strongest and most prudent of all social forces: the English constitution makes it responsible for assisting and directing the younger generations. In this way, the organization of the family and the transfer of property are strengthened. In contrast, their power is rapidly weakening in societies where laws promote the division of inheritances. Such laws cause a periodic dispersion of the property, industry, or clientele which previously insured the livelihood of each family. In a word, these laws allow each new generation to destroy the work of its predecessor. It is obvious to everyone familiar with the customs and economic systems of the two great Anglo-Saxon nations that the happy combination of individual freedom and paternal authority is the principal cause for this race's success wherever it has settled.

In summary, all European nomadic societies and social systems of obligatory work agreements are linked to a strong family organization. In the social systems of long-term work agreements and temporary work agreements, the family circle and paternal authority are diminished. In general, this weakening corresponds to an increase of individual freedom. However, there are limits to the extent of personal freedom that cannot be exceeded. As this study will often point out, the best social systems are those which wisely consider and preserve all the great principles which have provided up to today either stability or progress in European society. In particular, we must preserve those principles which reconcile the greatest development of individual freedom with the greatest amount of paternal authority.

21

INHERITANCE LAWS, FAMILY ORGANIZATION, AND SOCIAL REFORM

For all their individualistic tendencies, European nations have not forgotten the usefulness of maintaining a common center of direction and assistance for people related by blood. In all societies the father plays the role of guardian as long as he is alive; then, when his death deprives his children of this support, the deficiency is made up as much as possible by some arrangement for the distribution of his property. These arrangements vary not only according to the genius of each race but often even from one family to another. In the most common arrangement, the whole family's interest is thought to be best served by leaving the father's property intact; the ownership of his property is passed on to the child who will put it to the best use, both for the family and for society. But the heir takes over not only the rights of the head of the family but also his obligations. In well-organized societies, particularly in those where the practice of religion maintains among the rich such virtues as personal moderation and love for one's neighbor, the force of conscience and, when necessary, the pressure of public mores combine to assure that the heir will do his duty. When these social customs are not observed, when affection and benevolent guidance are not transmitted along with the father's property, when public opinion allows an heir to live luxuriously among brothers and sisters left

From *Les Ouvriers européens* (Paris: Imprimerie Impériale, 1855), pp. 286–87.

destitute and without prospects for marriage; then one can conclude that the loss of religion and the general corruption of public mores have already gone a long way toward undermining the society's foundations. But these scandals do not disqualify the principle of leaving the father's property intact; even the best institutions can only work with the aid of good public mores: the attempt to remedy abuses of this kind by mandating the indefinite divisibility of estates was a mistake. The laws only aggravated the problem and weakened this society's economic and moral order.

There are two principal ways to assure the transmission intact of paternal property. In one system, custom or the law determine the order of succession, conferring the father's property on the first, the second, or perhaps the last son; in the second system, the law entrusts this important mission to the father, giving him the power to extend the benefits of his foresight and concern beyond his own lifetime. The freest countries, where individual initiative is most powerful, prefer this second system, which is better suited than the rigidity of custom to the particular needs of each family, and which does a better job of reconciling the public interest with the principles of individual justice and affection. The head of the family, bound by no single law or custom, freely following his heart and his conscience, finds the solution in each case by drawing on his profound knowledge of his property, his profession, his clientele, and by studying the character of each of his children: he can divide his estate equally among his children if each is capable of putting his share of the inheritance to good use; otherwise, he can keep the family's wealth intact, to everyone's advantage. The right to bequeath, or freedom of testation, exerts a good influence at the two extreme limits of civilization: the nomads uphold this right as a necessary consequence of paternal authority; among English-speaking people in both hemispheres, it is seen as a consequence of the right to property and the right to individual liberty. Freedom of testation, when it has been exercised for some time without being thwarted by forced division of property or the practice of entailment, tends to assure that land, businesses, and workshops are all distributed in ways which suit the local requirements of the soil, climate, and the genius of the race. Under this system, aside from gradual changes due to the advance of civilization, agricultural, industrial, and commercial enterprises tend to establish themselves on permanent foundations. A division of national activity between large-scale and small-scale economic operations is thus maintained, or adjusted without serious disruption, in accordance with the nature of men and of things. This stability, based at once on conditions peculiar to each locale and the free will of society's most thrifty and experienced members, is the principal secret of the success achieved in every country in the world by the British and the North Americans.

These two ways of transmitting property intact were widely represented in prerevolutionary France; but the revolutionary assemblies, struck by the abuses engendered by such practices as entailment and mortmain, preoccupied by ideas of equality and natural right, fearing that freedom of testation left too much power over young people in the hands of heads of families and that it would hinder the establishment of the new social order, were naturally inclined to see any strength in the structure of the family as an obstacle to progress. Referring back to the deliberations which produced the laws of 1790, 1791, and of the year II, and also to the discussions which accompanied the drafting of the Civil Code, one notices that the new inheritance laws—that is to say, the very groundwork of the new society—were passed impulsively and without the aid of one of those public inquiries which, in England, are indispensable to the most minor institutional reform. In this way, our legislators, giving way to one of those obsessive preoccupations which violate the very principle of European civilization, strayed abruptly from national tradition. They almost completely abrogated both the right to freedom of testation, which had prevailed in several southern provinces, and the various ways of transmitting property intact which various northern customs established either in favor of the nobility or for the whole population. Exaggerating, in the opposite direction, the rigidity of these northern customs, and saving scarcely a single loophole for paternal authority, the new law established equal and indefinite divisibility of inheritances just as absolutely as some old European customs had established inequality and indivisibility.

The practical rules which were established earlier in connection with the assessment of social change now bring to mind very serious doubts; they give us reason to reconsider whether France is on the true path of civilization in matters of family organization. Inheritance laws are a foundation of society, one of the principal causes of a society's progress or decline; thus one must study with great care the arguments of those who founded the current system and the arguments of those who recommend changing it. While waiting for these questions to be treated by more competent authorities, we think it would be useful to summarize those arguments which we have asserted, or which became apparent to us in the course of our studies.

Public opinion today is still struck by the abuses, caused by the corruption of public mores, which afflicted the prerevolutionary organization of family property. The public would reject any change in the laws that would contain the seeds of a return to a system awarding wealth and social advantages to eldest sons and condemning younger siblings to poverty and unmarried lives. Most instinctively distrust large territorial holdings, thinking that such holdings must hinder the development of smaller holdings and of agriculture in general; in the same spirit, they sympathize with the forced division of property which the current laws require. They fear that the morals of heads of families are neither firm enough nor pure enough to resist, in their declining years, the temptation to cheat their legitimate heirs or maneuver to reestablish the practice of mortmain on a large scale. Finally, people dread the jealousy and dissension which a father's preferences can kindle among brothers and sisters.

Some people who favor the current inheritance law base their opinion on the fact that the current law, in effect for fifty years, has encountered almost no opposition from the public. They point out that the current law does allow fathers a certain latitude in making a will to pass on their property, and that fathers nevertheless rarely use this power. Certainly, the argument runs, such an enlargement of liberty cannot threaten our mores.

French people are generally convinced that the current system is more conducive to good relations between parents and children than the English system. In support of this opinion, they mention the incontestable fact that French parents are more openly affectionate with their children than their British and American counterparts are with theirs.

Another line of argument is that the idea of equal division of property among heirs goes far back in French history. Numerous precedents for the current practice can be found among our traditional customs; it was even adopted spontaneously in several provinces, in a reaction of public mores against traditional laws and customs. This practice was an expression of ancient Gaul's individualism, which neither Romans nor Franks, Christianity nor monarchy could ever subdue. The Gallic spirit resisted the collective forces personified by the head of the family, just as it resisted such collective encroachments as communes and the state.

Finally, the political preoccupations which gave birth to the current inheritance laws have maintained much of their strength right up to the present, particularly in public administration. It is widely believed that owners of large properties have not yet sufficiently steeped themselves in those egalitarian ideas which rule the land and provide the basis for our new civil institutions. Consequently, it is widely feared that the unrestricted restoration of freedom of testation would strengthen those very forces which proved so difficult to defeat at the end of the last century; public administrators also hope that the current law will hasten the disappearance of those last vestiges of resistance which could still spring up. There is a widespread conviction that the current law will significantly increase the power of the class of small landholders, a class with a definite stake in the consolidation of the new social organization.

These views are so entrenched and widespread in France that no legislator could even hope to modify the current laws before bringing about a major change in public opinion. He would have to get people to see that fifty years of progress have extinguished some of the dangers they fear, and that the dangers that remain could be avoided by judicious reform.

The reasons for changing the French inheritance laws will naturally escape the majority whose concerns were just discussed; but these reasons make clear sense to foreigners, who are less affected by the abuses of our ancien régime; and who devote less thought to considerations which have local interest for us than to those which have to do with permanent conditions of order and progress. It is always useful, if only for the purpose of getting a partial glimpse of the future of our society, to report the opinions of those—North Americans or British radicals, for example—who bring to their sympathy for the democratic spirit of our institutions a sincere desire to see these institutions strengthened. We will summarize some of these considerations, which it is particularly important to bring to the attention of the French public.

Troublesome consequences of our inheritance laws can be found in the current state of the family, of marriage, and of property. Children accustomed from early on to the thought that the simple fact of their birth entitles them to wealth generally show little inclination to work or to follow the direction their parents set for them. The efforts which a man must make to prove his worth are thus more likely to be found in poor families; hence the opinion, generally justified, that rich children rarely rise above mediocrity; hence also France's lack of those families, so common in other countries, which devote themselves over the course of generations to great practical, intellectual, and moral enterprises; hence, finally, an instability which encourages certain envious feelings, but which does not provide real benefits to any social class, and which, paralyzing the resources once developed by the hereditary transmission of traditions, is now a cause of France's social decline.

The French lower classes are less respectful and obedient to their superiors, an obvious sign that paternal authority, henceforth stripped of its legal safeguards, is in steady decline. For the young, nothing can replace the influence of their father, one of whose primary responsibilities in a well-ordered society is the moral education of his children. Examples of formal rebellion against parents are no longer rare. Public opinion justly condemns the conduct of rich young people who, falling prey to immoral passions, squander, with the help of usurers, the wealth earned by the thrift and hard work of their parents. Standards of public morality are even more seriously violated by certain attitudes which are surfacing among the class of small property-holders, especially among those who, taking custody of property which their parents are too old to administer, make no secret either of their scorn for the obligation to support their parents which this custody implies or of their impatience for their parents' deaths.

In today's upper-class families, parents are especially devoted to their children because only by the force of affection can they exert that influence, so indispensable to a family's strength, which was once simply assured by the very organization of society. This explains the importance (excessive, according to some) given to children in today's families, a circumstance which clearly distinguishes current mores from the old ones. With the best families, these affectionate attentions undoubtedly develop from genuine feelings; but there is reason to fear that their effect on the children is exactly the reverse of what their parents expect. It is certainly doubtful whether this influence is as beneficial as the judicious exercise of traditional authority used to be.

The right to an inheritance not only leads individuals to rely less on their own efforts; it also leads them to entertain such future prospects as a lucrative marriage or the death of one's parents. It deals the institution of marriage a severe blow, substituting calculation for the heart's inspiration; it allows the appearance in daily life of aspirations and wishes which would be considered reprehensible and disgraceful in societies where men are accustomed from earliest childhood to the idea that they must make their own fortune. The forced division of wealth between the two sexes even has a detrimental effect on the physical constitution of populations: Normandy and England both demonstrate that a race steadily improves itself in societies where each man who plans to marry takes into consideration a woman's physical and moral qualities rather than her fortune.

The very principle of property is jeopardized by a policy which, depriving everyone of the right to dispose of the wealth they have earned, ultimately reduces the property owner to the condition of a life-long tenant (usufructuary). The law which assures the right of inheritance to all children related by blood allows an opening for the opinions of those who, without fear of destroying both property and the family in one blow, want to extend this right to an even broader range of people. The systematic enemies of private property find additional arguments for their position in the defects of a system which, leaving inheritance to the accident of birth, multiplies the number of fortunes acquired by people incapable of managing them competently. It is worth noting that the unrest spurred by these resentments and doctrines occurs primarily in Western countries which have adopted the French laws, whereas the same tendencies remain powerless, in spite of the extraordinary degree of freedom of thought, in English-speaking countries, which uphold the principle of private property by protecting freedom of testation, that is, an intelligent system of succession in which a child's birthright is sensibly balanced by the father's discretion and affection. Under this system, where a family's wealth is transmitted intact, the heir, if he is not corrupted by ambition or a weakness for luxury, stays on the land which he has been managing for years under his father's direction; he learns early on to fulfill his duties and to respect the obligations which ownership imposes; affection, more than self-interest, binds him to the agricultural laborers working his land; the inclination to stay in one place and put down roots, so rare under a system of forced division of property and yet so important to social stability and agricultural progress, springs naturally from the very fact of possession.

The French law, awarding each heir a right to a share of an inheritance, regardless of the wishes of his father or the other heirs, awards to the least foresightful and experienced members of society the power to undo the accomplishments of the most skillful members of the previous generation; therefore, it should not be surprising that in several provinces families, particularly the agricultural interests, are still resisting the inheritance laws. Fathers, no longer able to get their children to follow in their footsteps, and soon losing hope that their children will be associates and eventually successors in the business, are not encouraged to undertake agricultural improvements which will mainly benefit future generations; ordinarily they withdraw from industrial and commercial ventures at the moment when they could have made them more productive than ever, if they had had the help of a son who had begun to learn the business. A nation where the family is constituted in this way can distinguish itself in enterprises which require only a preliminary idea or a brief effort; but it is necessarily handicapped in undertakings in agriculture, mining, industry, and commerce which require a kind of commitment and sense of family tradition developed over generations. Things are different in countries where the law does not curtail freedom of testation: fathers are pleased to devote all their energy to their business, except to delegate bit by bit the more menial chores to their sons. During this long period of shared labor, the father can accumulate enough wealth to be able to provide for all of his children without dividing up the property, and he can learn which of his sons is best qualified to take over the property.

Many French people instinctively connect freedom of testation with primogeniture, an association which can be explained by memories of a past which has been destroyed; but this opinion will not withstand close scrutiny when we turn our attention to the new social order. The liberty of the head of the family is a principle which is not confined exclusively to any legal system; in fact, it works in concert with the particular genius of each people, leaving the law to settle those cases where the father does not express his will. In England, where primogeniture plays an important role in the inheritance laws, the father ordinarily favors his eldest son in his will, on condition that this son preserve, for his brothers and sisters and for the sake of family property, a common center for direction and assistance. The United States, which before their revolution had followed English law, set off in the opposite direction after new laws mandated the equal division of family property. But in both countries fathers ordinarily use their rights simply as a check against overly rigid application of the laws—in America the principle of equality, in England primogeniture. Even France resembles the Anglo-Saxon race in this respect. Freedom of testation, which guaranteed the privileges of the eldest sons of the nobility throughout most of France, also performed the same function before the Revolution for the bourgeoisie and the peasantry in the southern provinces. On the other hand, since the principle of equal division of property has been applied to every social class, fathers are hardly using any of the power which the law has left them. Freedom of testation, granted to fathers of all social classes, would not jeopardize the principle of equality, which is so precious to the French, any more than it has in the United States; on the contrary, it would even protect that principle in certain cases where today's laws are too rigid. But freedom of testation, if it functioned throughout the entire society as the ultimate sanction for paternal authority, would develop those attitudes of respect and obedience which form the indispensable ballast for a free constitution, for the development of primary education, and for a spirit of progress and innovation; finally, it would protect the rights of property and the family from the troubling and frequently demoralizing encroachment of a certain class of lawyers, which has gained inordinate power among us since the establishment of the Civil Code.

The examples of England and the United States both demonstrate that a father's freedom of testation does not generate jealousy among his children during his lifetime. It is even clear that such dissension would be nipped in the bud under a system where every child, considering the mere thought of an eventual inheritance indelicate, accustoms himself to relying on nothing but the fruits of his own labor. In France, on the contrary, it is clear that jealousy and hatred are often caused by a father's maneuvering to circumvent the law; the suspicions aroused by the difficulty of dividing up property are equally notorious, leading too often to legal proceedings and the rupture of family ties. Small landholders are particularly prone to these family disputes, which are often incited by local administrators in our rural provinces who exercise under our current law an influence unequalled anywhere in the civilized world. It is a confirmed fact in rural districts that this influence inevitably ruins families, particularly when the presence of underage children among the group of prospective heirs increases the delays and costs of each inheritance case. Contrary to the proven sympathies of legislators and to the purposes of our institutions, it is our peasant landowners who suffer the most from abuses of our current laws.

Freedom of testation, established to provide support for the principles of property and the family, can, like other freedoms, precipitate abuses which undermine those principles. In countries where fathers have this freedom, the legislator must provide special safeguards, suitable to the particular characteristics of each people, against abuses. Accordingly, England and the United States have adopted special measures for keeping the practice of entailment within reasonable limits; the measures which France has adopted to restrict the accumulation of property in mortmain could be further strengthened if, as is widely feared, the spread of this practice will be found to weaken private property and the family. Several American states have adopted reforms of this type, particularly New York.

The disgraceful compulsion to plunder the inheritance of legitimate heirs would be a real danger in societies where few citizens were imbued with a sense of duty. An immoral society is no more worthy of freedom of testation than of any other liberty; but though this liberty was justifiably curtailed by the laws of an earlier epoch in our history, we would hinder civilization's growth if we did not restore this liberty in acknowledgment of the progress which we have seen in our public mores.

The effects of the current inheritance laws are not the same as they were in the years immediately following the Revolution of 1789; today, for example, it rarely causes the actual division of farms organized as medium-sized and large landholdings. The heirs ordinarily limit themselves to splitting the profits from the sale of the proceeds; as a result, the law does not disrupt agricultural production, although it does disrupt relations among the heirs, with bad consequences for the relations which should be maintained between the co-owners and the farm laborers. The small holdings of the peasant, on the other hand, are divisible seemingly unto infinity, and production suffers along with family relations. Here again we see that the legislation's bad consequences weigh most heavily on the class of peasant landowners: the view that forced division of inheritances favors the interests of the owners of small holdings may have been true for a while after the Revolution; today, throughout most of France, it is in direct contradiction with the facts.

One of the circumstances which weighs most heavily on the small landholder is his need to borrow to supplement the truncated and insufficient plots of land which he has inherited. For example, a peasant, endowed with the necessary skill for an agricultural undertaking that requires only traditional farming methods, gets into trouble when he has to borrow to acquire a new holding. This is when he falls prey to usurious loans.

Any effort to reform the practice of moneylending would be in vain; the extension of agricultural credit, if it were not done on a small scale and with a profound knowledge of the population of each district, would certainly hasten the ruin of the class of peasant landowners, a class whose members unhappily lack the inner resources necessary for success. In summary, the system of forced division of property functions as a kind of bait which, with the help of loans, draws the individual into a state of affairs where he can no longer support himself, where he retains only the appearance of ownership; under these conditions, mortgages and usurious loans have become common transactions in several of our rural provinces.

Thus the inheritance laws, adopted at first for a political purpose and trained like artillery at the nobility, now damage our entire society. They have taken their toll on the family, on property, and consequently on the health of the state. Without paternal authority, the experience acquired by each generation has little impact on the opinions and actions of the next generation; it is small wonder that, in the midst of all the groping we have had to do in the sixty years after our Revolution, our society fetches up every fifteen years on the same reef.

Deprived of the power necessary to direct and motivate the younger generation, fathers henceforth can only assure the well-being of their descendants by limiting their number. The consequence of this emphasis on foresight is that sterility afflicts those social classes which any well-organized society would encourage to multiply; this tendency grows more pronounced every day among our most distinguished families, while the populations of our most improvident and more or less degraded classes are multiplying more rapidly than ever. This is why it is becoming so difficult to recruit a group of strong men in France and to establish a system of emigration like the ones which populated Canada,

Louisiana, and the Antilles in the last two centuries, and like the ones which are now doing so well in England and Germany.

This deficiency also may explain why the French race, which possesses intelligence, energy, and initiative to such a high degree, struggles to maintain its longtime borders, while other races which surpass the French in none of these fundamental qualities expand their interests all over the world....

In summary, are France's inheritance laws peculiarly suited to the qualities (or, if one prefers, the faults) of the French race, and do they meet the needs of our national development? Or, on the contrary, should we see in this system the never-dying worm that secretly undermines our society; that precipitates periodic crises in our affairs of state; finally, that provokes in the condition of the family and of property the decline that everyone is aware of, but whose cause no one knows?

Without claiming to settle such serious questions, whose solutions lie beyond the scope of our present study, we believe that these questions must henceforth engage the public's attention. As the preceding discussion shows, the considerations which would lead us either to retain or to reform our current inheritance laws should rest on facts, not on speculations. These considerations will only change the long-held convictions of those who will be able to verify the facts by a comparative study of France and other countries. A public inquiry into the laws of inheritance, if its value were demonstrated by the results of the research studies which we propose, would do for France what a public inquiry into factory working conditions did for England twenty years ago. The English inquiry, by testing deeply rooted economic opinions and demonstrating their inadequacy, saved England from the imminent danger of social disintegration.

There are other reasons for an inquiry. The laws of the year II and of 1803 were meant by their authors to solve essentially temporary problems. The illustrious founder of the Civil Code, moreover, soon recognized the need to balance the corrosive impact of these laws on the nobility by means of entailments, which egalitarian interests later abrogated. In order to know the sequel of the traditions of the Revolution and the empire, there is reason to inquire whether these problems have ended, and whether property, definitely emancipated from the bondage of perpetual entailments, can also be freed from the grip of forced divisions. Now, it is clear that the conditions which motivated our legislators have today lost their importance. For example, there is no longer reason to fear that the influence of fathers will inhibit the spirit of innovation of the young; it may even be true that such fears, so often expressed during the Revolution, have been replaced by fears of an opposite kind. If it were recognized that private mores and social trends have sufficiently changed, then it might be time to return, after a half-century of trials, to the path of progress, which was temporarily closed during the moral degeneration of the eighteenth century. The legislator who will retrieve our national tradition in this way, without threatening the spirit of progress or giving way to the spirit of reaction, will have truly established on the European continent that new order which so many good men had hoped to see arise from the great reforms of 1789.

VII. SOCIAL REFORM

22

THE SCIENCE OF SOCIETY AS A THEORY OF SOCIAL REFORM

A few general considerations will enable us to establish the principles which underlie the observations revealed by a comparative study of the workers of Europe. We will now present those observations which are particularly relevant to the reforms necessitated by the present situation in the West.

The diversity of proclivities and aptitudes in Europe is part of human nature; but it is also linked to the spirit of initiative and freedom fostered by Christianity which has so strongly marked the European character. In effect, European civilizations differ from Asian societies (those which survive today or merely remain in name alone) by the fact that European society was not bound by a single social system. Like all primitive entities, European society provided ample ground for human failings; but at the same time, it was ever ready to draw profit and glory from the great potential of the human mind. This has been an outstanding characteristic of Europe for centuries, and it becomes more pronounced every day. Because of this tendency, the peoples of Europe were able to firmly maintain order and stability without falling into the excesses of despotism or a caste system. They raised religious feeling to greater heights than had any other people without bowing to a theocratic regime or hampering freedom of thought; while preserving the concepts of governmental

From *Les Ouvriers européens* (Paris: Imprimerie Impériale, 1855), pp. 281–82.

authority and collective action, they granted much more individual freedom than had any other race. By favoring the development of democracy, they accelerated the progress of the popular classes and affirmed the influence of the middle classes without stifling the sources of greatness which flow from an aristocracy. Finally, today more than ever, the peoples of Europe are clearly continuing their long-time progress toward unity of thought and action without forsaking the processes of emulation and achievement which are fostered by nationalism. History clearly teaches that no member of the European family has remained constantly faithful to these trends; nearly all have succumbed to some accidental deviation and have exaggerated the development of one of these principles, thus momentarily disrupting the harmony which is an indispensable condition of progress; but these states immediately entered a period of decadence, and the ascendance of other nations, together with their trying ordeals, quickly brought them back to the true path of civilization.

The elasticity and abundant variety of the peoples of Europe explain the diversity of the means which they have employed to avert or remedy the evils engendered by improvidence; the *Atlas* contains a faithful description of these efforts, and incontrovertible proof of their efficacy is often established by the well-being and tranquility of the populace. But this very diversity seems to give rise to a new difficulty, particularly in the manufacturing countries of Western Europe. Among so many solutions borrowed from so many different civilizations and races imbued in varying degrees with the spirit of tradition, how can we choose solutions appropriate for nations which typify the modern spirit and where, in an apparent contradiction, we see the most advanced civilization as well as the most urgent need for reforms?

To this end we need only rely on common sense and experience: let us carefully consider societies where the traditional system reigns and be guided by societies whose mission today is to lead other nations toward progress. Nevertheless, enlightened by observation and knowing that no social system is free from a mixture of good and evil, we will give separate treatment to the important questions which deal with the principles of preservation and progress; and for each question we will indicate the solution recommended by previous success.

There is no doubt as to the choice of which societies to honor with the role of guide. Notwithstanding national rivalries over secondary issues, public opinion unanimously recognizes a gradual amelioration of men and things from the far reaches of Europe to the territory of the richest provinces of Germany, France, and England. Several nations located outside the center of European civilization, although justifiably conscious of their own grandeur, nevertheless recognize the superiority of Europe's innovative peoples and follow their lead in the sciences, arts, industry, and even in the smallest details of social life. European superiority is revealed in all the forms and manifestations of human activity; it is evident in the classes of the population specifically studied in this work; to contest this fact would be paradoxical. Terms of comparison and the approximate rank of each nation can be established without a lengthy investigation; one would surely comply with standard measures of civilization—either certain purely physical facts, such as the extent of means of communication in each country, or elements of intellectual activity, such as the importance of schools or the number of books published each year.

In keeping with the preceding considerations, we have closely followed the development, abrogation, and especially the gradual transformation of the tutelary institutions and customs which are specifically related to the moral imperfections of populations at various stages of civilization. The general trend of civilization—carefully verified by the facts—will indicate a practical solution for each important question facing European society today. Thus, if observation demonstrates that an institution which thrives in primitive societies gradually weakens or disappears entirely in more advanced societies, it can scarcely be expected that such an institution would be of great help for the future of civilization; any effort to reestablish this institution in disregard of general social trends would simply be a sterile return to the past and would only add a new source of malaise to society's existing ills. In contrast, just the opposite would be true of an institution which was unknown or only latent in less developed societies but which followed the same phases of development as the civilization itself. There would be all the more reason to base hopes for fruitful reform on an institution which had been maintained intact among most nations, even though it had been momentarily abandoned by the people under study; an institution which, for example, was still a fundamental base of the social structure among the nomads of the East, where authority and tradition prevail, as well as among peoples of the West who have given rise to the greatest development of the spirit of innovation and individual freedom.

The practical rules which we have just established justify the point of view which guided the consideration of various European civilizations in this work. Since our principal aim was to treat the social questions of importance to Western Europe, we have stressed the most outstanding characteristics of inferior civilizations and the most deserved criticisms of the more advanced civilizations. Thus, while tracing the thirty-six descriptions collected in the *Atlas* as accurately as possible, we took care to point out in the notes appended to the first monographs the elements of well-being and security characteristic of the social systems of the North and East; while in the notes appended to the later monographs we stressed the dangers of isolation for the improvident populations of the West, and, in particular, the sinister influence exercised on their lives by the ever-growing spirit of individualism and unfettered competition. Nevertheless, we also indicated the considerations which establish the incontestable superiority of Western civilization and which preclude any reversal of this trend. The stability and well-being which we admire in Eastern peoples are only the first step in the path of civilization; the vices we observe in the social systems and customs of the West are blemishes in a social order which is incomparably more advanced; they are a temporary consequence of human imperfection, an accidental deviation from society's principles of self-preservation. Even though we have been obliged to praise various consequences of social systems based on tradition and authority, we are far from proposing such a system as a model. The sole lesson we would draw from the example of these systems is to recall the basic principles which they, in particular,

A Theory of Social Reform

have preserved and which other peoples have momentarily forgotten in their sometimes disorderly march towards progress. Countries where these social systems are still vigorous cannot be considered an impetus spurring all of Europe to a better order of things; but like the parts which regulate the movement of machines, their role lies in controlling the action of that force; and from time to time they must intervene by bringing the innovators back to the true path from which they have strayed.

These rules are delicate but necessary for the examination which we have envisaged. It will now be easy to use the facts presented in this work as the basis for a careful consideration of the institutions and customs with which various civilizations compensate for individual improvidence and the unforeseen misfortunes which may strike without warning. As we present these considerations in the following paragraphs, we will give special emphasis to those which are pertinent to the situation in France today.

23

PROPOSALS FOR REFORM

In summary, the reforms which are so urgently needed in the manufacturing countries of the West are not derivable from a general axiom, from a systematic formula of progress, or from any kind of universal panacea. If we follow the example which England has set for the last thirty years, these reforms will result from exhaustive inquiries whose goals will be to observe social facts, to determine which improvements are warranted by experience, and above all to destroy ignorance and prejudice, which, even more than selfishness and bad mores, are the principal obstacles to progress.

For France, in particular, where national tradition has been shaken by the impact of revolutions; where, to check the abuses of the old order, it has been necessary to exaggerate the principles of the new order; finally, where European traditions are not better known than those of our own country, these inquiries should always contrast actual facts observed on our territory with facts about the ancien régime and facts about foreign countries.

These inquiries should first of all be undertaken by a free organization, each of whose members would be required to study firsthand the actual conditions of the population. Only a picture of the facts and debate about their consequences that can be derived from studies like this can put an end to those differences of opinion which, in today's society, separate so many well-intentioned

From *Les Ouvriers européens* (Paris: Imprimerie Impériale, 1855), pp. 292–94.

Proposals for Reform 289

and eminent men; this is the only way to bring about the strong convictions and unanimity needed to overcome the inattention and preconceived ideas which too often stand in the way of individual efforts. Such a group would accomplish its program of studies of social economy and of practical reforms with the speed which individual initiative makes possible and with the guarantees provided by cooperation of intellects and wills. Composed mainly of landowners and captains of industry who are in intimate contact with the working classes, this organization would find within itself the resources needed to apply the practical results of its studies. Moreover, the conclusions, when they had been ripened by debate and further observation, would be placed at the disposal of the government, to which the organization would attach itself (following the English custom) under the aegis of some influential personage.

The study of the ways in which the various European countries have sought to aid and direct their improvident classes does not provide reason to believe that Western nations will be able to get much use out of institutions which are either essentially hostile to individual liberty or too encumbered with restrictions and regulations. Indentured labor, a practice still in effect in Slavic states, and the craftsmen's and artisans' guilds of southern Germany are considered, even in the countries where these institutions survive, to be incompatible with the progress of civilization. Germany's mining guilds and Sweden's *bergslags,* though they exert a good influence on the working class, are nevertheless looked upon impatiently by many enlightened men. The conservation of communal property and commons is often a temporary necessity, but it is invariably a symptom of a backward civilization, and as soon as the people have become moral and intelligent enough, they can serve progress by dispensing with this form of security. Russian customs which prescribe, at short intervals, the equal division of land among the families of a rural commune are well suited to a system whose main purpose is to assure the security of the improvident masses; these customs would be incompatible with Western social practice, which is founded on the rapid advancement of individuals who distinguish themselves by their virtues and talents. Individual preferences notwithstanding, the French inheritance law also causes the division of land, workshops, and businesses, although it does so in a less direct way and with a greater awareness of those inequalities that are produced by intelligence and industry; and this also cannot be reconciled with sound industrial, commercial, and agricultural organization. Nor is there any merit to the proposals, urged by radical English economists, which would set a maximum limit on the amount any individual could inherit.

Nations whose progress has cleared away most of these obstacles have often encountered still another stumbling block: the development of pauperism. They have had to resort to a special kind of regulatory measure to correct those ills which improvident families bring on themselves by the simple exercise of their free will. The institutions serving this function include the systems of parochial assistance which Germany and England have adopted, the distribution of aid administered by Catholic convents in Italy and Austria, the hospitals and poorhouses in most towns in Western countries, etc. Closely related to these programs are Germany's regulations restricting marriage among the working class and the poor, and the English regulations which disperse the members of needy families to workhouses. All enlightened men recognize the drawbacks of these forms of assistance and these emergency measures; they know that civilization, in order to progress, must render these measures unnecessary.

The inherent defects of these institutions, whose programs are mostly temporary expedients useful only within particular regions, are not to be found among three other tutelary institutions, whose characteristics in Europe's principal regions have been set forth with particular care in the present work. The family, associations, and patronage play an integral role throughout society, because they result from human nature's most powerful instincts. These institutions today are capable not only of protecting improvident individuals but also of assuring the progress of every class in every European society. They adapt themselves with admirable flexibility to every one of civilization's demands. Their authority in such matters works upon people's feelings and moral attitudes; they can therefore remedy social ills or assist and direct individuals with a minimum of restrictions and regulations. In summary, these are the institutions which will bring us to civilization's ultimate goal: a just and good society dedicated to the principle of freedom of the will; society's mission consists in establishing justice and goodness without compromising the requirements of individual liberty. In France, associations decline or grow according to the same laws which were found earlier to apply to the whole of Europe. The communities which suppress individual initiative and activity in the name of the collective enterprise are in steady decline. Those organizations, on the other hand, which are able to achieve useful goals while respecting individual liberty both in one's private life and in one's work prosper more and more. The freest corporations are at the same time the most productive, and their growth will always be one of the best measures of civilization's progress; but they play an important role only in those relatively rare societies whose people have reached a fairly advanced level of intellectual and moral development.

Patronage, which affects all the interests of the working class (and often even the interests of associations), exerts a more general influence on a larger portion of the population. The current decline of this institution explains most of the difficulties which have arisen in Western societies. In England, in spite of the undeniable improvements which have taken place in the mores of the upper classes, the patronage exercised on behalf of factory workers has been weakened by the unruly impact which the steam engine and the use of coal have had on manufacturing. In France, these same influences have had their effect, albeit on a smaller scale, in our coal regions and industrial centers; but the main causes of our disorganization developed a long time ago in the class of large landholders and affected the entire rural population. This disastrous influence must be attributed to governments which, from the seventeenth century on, encouraged absenteeism and a fondness for luxury; to that weakening of mores and beliefs which took place between the end of the seventeenth century and the Revolution of 1789; and finally, to a certain degree, to our new civil laws which, in order to clean up this corruption, have for the time being disrupted the stability of families and their property.

On the subject of reforms in manufacturing, France would do

well to study the principles which the English established in 1833; but the details on which the French must concentrate are generally different from the ones which engaged the attention of the English parliament. In France, the government must above all prevent an imbalanced distribution of manufacturing centers and provide the initial impetus toward the establishment of a good system of emigration. For the sake of equity and the public interest, the government must intervene by means of a preliminary inquiry—or if necessary by regulation—in localities where imprudent industrial development might endanger or harm neighbors. It must not remain neutral in those cases where the principles of fair competition are violated by acts which are inimical to morality and humanity. As the experience of the past twenty years has already proven, the enforcement of restrictions of this type would in no way attack the principle of competition: on the contrary, the principle would be protected by a return to the system of patronage that has remained in effect among the most honorable factory owners and even in certain advanced manufacturing countries, where the force of public opinion has been sufficient to prevent the abuses which have been particularly severe in England and France. The establishment of institutions whose purpose would be to prevent fluctuations in grain prices would also have a most beneficial effect on France's economy. But to obtain these results, it is necessary to do more than just promulgate laws; following England's example, France must assure the enforcement of these laws by publicizing them and by providing an effective system of record-keeping and sanctions.

On the subject of upper-class mores, reform has gradually resulted from the beneficial effects of the trials which France has undergone in the past sixty years; reform is evident in the way people have returned to the ideas and sentiments which are the basis of all civilization. The most eminent thinkers are abandoning bit by bit the preoccupations which gave strength and glory to those who destroyed the ancien régime, and they are now offering their influence to the new movement. The initial impetus has been provided; with the passage of time it will bear fruit and, most important, it will exorcise the danger of new revolutions. But even in this direction, it is important to guard against a certain thoughtless impulse: the kind of pressure to be exerted must be exclusively moral pressure, whose sole weapon is public opinion. The social authorities who must preside over these matters must repress with vigilant care those coercive tendencies and intolerant habits which the desire for the good can encourage in certain minds which are more passionate than enlightened. In this connection, extreme caution is especially necessary in a Catholic country where there are admirable means for achieving progress but where it is particularly important to guard against the excesses and the abuses which brought on the Protestantism and the antireligious reaction of the eighteenth century.

In France, and in other countries which have adopted the inheritance laws from our Civil Code, the family is growing weaker and weaker, with bad consequences for paternal authority, individual well-being, and the public interest. The troublesome consequences of this state of affairs are especially evident in the instability of agricultural, commercial, and industrial enterprises, in the indolence of the young members of most well-to-do families, in the difficulties France is having recruiting an army and setting up a good emigration program, in the powerlessness of our colonial system. These consequences seem to be attributable to the prolonged impact of legislation which should only have been a temporary expedient. But this conclusion, which the English and the Americans have always accepted as self-evident, is still contradicted by French public opinion. Therefore, it is on this problem that an organization for social research should first form a consensus of well-reasoned convictions, and then use the force of evidence (if it is available) to destroy prejudice and error. As soon as the cause of the illness has been stated, as soon as it has been proven that French mores no longer require the pressure of restrictive laws, then the remedy will be easy to find: it will suffice to return to European tradition, to follow the example of those two countries whose current success is most striking—in other words, to return to fathers the freedom to dispose of their property as they choose. This family reform would have a most beneficial effect on the working classes, not only by strengthening the institution of patronage but more importantly by guaranteeing the survival and growth of the class of small landholders.

The conclusions which I have just summarized prove that, given civilization's actual state of affairs, reforms cannot succeed without the support of good mores; even in those cases where government must provide the initial impetus, the goal will only be achieved by individual initiative. One important portion of society, by distinguishing itself intellectually and morally, must prepare itself for the challenge of this mission, and herein lies the most delicate aspect of the problem of social reform. Since improvidence, as we have often stated, is the universal and distinctive characteristic of the masses, one segment of society must be responsible for seeing to the well-being of the masses. In the least perfect civilizations, the law commands one class to perform this duty at the same time as it demands obedience from the masses. In civilizations where free will is not fettered at either end of the social scale, eminent individuals adapt to the role of guardian, inspired by conscience and a heightened awareness of social interests. True nobility and superiority are characteristics to be found in the moral attitudes of those families that rise to the challenge of this lofty task. This is the essence of the distinction which has been drawn frequently over the course of this study, a distinction which must be established in every civilization between classes at the two ends of the social scale. It is vain to hope for the maintenance of this distinction when the upper class, losing its sense of obligation and distancing itself from the class it should be protecting, betrays its mission; history has sufficiently shown that in such cases the public, inspired by the prospect of a better order of things, extinguishes prestige that is based upon tradition.

At the same time, it is also true that a nation has not been truly established until a class of substantial size has distinguished itself from the masses by its virtues and talents: those very societies which most strenuously reject any legal classification of individuals are precisely those where the natural distinctions between the two classes are most formally drawn by mores, public opinion, and especially by popular acclaim. In democratic societies, which are so favorable to the development of free will, one sees a multitude of individuals rise, by virtue of industry and thrift, from the lowest ranks of the working class; many are able to achieve

Proposals for Reform 295

wealth, although public opinion does not classify them in society's top ranks right away. Indeed, the qualities which have assured their success are almost always the exact opposite of the qualities which would earn them this final promotion. An excessive commitment to manual labor and an incessant preoccupation with profit and thrift are to a certain extent incompatible with the normal development of intelligence and moral sentiments; they leave an imprint of harshness on most people, a consequence which only an elite few are able to resist; under these conditions, for example, we see the development, particularly in the middle levels of the social hierarchy, of such types as the miser and the usurer. Those who, by force of will and energy, have climbed beyond the lowest ranks of the social hierarchy rarely retain the instinctive generosity (that most affecting trait of the improvident masses) which impels one to help the weak or the destitute. The numerous analyses which are summarized in the *Atlas* even enable us to state that those workers who have worked hard and stubbornly to become bosses often impose their authority on subordinates with a harshness that is very rare among those whose authority stems from the simple fact of their birth. In most manual trades, the common laborers themselves treat young apprentices with a severity that sometimes degenerates into inhumanity. The virtues which enable one to get beyond the lowest ranks of the social scale are thus mutually exclusive, in all but the most distinguished souls, with those virtues which entitle one to admission into the upper class. Accordingly, even among the most advanced peoples, the natural movement of progress usually requires more than a single generation to produce those superior individuals who are indispensable to the maintenance of social harmony. These same superior individuals, lacking the privileges which belonged to them under the old European social systems, can only maintain and further their interests by indirect means, especially the protection which their property affords; it should come as no surprise that public attention has focused on those families which, under these difficult conditions, have succeeded in preserving their honorable tradition of moral preeminence.

Free societies therefore have a definite stake in strengthening the organization of property and of the family, in order to establish a class whose noble habits of patronage can be transmitted without danger of being compromised by self-interest. But to attain this goal without betraying their principles, these societies must see to it that two goals are met. The natural aristocracy, whose authority is based on property and intelligence, must never take advantage of its authority and well-being, thereby losing those moral qualities which are the very reason for its existence. At the same time, the influence of this class must be constantly kept in balance; its very membership must change constantly, stimulated by contributions from all segments of society; consequently, the lower class must be allowed to pass the moral barriers separating it from the uppermost class as quickly as human nature and the conditions of civilization allow. In other terms, free societies, in order to assure progress and harmony, must avail themselves of that power which can keep the class exempted from industrial labor from forgetting its duty and turning corrupt, and which can keep the class dedicated to gain and thrift from turning harsh and selfish. This power, which must supersede even liberty, which in society is concerned mainly with individuals, can be found only in religion. Religion not only raises societies to moral perfection, civilization's ultimate goal; in addition, it is the most powerful means of achieving economic success. This is the explanation of the fact that is so apparent in our epoch: the development of work, wealth, and liberty among the different peoples is closely linked to the progress of those firm and austere mores, of that spirit of justice, conciliation, and shared benevolence which are the surest manifestations of religious belief.

Thus, when one analyzes the resources which each nation must draw on to accomplish the reforms which its system demands, and when one looks to the future, one is always led to that conclusion glimpsed by every thinker and expressed a thousand different ways. The rank which each nation occupies undoubtedly depends on its material circumstances and on the institutions which govern it, but the elements essential to preeminence belong to the moral order; and if, to conclude the analysis which has been the purpose of this work, it were necessary to indicate that force which, affecting both ends of the social scale, would be in itself sufficient to assure progress, we would not hesitate to give the least prominence to foresight and the greatest prominence to religion. Let science multiply its discoveries, let liberty display its resources and authority its power, let all of civilization accumulate grandeur and splendor—all their labor will be useless if, even without abandoning the rights guaranteed by reason, people fail to uphold God's dominion in their souls. By analyzing facts and manipulating figures, social science thus furnishes the same conclusions that ethics does. In this way, the unity of the supreme truth reveals itself in every form, and human thought in its most varied endeavors is led back to the sovereign principles of justice and goodness.

NOTES

All monographs have been cited from the 1877–79 edition of *Les Ouvriers européens*, for several reasons. The 1877–79 edition contains all the monographs from the 1855 edition, in unchanged form, as well as many new monographs prepared for the second edition. It therefore seemed less confusing to cite only from the 1877–79 edition. Moreover, the later edition is more readily available in American libraries.

It should also be noted that the first citation of a monograph gives the full title in French and the translation. All subsequent citations give only a shortened form of the French title. This same procedure has been used for the rest of Le Play's works, principally because of the extreme length of his titles.

Introduction

Le Play and Social Science

1. Frédéric Le Play, *La Constitution essentielle de l'humanité: Exposé des principes et des coûtumes qui créent la prosperité ou la souffrance des nations* [The essential constitution of humanity: presentation of the principles and customs which lead to prosperity or suffering of nations], pp. 1–16.

2. Le Play's contribution has been ignored or dismissed by Marxists and Durkheimians alike, even in such well-known histories of sociology as Raymond Aron's *Main Currents in Sociological Thought* (1968), Lewis Coser's *Masters of Sociological Thought* (1971), and Gaston Bouthoul's *Traité de sociologie* [Treatise on sociology] (1959). This oversight by such distinguished authors shows how thoroughly Le Play's achievement has been forgotten. One partial exception is Georges Gurvitch's acknowledgment of Le Play's work as the first attempt to study

the working classes empirically. See his "Brève esquisse de l'histoire de la sociologie" [Brief outline of the history of sociology], in G. Gurvitch, ed., *Traité de sociologie,* p. 45. Howard Becker and Elmer Barnes, in *Social Thought from Lore to Science* (1961), also acknowledge Le Play as a founding father of sociology, but unfortunately their description and analysis are often misleading.

The following histories mention Le Play in passing: Nicholas S. Timasheff, *Sociological Theory: Its Nature and Growth* (1959), and Albion W. Small and George E. Vincent, *An Introduction to the Study of Society* (1894) (the first sociology "textbook"). To my knowledge, only a few histories of sociological thought have presented his contributions at any length: John Madge, *The Origin of Scientific Sociology* (1962); Ronald Fletcher, "Frédéric Le Play," in *The Founding Fathers of Social Science* (1969), ed. Timothy Raison; and Pitirim A. Sorokin, *Contemporary Sociological Theories* (1928). One should also mention Matilda Riley's inclusion of Le Play's monographic method in her *Sociological Research* (1963). Unfortunately, even these accounts give incomplete or distorted pictures of Le Play.

3. See, for example, Alvin W. Gouldner, *The Coming Crisis in Western Sociology* (1970).

4. For a discussion of this issue, see ibid., chaps. 2 and 3. See also Anthony Giddens, *Positivism and Sociology* (1974).

5. The full title of Le Play's book is *Les Ouvriers européens: Etudes sur les travaux, la vie domestique et la condition morale des populations ouvrières de l'Europe, et leur relations avec les autres classes* [European workers: studies on the labor, domestic life and moral condition of the working classes of Europe and their relationship with other classes]. Despite the title of this volume, the first edition includes the study of a Siberian family and the second edition adds studies of Central Asian families.

6. The study of the history of empirical social research was begun by Paul Lazarsfeld in a seminar at the Sorbonne in 1962–63 and continued in subsequent years at Columbia University under the joint sponsorship of Lazarsfeld and Robert Merton. From these seminars, a number of papers and books on the subject were published. Lazarsfeld describes the beginnings of this study of empirical research in his foreword to Anthony Oberschall, ed., *The Establishment of Empirical Sociology,* pp. vii–xv.

7. A number of authors examine the role of empirical research during the incipient phase of sociology. See Philip Abrams, *The Origins of British Sociology* (1968); Terry N. Clark, "Discontinuities in Social Research: The Case of the *Cours Elémentaire de Statistique Administra-*

tive," *History of Behavioral Sciences* (1967), and *Prophets and Patrons: The French University and the Emergence of the Social Sciences* (1973); Michael J. Cullen, *The Statistical Movement in Early Victorian Britain* (1975); Nathan Glazer, "The Rise of Social Research in Europe," in *The Human Meaning of the Social Sciences*, ed. Daniel Lerner (1959); Paul Lazarsfeld, "Notes on the History of Quantification in Sociology," *Isis* 52 (pt. 2) (1961); Gérard Leclerc, *Observation de l'homme* (1978); Bernard Lécuyer and Anthony Oberschall, "The Early History of Social Research," *International Encyclopedia of the Social Sciences*, 15:36–53; Daniel Lerner, "Social Science: Whence and Whither?" in *The Human Meaning of the Social Sciences*, ed. Daniel Lerner (1962); and Anthony Oberschall, ed., *The Establishment of Empirical Sociology* (1972).

8. *La Réforme sociale en France, déduite de l'observation comparée des peuples européens* [Social reform in France, deduced from the comparative observation of different European countries].

9. *L'Organisation du travail, selon la coûtume des ateliers et la loi du Décalogue, avec un précis d'observations comparées sur la distinction du bien et du mal dans le régime du travail, les causes du mal actuel et les moyens de réforme, les objections et les réponses, les difficultés et les solutions* [The organization of work, according to the custom of workshops and the law of the Decalogue, with a summary of comparative observations on the distinction between social well-being and social ills, the causes of current ills and the means of reform, objections and answers, problems and solutions].

10. *L'Organisation de la famille, selon le vrai modèle signalé par l'histoire de toutes les races et de tous les temps* [The organization of the family, according to the true model indicated by the history of all races and all periods].

11. Carle C. Zimmerman and Merle E. Frampton, in *Family and Society* (1935), present a translation of part of volume 1 of the second edition of *Ouvriers européens* (1877–79), a portion of Le Play's work which emphasizes his nonempirical concerns. Jesse R. Pitts presents a translation of a short passage from *Ouvriers européens* dealing with household economy, in *Theories of Society*, ed. Talcott Parsons et al., pp. 457–59. C. A. Ellwood was the first to translate Le Play's "Instruction sur la méthode d'observation dite des monographies de famille" [Instruction in the observation of social facts according to the Le Play method of family monographs]. This translation was published in the *American Journal of Sociology* 2 (1897):662–79.

12. Both Paul Lazarsfeld and Robert Nisbet have acknowledged the originality of Le Play's sociological method. See Robert Nisbet, *Tradi-*

tion and Revolt, pp. 73–89; and Paul Lazarsfeld, "Notes on the History of Quantification in Sociology," *Isis* 52 (pt. 2) (1961):277–333.

13. Emile Durkheim, *Rules of Sociological Method* (1966), pp. 78–81.

14. The "tableau" is presented in this volume, p. 99. See *Ouvriers européens* (1855), p. 17.

15. For a discussion of the role of classificatory devices in theory construction, see Paul Lazarsfeld, *La Philosophie des sciences sociales* [The philosophy of the social sciences], pp. 361–74.

16. A good illustration of the connections between theory and research in Le Play's work can be found in *Ouvriers européens* (1877–79), 2:368–71.

17. Nisbet, *Tradition and Revolt,* pp. 85–86.

18. Sorokin, *Contemporary Sociological Theories,* p. 63.

19. Zimmerman and Frampton, *Family and Society,* and Zimmerman, "Frédéric Le Play as a Social Change Theorist," in *Recueil d'études, sociales publié à la mémoire de Frédéric Le Play* [Collection of studies of society published in memory of Frédéric Le Play], pp. 99–107.

20. Nisbet discusses Le Play's empirical method in *The Sociological Tradition,* p. 61. He clearly sees Le Play as a major figure in the study of communities and as a precursor to Durkheim.

21. Nisbet, *Social Change and History,* pp. 195–269.

22. Walter Goldfrank, "Reappraising Le Play," in *The Establishment of Empirical Sociology,* ed. Anthony Oberschall, pp. 130–51.

23. Lazarsfeld, "Notes on the History of Quantification," pp. 311–33.

24. See Jesse R. Pitts, "Le Play, Frédéric," *International Encyclopedia of the Social Sciences,* 9:84–91; Philip Abrams, *Origins of British Sociology* (1968); Michel Dion, "Science sociale et religion chez Le Play" [Social science and religion in the work of Le Play], *Archives de sociologie des religions* 24 (1967):83–101.

Two social historians have devoted theses to Le Play's life and work: Hans D. Kellner, "Frédéric Le Play and the Development of Modern Sociology" (Ph.D. dissertation, University of Rochester, 1972), and Lois H. Rogers, "Frédéric Le Play" (M.A. thesis, Columbia University, 1950).

25. M. Z. Brooke, *Le Play: Engineer and Social Scientist.*

26. Le Play is discussed as a Catholic and a conservative thinker without reference to his empirical work in Andrée Michel, "Les Cadres sociaux de la doctrine morale de Frédéric Le Play" [Social frameworks of Le Play's moral doctrine], *Cahiers internationaux de sociologie* 34 (1963):47–68; and in Jean-Baptiste Duroselle, *Les Débuts du catholicisme social en France, 1822–1870* [The origins of social Catholicism in France, 1822–1870], pp. 673–85.

27. These aspects of Le Play's work are most clearly expressed in *Réforme sociale* (1864); in *Constitution essentielle*, 2d ed. (1893), pp. 215ff.; and in *Ouvriers européens* (1877–79), vol. 1.

28. Le Play influenced such economists as Charles Gide and Charles Rist, and such conservatives as la Tour du Pin and Vicomte Alfred de Mun. He also influenced progressive Catholics, including Lamennais.

29. Louis Baudin, ed., *Le Play: Textes choisis*.

30. Neither Tarde nor Durkheim recognized Le Play as an influence on his work.

31. Durkheim, "La Sociologie en France pendant le 19ᵉ siècle" [Sociology in France in the 19th century], *Revue politique et parlementaire* 19 (May 1900):651.

32. Pierre Joseph Proudhon, *De la justice dans la révolution et dans l'église* [On justice in the revolution and in the church], 3:132.

33. Comte Léon de Montesquiou, a well-known Monarchist, attacked Le Play on these grounds and deplored what he considered Le Play's lack of strong political commitment in *L'Oeuvre de Frédéric Le Play* [The work of Frédéric Le Play], p. 39.

34. A complete list of the 339 contributors to the Société internationale des études pratiques d'économie sociale in 1862 is available at the Bibliothèque Le Play, Institut catholique de Paris.

35. For a description of the French university system and the institutionalization of sociology in France, see Clark, *Prophets and Patrons*, pp. 13–65.

36. Karl Mannheim, *Ideology and Utopia*, pp. 211–15.

Life of Le Play

1. Le Play draws connections between his life and his work in the following passages: *Ouvriers européens* (1877–79), 1:vii–viii, 1–41; ibid., chap. 13, sec. 2. See also *Constitution essentielle* (1893), pp. 4–13.

2. See "The Apprenticeship of a Social Scientist," pp. 137–47 in this volume, and Le Play, *Ouvriers européens* (1877–79), 1:17–48.

3. Le Play, *Ouvriers européens* (1877–79), 1:41.

4. Le Play was highly praised by such contemporaries as Montalembert, Sainte-Beuve, Schäffle, and Renan. Excerpts from these authors are found in the introduction of *Réforme sociale* (1878), pp. xxii–xl. Le Play received a statistical award for *Ouvriers européens*, but these contemporaries concentrated instead on praising his moral courage and leadership.

5. Cited in Charles de Ribbe, ed., *Le Play, d'après sa correspondance* [Le Play's correspondence], p. 85.

6. I have drawn information about Le Play's life from biographical and autobiographical sources. The most complete and accurate biography is

Brooke's *Le Play*. I have also drawn upon the autobiographical portions of Le Play's *Réforme sociale* and the second edition of *Ouvriers européens*. Though some of Le Play's information may be questionable, these works clearly convey his perceptions of the links between his life and work. In addition, I have consulted the documents about his life and the portions of his correspondence located in the Bibliothèque Le Play at the Institut Catholique.

7. A. J. Tudesq and A. Jadin, "Les Pays de l'ouest" [The western regions] in *La France des notables, 1815-1848* [The France of the notables, 1815-1848], 1:18-28.

8. Le Play, *Ouvriers européens* (1877-79), 1:24.

9. Le Play, *Réforme sociale* (1864), 1:15 and 2:34.

10. A number of eminent scientists taught at the Ecole Polytechnique, including Lagrange, Monge, Fourier, Poisson, and Bertholet. For an analysis of this school, see Friederich A. von Hayek, *The Counter-Revolution of Science,* pp. 110ff.

11. Le Play, *Constitution essentielle,* pp. 3-4.

12. These interpretations of Saint-Simon's work are discussed in Armand Cuvillier, "Les Antagonismes de classes dans la littérature française de Saint-Simon à 1840" [Class antagonisms in French literature from Saint-Simon to 1840], *International Review of Social History* 1 (1956):433-63, and Armand Cuvillier, *Les Doctrines sociales de 1840* [The social doctrines of 1840], pp. 109-38. See also Durkheim's *Socialisme,* pp. 298-336.

13. See Saint-Simon, *Mémoire sur la science de l'homme* [Notes on the science of man], vol. 5 in *Oeuvres de Claude-Henri de Saint-Simon* [Works of Claude-Henri de Saint-Simon] (Paris: Editions Anthropos, 1966).

14. Le Play, *Ouvriers européens* (1877-79), 1:4.

15. Le Play's pioneering interest in the human side of industrial organization was acknowledged by Elton Mayo in *The Human Problems of an Industrial Civilization*.

16. For an analysis of the processes of institutionalization of the social sciences in France, see Clark, *Prophets and Patrons,* pp. 99-116.

17. Among the members of the political and social elite who convinced him to publish his results, Le Play mentions Arago, Lamartine, Carnot, de Tocqueville, J. B. Dumas, Sainte-Beuve, and Cochin. See *Constitution essentielle,* p. 239.

18. Ibid.

19. Le Play, *Réforme sociale* (1878), 1:v.

20. He used his monograph on the miners of the Harz Mountains to prove this point. See *Ouvriers européens* (1877-79), "Mineur des corporations de mines d'argent et de plomb de Haut-Hartz," [Silver and lead miner of the Harz Mountains], 3:99-152.

21. Brooke, *Le Play,* pp. 49-54.

22. Le Play, *Constitution essentielle*, p. 257.
23. Quoted in Brooke, *Le Play*, p. 14.
24. This opinion was widely shared by liberals and socialists alike in the first part of the nineteenth century. Karl Marx was the first to express the idea that the emancipation of the working class should be undertaken by the workers themselves.
25. The Conseil d'Etat is a consultative body, not a legislative one. Its main role is to study and prepare laws which are voted on by the Chamber of Deputies.
26. Cited in de Ribbe, *Le Play, d'après sa correspondance*, p. 97.
27. Ibid.
28. For a description of Le Play's role as an organizer of the international exhibitions of 1841, 1851, 1862, and 1867, see Brooke, *Le Play*, pp. 59–71.
29. Ibid., p. 71.
30. The law which was passed stipulated that only a certain portion of a man's estate could be bequeathed as he wished. The rest had to be equally divided among his children. The law, which was an attempt to break up the big estates, also had a devastating effect on small holdings. See ibid., p. 74.
31. Le Play, *Ouvriers européens* (1855), sec. 43, p. 36.
32. Le Play, *Ouvriers européens* (1877–79), 1:149; see also *Constitution essentielle*, pp. 215–19.
33. Cited in *Réforme sociale* (1872), 1:xxxi. The British journal *Saturday Review* praised the book in its issue of June 3, 1871.
34. Le Play, *La Réforme en Europe et le salut en France* [Reform in Europe and the salvation of France], p. 36.
35. *La Constitution d'Angleterre considerée dans ses rapports avec la loi de Dieu et les coûtumes de la paix sociale, precedée d'aperçus sommaires sur la nature du sol et l'histoire de la race* [The English constitution, understood in its relationships with the law of God and the customs of social peace, preceded by a summary regarding the nature of the soil and the history of the race].
36. See "The Three Ages of Work" in this volume (IV, 8).
37. Le Play, *Constitution essentielle*, p. 83.
38. Le Play, *Réforme sociale* (1872), 2:412.
39. Le Play, *Ouvriers européens* (1877–79), 6:xxxix.
40. Ibid., 1:16–17.

Le Play and the Sociological Orientations of His Time

1. In chemistry, the 1820s saw the introduction of "crystallo-chemical" classificatory schemes, which concentrated on the chemical components as well as the interior structure of atoms. Le Play, who studied chemistry at that time, later compared the study of families and

societies to the analysis of the structure and components of a chemical. For a history of classificatory devices in mineralogy, see John G. Burke, "Mineral Classification in the Early 19th Century," in *Toward a History of Geology*, ed. Cecil Schneer, pp. 63–77.

2. For an analysis of the political and social changes that occurred in France, see Theodore Zeldin, *France, 1848–1945*, vol. 1: *Ambition, Love, and Politics*. See also J. H. Clapham, *The Economic Development of France and Germany, 1815–1914*, chap. 3.

3. My discussion of the influence of conservative thinkers on Le Play's work corroborates Nisbet's analysis—in *The Sociological Tradition*—of the influence of the conservative tradition on French sociology in general.

4. The elaboration of conservative thought and its impact on emerging social theories is discussed in Nora Hudson, *Ultra-Royalism and the French Restoration*, pp. 20–30, 190–92; in Robert R. Locke, *French Legitimists*, p. 134; and in René Rémond, *La Droit en France, 1815–1848* [The right in France, 1815–1848], vol. 1:25–94.

5. A discussion of the system of ideas accepted by French elites during this period can be found in Emile Levasseur, *Histoire des classes ouvrières en France depuis 1789 jusqu'à nos jours* [History of the working classes in France from 1789 to the present day], 1:470–560. See also Charles Morazé, *The Triumph of the Middle Classes: A Study of European Values in the 19th Century*, pp. 192–225.

6. Louis Chevalier, *Laboring Classes and Dangerous Classes in Europe during the First Half of the Nineteenth Century*, p. 360. See also "The Subject Matter of the Science of Society" in this volume (II, 6).

7. De Bonald, "De la famille agricole et de la famille industrielle" [On the agricultural family and the industrial family], *Oeuvres complètes*, 2:280.

8. In the first half of the nineteenth century, capitalism in France was a much more flexible and open system than it was to become during the reign of Napoleon III. Professional and social mobility were more common before France became fully industrialized. See Georges Duveau, *La Vie ouvrière en France sous le Second Empire* [The worker's life during the Second Empire], p. 415.

9. Aron, *Main Currents in Sociological Thought*, vol. 1; Coser, *Masters of Sociological Thought;* Henri Sée, *Histoire économique de la France des temps modernes, 1789–1914* [Economic history of France in modern times, 1789–1914], pp. 144–247; and Gouldner, *The Coming Crisis in Western Sociology*, pp. 98–108.

10. Philippe Ariès shows that in France industrialization did not necessarily uproot families, that there was a slow and gradual migration from rural to urban centers, that most of the workers were not proletarians, and that cooperation between workers and the bourgeoisie was more common than antagonism; see *Histoire des populations françaises* [His-

tory of the French population], pp. 228–30. J. H. Clapham, in *Economic Development of France and Germany, 1815–1914,* p. 53, argues that in France, unlike in England, there was no real industrial revolution or clear passage from one system of economic organization to another.

11. Karl Polanyi analyzes England's industrialization in *The Great Transformation,* pp. 130–219.

12. By studying the property records of a French village during the first half of the nineteenth century, Harvey Smith has shown that more small landholders acquired property even while agriculture was becoming more specialized—a trend which continued into the 1870s. Though the village Smith studied may not have been representative of most French communities, Smith did demonstrate that its peasants were able to cling to their communities in the face of industrialization. See his "Work Routine and Social Structure in a French Village: Cruzy (Hérault) in the 19th Century," a paper delivered at the Brockport Conference, Brockport College, State University of New York, September 29–30, 1972.

13. Tudesq, *Les Grands notables en France, 1840–1849: Étude historique d'une psychologie sociale* [The great notables in France, 1840–1849: a historical study of a social psychology].

14. De Bonald's ideas on industrialism are analyzed in D. K. Cohen, "The Vicomte de Bonald's Critique of Industrialism," *Journal of Modern History* 41 (1969):475–84.

15. De Bonald, *Considérations politiques sur l'argent et le prêt à interêt* [Political considerations on money and money-lending], *Oeuvres complètes,* 2:280.

16. Le Play, Preface to *Programme de gouvernement et d'organisation sociale d'après l'observation comparée de divers peuples* [Program of government and of social organization based on the comparative observation of various countries], p. vi.

17. Abrams, *Origins of British Sociology,* pp. 31–52.

18. Le Play, *Réforme sociale* (1872), pp. 5–8.

19. Le Play, *L'Organisation de la famille,* pp. xvii–xx. See also "Family Organization in the Four Social Systems of Europe" in this volume (VI, 20).

20. Raymond Deniel analyzes the renewed importance of the family in conservative thought after the Revolution in *Une Image de la famille et de la société sous la Restauration* [A picture of the family and of society during the Restoration], pp. 95–128. Traditionally, the church had claimed primary responsibility for the moral education of the young, thinking it too important a task to be left to the family. Also, the church had often looked upon the family with ambivalence, as the center of permissible sexual activity. See John Bossy, "The Counter-Reformation and the People of Catholic Europe," *Past and Present,* no. 47 (1970): 68–70.

21. Le Play, *Organisation de la famille*, p. 260.
22. Nisbet, *Tradition and Revolt*, p. 81.
23. Le Play was criticized by Catholic thinkers for undermining Catholic ideas and minimizing religion as a factor in social stability. See Paul Ribot, *Du role social des idées chrétiennes* [On the social role of Christian ideas], p. 398.
24. Le Play, *Ouvriers européens* (1877–79), "Forgeron Bulgare des usines de fer de Samakowa" [Bulgarian ironworker in the factories of Samakowa], 2:231–65; "Fondeur au bois de Hundsrucke" [Iron smelter of Hundsruck], 4:68–120; "Chiffonier de Paris" [Ragpicker of Paris], 6:257–326; "Manoeuvre à famille nombreuse de Paris [Parisian laborer with a large family], 6:327–86.
25. After the revolution of 1830, qualified and intelligent men had greater access to important social positions. See Rémond, *La Droite en France, 1815–1848*, 1:87.
26. A study of a rural district near Grenoble in 1847 shows that only 27 percent of the population did not own property. See Jesus Ibarrola, *Structure sociale et fortune dans la campagne proche de Grenoble en 1847* [Social structure and wealth in the country near Grenoble in 1847], p. 17.
27. Duveau, *La Vie ouvrière en France sous le Second Empire*. See also Henri Sée, "Quelques aperçus sur la condition de la classe ouvrière de 1815 à 1848" [A few insights into the condition of the working class from 1815 to 1848], *Revue d'histoire économique et sociale* 12 (1924):493–521; also Levasseur, *L'Histoire des classes ouvrières*, p. 562.
28. Le Play, *Ouvriers européens* (1877–79), 6:386 and 3:12. See also *Constitution essentielle*, p. ix.
29. Le Play pointed out a curious contrast: England, the first nation to develop a laissez-faire market economy, retained traditions and political mechanisms which enabled her to contend with the destructive effects of the industrial revolution. France, on the other hand, which had had a long tradition of state regulation and intervention, was much less successful at containing the impact of these economic changes. For a further discussion of this contrast, see Morazé, *The Triumph of the Middle Classes*, pp. 139–82. See also Le Play, "La Superiorité des sociétés Anglo-Saxonnes" [The superiority of Anglo-Saxon societies], in *Ouvriers européens* (1877–79), 4:492–93.
30. For an analysis of the increasing privatization of the family, see Philippe Ariès, *Centuries of Childhood*, especially pp. 15–136.
31. For an analysis of the concept of freedom in conservative and liberal thought, see Tudesq, *Les Grands notables*, 1:598–605; and Levasseur, *L'Histoire des classes ouvrières*, p. 479.
32. Le Play, *Réforme sociale* (1878), 1:38–62.
33. Le Play, *Ouvriers européens* (1877–79), "Mineur du Haut-Hartz," 3:134–43.
34. Le Play, "L'Organisation du patronage" [The organization of pa-

tronage], *Ouvriers européens* (1855), pp. 19–20.

35. Cited in Cuvillier, "Les Antagonismes de classes," p. 438.

36. Le Play, *Ouvriers européens* (1877–79), "Paysans, Portefaix et Bateliers émigrants du Bassin de l'Oka (Russie)" [Peasants and migrant porters and boatmen of the Oka Basin (Russia)], 2:201–7.

37. Ibid., 1:149.

38. Ibid., 1:194–95n.

39. Le Play, *Réforme sociale*, 2:413.

40. Ibid.

41. Le Play, *Organisation de la famille* (1884), pp. 108–9; *Réforme sociale*, pp. 28 and 47; and *Constitution essentielle* (1893), chaps. 1, 4. See also Luigi Einaudi, "The Doctrine of Original Sin and the Theory of the Elite in the Writings of Frederic Le Play," *Essays in European Economic Thought*, trans. and ed. Louise Sommer, pp. 162–217.

42. St. Augustine's *Confessions*, pp. vii–xix.

43. Le Play, *Constitution essentielle*, pp. 18–22.

44. Le Play, *Ouvriers européens* (1877–79), 2:xxviii.

45. Ruggiero, "Positivism," in *Encyclopedia of Social Sciences*, 12:260–66.

46. Mannheim, *Ideology and Utopia*, p. 232.

47. Le Play, *Ouvriers européens* (1877–79), 1:33.

48. Le Play, *L'Organisation du travail*, p. 272.

49. Le Play, *Réforme sociale*, 1:9ff. and chap. 3.

50. Saint-Simon, *La Physiologie sociale* [Social physiology], in *Oeuvres*, 10:195.

51. See "The Comparative Study of European Workers" in this volume (II, 5).

52. Le Play, *Ouvriers européens* (1877–79), 1:203–4.

53. Ludwig Buchner (1824–99) proposed a new materialism. His works include *Kraft und Stoff* (1855) [Spiritual force and physical matter]; *Natur und Geist* (1857) [Nature and spirit]; and *Darwinismus und Socialismus* (1894) [Darwinism and socialism].

54. Abrams, *Origins of British Sociology*, p. 60.

The Science of Society

1. Le Play explicitly refused to use the term "sociologie" because he distrusted the creation of new words. See *Réforme sociale* (1872), 1:xvii and 380.

2. Lazarsfeld, "Notes on the History of Quantification," pp. 279–94, and Bertrand Gille, *Les Sources statistiques de l'histoire de France des enquêtes du 17" siècle à 1850* [The statistical sources for the history of France from the inquiries of the 17th century to 1850].

3. Le Play, *Vues générales sur la statistique* [General considerations on statistics], p. 10.

4. Lazarsfeld, "Notes on the History of Quantification," pp. 283–91.
5. Le Play, *Vues générales de statistique*, pp. 10–14.
6. Ibid., p. 11.
7. For a description of these official inquiries, see Lécuyer and Oberschall, "Early History of Empirical Social Research," *International Encyclopedia of the Social Sciences*, 15:36–53.
8. Le Play, *Ouvriers européens* (1855), Foreword, p. 4.
9. For more information on the survey of 1848, see Hilda Weiss-Rigaudias, *Les Enquêtes ouvrières en France entre 1830 et 1848* [Labor inquiries in France between 1830 and 1848], pp. 184–246. The complete text of the questionnaire is reproduced in ibid., pp. 214–15.
10. Ibid., pp. 214–18.
11. Unlike the English, the French conducted their social surveys under the pressure of highly charged political circumstances, including the events of 1815, 1830, and 1848. This situation may have undermined for some time the role of empirical research in France.
12. Le Play, *Ouvriers européens* (1855), sec. 38, p. 11.
13. Joseph Lottin, *Quetelet, statisticien et sociologue* [Quetelet, statistician and sociologist].
14. F. A. Isambert, "Les recherches statistiques d'Ange-Michel Guérry (1802–1866)" [The statistical research of Ange-Michel Guérry (1802–1866)], *Cahiers internationaux de sociologie* 47 (1969):36.
15. "Statistics versus Direct Observation" in this volume (II, 4).
16. Le Play, *Ouvriers européens* (1855), sec.3, p. 11.
17. The first British census undertaken with the help of a statistical society was conducted in 1851.
18. See David Elesh, "The Manchester Statistical Society: A Case Study of Discontinuity in the History of Empirical Research," in *Establishment of Empirical Sociology*, ed. Anthony Oberschall, pp. 31–72. For a broader discussion of statistical societies in England, see Abrams, *Origins of British Sociology*, pp. 13–23.
19. Le Play was emulated by his friend Porter, a leading member of the Statistical Society of London, who both engaged in independent social research and provided information to royal commissions and select committees.
20. Clark, "Discontinuities in Social Research: The Case of the *Cours elémentaire de statistique administrative*," *History of Behavioral Sciences* 3 (1967):3–16.
21. Le Play, *Ouvriers européens* (1855), pt. I, sec. 10, p. 21. See also "The Study of Working-Class Families" in this volume (III, 8).
22. Hohenberg's study of French and English elites seems to corroborate Le Play's analysis. Hohenberg observed that "while England was becoming an urban country whose elites retained rural values, France remained a rural country with highly urbanized elites." He further observed that the more rapid progress of agriculture in England was due to

the greater cooperation and trust between landlords and tenants, while France tended to oscillate between "paternalism and capitalist tenancy." English leadership was at the same time more personal and more efficient. See Paul Hohenberg, "Change in Rural France in the Period of Industrialization," *Journal of Economic History* 32 (1972): 219–40.

23. Le Play, *La Méthode sociale* [The social method] (1879).

24. Le Play, *Ouvriers européens* (1855), sec. 10, p. 21.

25. Ibid., pp. 11–12. See also "The Use of Direct Observation" in this volume (II, 3).

26. Frégier equates the working classes with the dangerous classes in *Des classes dangereuses de la population dans les grandes villes* [On the dangerous classes of the population in the big cities], (1840); similarly, the Comte J. M. de Gérando, in *De la bienfaisance publique* [On public charity], shows no understanding of the difference between criminals, the poor, unemployed workers, and beggars.

27. Cited in Henri Sée, *Histoire économique de la France des temps modernes, 1789–1914* [Economic history of France in modern times, 1789–1914], p. 340.

28. See, for example, Baron Bigot de Morogues, *Recherches sur les causes de la richesse* [An investigation into the causes of wealth] (1834); Comte J. M. de Gérando, *De la bienfaisance publique* (1849); Vicomte Alban de Villeneuve-Bargemont, *Economie politique chrétienne, ou recherches sur la nature et les causes du paupérisme en France et en Europe et sur les moyens de les soulanger et de les prévenir* [Christian political economy, or an investigation of the nature and the causes of pauperism in France and in Europe and of the ways to alleviate and prevent them] (1837); and Armand Audiganne, *Les Ouvriers d'à présent et la nouvelle économie du travail* [Workers today and the new economy of work] (1865).

29. See Alexandre Jean Baptiste Parent-Duchâtelet, *De la prostitution dans la ville de Paris* (1857).

30. Louis René Villermé, *Tableau de l'état physique et moral des ouvriers employés dans les manufactures de coton, de laine, et de soie* [Portrait of the physical and moral state of workers employed in the cotton, wool, and silk mills].

31. Ibid., 2:6ff.

32. The *livret* was a book in which a record was kept of whom the worker had worked for, how long, for what wages, and, if he had been discharged, for what reasons. The *livret* was mandatory for all workers and no one could be hired without it. The initial intention of the *livret* was to organize and stabilize the working class. However, it became a weapon against the working class, one deeply resented by the workers.

33. Villermé's conclusions were similar to Le Play's—especially his emphasis on the role of associations and patronage and the role of work and thrift in improving the lot of the working classes.

34. Le Play, *Instruction sur la méthode d'observation*, p. 1.
35. The full title is *Description des procédés métallurgiques employés dans le pays de Galles pour la fabrication de cuivre et recherches sur l'état actuel et sur l'avenir probable de la production et du commerce de ce métal* [Descriptions of metallurgical procedures used in Wales for the manufacture of copper and findings on the current state and probable future of the production and trade of this metal].
36. Ibid., p. 17.
37. Le Play, *Ouvriers européens* (1877–79), 1:391. See also "The Comparative Study of European Workers" in this volume (II, 5).
38. Le Play, *Ouvriers européens* (1877–79), 1:15.
39. Le Play, *Méthode sociale*, "Le Vocabulaire social" [Social vocabulary], pp. 444–548.
40. Le Play, *Ouvriers européens* (1855), p. 12.
41. Le Play, *Ouvriers européens* (1877–79), 1:446.
42. Ibid., 1:388. For a discussion of the role of social authorities see H. D. Kellner, "Frédéric Le Play and the Development of Modern Sociology," pp. 102–5.
43. Le Play, *Descriptions des procédés métallurgiques*, pp. 12–15.
44. Von Hayek, *The Counter-Revolution of Science*, pp. 105–7.
45. See J. K. Finch, *The Story of Engineering*, p. 524.
46. C. Wright Mills, *The Sociological Imagination*, p. 65.
47. Le Play, *Constitution essentielle*, pp. 8–9.
48. Le Play, *Ouvriers européens* (1855), sec. 2, p. 11.

The Monographic Method

1. Le Play, *Instruction sur la méthode d'observation*, p. 3.
2. Le Play, *Constitution essentielle*, p. 235.
3. Le Play, *Réforme sociale* (1878), 2:1–2.
4. Ibid., 2:9.
5. Le Play, *Ouvriers européens* (1877–79), 1:208. See also *Ouvriers européens* (1855), chap. 1, sec. 5, p. 17.
6. See "The Study of Working Class Families" in this volume (III, 8).
7. Le Play, *Réforme sociale* (1878), 1:60.
8. Duveau, *La Vie ouvrière en France sous le Second Empire*, pp. 436–37, 545.
9. Ibid., p. 415. Duveau reports that a survey of the population published in the *Journal officiel* of 1872 showed that 80 percent of property owners were former workers, and 15 percent were sons of workers.
10. Le Play, *Ouvriers européens* (1855), sec. 10, p. 21.
11. Ibid.
12. See "The Monographic Method" in this volume (III, 10).
13. Le Play, *Ouvriers européens* (1877–79), 5:375. For additional examples, see "Manoeuvre-agriculteur du Morvan" [Farm laborer of

Morvan], 5:259–322, and "Tailleur d'habits de Paris" [Tailor of Paris], 6:387–441.

14. Ibid., "Coutelier de la fabrique urbaine collective de Sheffield" [Cutler in the urban collective factory of Sheffield], 3:318–63.

15. Ibid., 1:380.

16. A detailed description of all the sections and subsections of the family monographs can be found in Le Play's *Instruction sur la méthode d'observation*, pp. 17–30.

17. Augustin Cochin, *Les Ouvriers européens: Résumé de la méthode et des observations de Le Play* [European workers: a summary of Le Play's method and observations], pp. 7–8.

18. Le Play, *Ouvriers européens* (1877–79), 1:223.

19. Ibid.

20. Le Play, *Instruction sur la méthode d'observation*, p. 16. See also "The Rules of Social Investigation" in this volume (III, 9).

21. Le Play, *Instruction sur la méthode d'observation*, p. 16.

22. The table summarizes the guidelines presented by Le Play in ibid., pp. 20–23. Actually, he gave many more details within each category about the kinds of facts that he wanted the researcher to observe.

23. Ibid., p. 20.

24. Ibid., p. 21.

25. Le Play, *Ouvriers européens* (1877–79), 1:211–12n.

26. Le Play, *Ouvriers européens* (1855), p. 25.

27. Le Play, *Ouvriers européens* (1877–79), "Chiffonier de Paris," 6:257–326.

28. Ibid., "Coutelier de la fabrique urbaine collective de Londres" [Cutler in the urban collective factory of London], 3:273–317.

29. Ibid., 5:39.

30. Ibid., 3:157.

31. Ibid., "Bordier-émigrant du Laonnais" [Day-laborer of Laon], 6:84–142.

32. Ibid., "Métayer de la Vielle-Castille" [Tenant-farmer of Castille], 4:247–90.

33. Ibid., "Chiffonier de Paris," 6:257–326.

34. In 1853, the participants in the First International Congress of Statistics (which was presided over by Quetelet) decided to complete budgets for working-class families. Ducpétiaux, an assistant of Quetelet's, published 199 family budgets in 1855, the year *Ouvriers européens* appeared. Ernst Engel used the family budgets collected by Ducpétiaux and Le Play as a basis for his famous consumption law. Maurice Halbwachs, a disciple of Durkheim, also used Le Play's family budgets in his book *La Classe ouvrière et les niveaux de vie* [The working class and standards of living], pp. 157–75.

35. Le Play, *Ouvriers européens* (1877–79), 1:224.

36. Ibid., 1:237.

37. Le Play, *Ouvriers européens* (1855), pp. 142, 143.

38. The figures in table 2 and table 3 are only a schematic outline of Le Play's budgets. For a comprehensive description of the two budgets of receipts, see pp. 195–98 in this volume.

39. Ibid., 1:240–89.

40. Ibid., 1:291.

41. Lazarsfeld, "Notes on the History of Quantification," p. 327.

42. Charles Booth, in *Life and Labour of the People in London* (17 vols.), tried to measure the extent and distribution of poverty in London by elaborating measures of poverty levels.

43. For an analysis of the four sources of receipts, see Le Play, *Ouvriers européens* (1855), pp. 23–24.

44. See ibid., pp. 24–27, for an analysis of the four types of revenue.

45. The average wage rates for each occupation and the wages in kind and in cash received by each family member for each occupation have been omitted from the tableau for clarity's sake. The full tableau can be found in "Monograph on the Miner of the Upper Harz Mining Corporation" in this volume (III, 11).

46. For an analysis of the five types of expenditures, see Le Play, *Ouvriers européens* (1877–79), 1:290–379.

47. Le Play, *Ouvriers européens* (1877–79), 1:226.

48. Ibid., "L'Armurier de la fabrique demi-rurale collective de Solingen" [Swordsmith in a semirural collective factory of Solingen], 3:165–66.

49. Ibid., "Ferblantier-Couvreur d'Aix-les-Bains" [Builder of Aix-les-Bains], 4:183–246.

50. Ibid., 3:329.

51. Ibid., 1:293.

52. Goldfrank, "Working Paper on Le Play and His Followers," seminar paper, Columbia University (1965), pp. 27–28.

53. See "Monograph on the Miner of the Upper Harz Mining Corporation" in this volume (III, 11).

54. Le Play, *Ouvriers européens* (1877–79), 1:114–17.

55. Eduard Julhiet, "Le Mineur du Hartz 50 années après Le Play" [The Harz miner fifty years after Le Play], *La Réforme sociale* 33 (1897):73–84.

56. The Le Play monograph on which Alfons Reuss based his analysis is "L'Armurier de Solingen" [Gunsmith of Solingen]. Le Play, *Ouvriers européens* (1877–79), 3:153–203.

57. Le Play, *Ouvriers européens* (1855), p. 287.

58. Le Play, *Ouvriers européens* (1877–79), "Fondeur des usines à cobalt de Buskerud (Norvège)" [Cobalt smelter of Buskerud (Norway)], 3:54–98. See also Thomas D. Eliot et al., *Norway's Families*, pp. 3–35.

59. Georges Duveau, *La Vie ouvrière en France sous le Second Empire*.

60. Louise A. Tilly and Joan W. Scott, *Women, Work and Family*.

Family Types

1. See, for example, George Homans, *English Villages of the Thirteenth Century;* Carle C. Zimmerman and Merle E. Frampton, *Family and Society: A Study of the Sociology of Reconstruction*.
2. H. J. Habakkuk, "Family Structure and Economic Change in Nineteenth-Century Europe," *Journal of Economic History* 1 (1955):1-12.
3. See "Family Organization in the Four Social Systems of Europe" in this volume (VI, 20). See also "Family Types: Patriarchal, Stem, Unstable" in this volume (VI, 19).
4. Le Play, *Ouvriers européens* (1877-79), 2:xvii-xxiii; 368-71.
5. Le Play, *Constitution essentielle*, p. 112.
6. Le Play, *Ouvriers européens* (1877-79), "Bachkirs, pasteurs deminomades de l'Oural" [Seminomadic shepherds from the Urals], 2:1-46.
7. Ibid., 2:43.
8. Le Play, *Constitution essentielle*, pp. 31-34.
9. Le Play, *Ouvriers européens* (1877-79), 3:133-43; and "Mineur des filons argentifères de Pontgibaud (Auvergne)" [Silver miner of Pontgibaud (Auvergne)], 5:164. See also Le Play, "Histoire de la famille souche" [History of the stem family], in *Organisation de la famille*, pp. 29-39.
10. Le Play, *Réforme sociale* (1872), 2:12.
11. See Le Play, *Organisation de la famille*, p. 258; see also "Paysans à famille-souche du Lavedan" [Peasants in a stem family from Lavedan], *Ouvriers européens* (1877-79), 4:445-510.
12. For a discussion of the stem family and its distribution in Europe, see Lutz K. Berkner, "Recent Research on the History of the Family in 19th Century Europe," *Journal of Marriage and the Family* 35 (1973):395-405. See also Michael Anderson, *Family Structure in 19th Century Lancashire*, p. 84.
13. Le Play, *Ouvriers européens* (1855), pp. 286-87, and "Inheritance Laws, Family Organization, and Social Reform" in this volume (VI, 21).
14. See Le Play, "Paysans à famille-souche," *Ouvriers européens* (1877-79), 4:445-510, especially 485-94. Le Play presents the family described in this monograph, the Melouga family, as a "model" of family organization.
15. Michael Anderson agrees with Le Play's analysis of the consequences of the different types of inheritance patterns on family solidarity. In Ireland and Lancashire, Anderson found that the father's right to bequeath his property as he chose gave him a better chance to control his

children's futures than French fathers had. See his *Family Structure in 19th Century Lancashire*, p. 93.

16. Le Play, *Ouvriers européens* (1877–79), "Menuisier de la ville de Sheffield" [Joiner of Sheffield], 3:364–99.
17. Ibid., "Paysans à famille-souche," 4:485–94.
18. Emile Cheysson, epilogue to Le Play's *Organisation de la famille* (1884), pp. 215–58.
19. Michael Anderson, "Family, Household, and Industrial Revolution," in Michael Gordon, ed., *The American Family in Social-Historical Perspective*, pp. 59–75.
20. Le Play, *Réforme sociale* (1878), 2:9.
21. Le Play, *Constitution essentielle*, p. 42.

Theory of Social Mobility

1. See "Intragenerational Mobility" in this volume (IV, 13).
2. Le Play, *Ouvriers européens* (1855), sec. 9, p. 50.
3. See "Comparing Occupational Styles" in this volume (IV, 14).
4. Le Play, *Ouvriers européens* (1877–79), 6:290.
5. Ibid., "Maître Blanchisseur de Clichy (Banlieus de Paris)" [Master laundryman of Clichy (outskirts of Paris)], 5:372–423.
6. Ibid., "Fondeur au bois," 4:68–120.
7. Ibid., "Horloger de Genève" [Geneva clockmaker], 6:34–73. See also "Maître Blanchisseur," 5:372–73.
8. Ibid., "Chiffonier de Paris," 6:296.
9. Ibid., 6:257–326.
10. See "Intragenerational Mobility" in this volume (IV, 13) and "Constructing a Social Hierarchy" in this volume (IV, 12). See also Le Play, *Ouvriers européens* (1877–79), "Maître Blanchisseur," 5:372–423.
11. Le Play's definitions of these categories can be found in the footnotes to the two-dimensional table in the 1855 edition of *Ouvriers européens*. See "Constructing a Social Hierarchy" in this volume (IV, 12). In the second edition of *Ouvriers européens*, Le Play used only six types of workers, dropping the category of worker-manager.
12. This is a simplified version of Le Play's social hierarchy, whose original presentation offered a short description of each category of workers. The numbers, letters, and roman numerals were added to clarify Le Play's presentation. See Le Play, *Ouvriers européens* (1855), p. 17.
13. Raymond Deniel, *Une Image de la famille et de la société sous la Restauration*, pp. 70–71.
14. Le Play, *Ouvriers européens* (1877–79), 1:230.
15. Le Play, *Ouvriers européens* (1855), sec. 9, p. 20.
16. Le Play, *Ouvriers européens* (1877–79), 1:281. See also *Ouvriers européens* (1855), sec. 41, pp. 293–94.
17. Le Play, *Ouvriers européens* (1855), sec. 9, p. 20.

18. Le Play, *Ouvriers européens* (1877–79), 1:219–39.
19. Ibid., 1:281.
20. See "Intragenerational Mobility" in this volume (IV, 13).
21. Le Play, *Ouvriers européens* (1877–79), 1:282.
22. Le Play, *Ouvriers européens* (1855), p. 29.
23. Le Play, *Ouvriers européens* (1877–79), 1:281.
24. Ibid., 1:270–75. See also *Ouvriers européens* (1855), pp. 29–30.
25. Le Play, *Ouvriers européens* (1877–79), 1:354.
26. See "Conditions of Social Mobility" in this volume (IV, 15).
27. Le Play, *Ouvriers européens* (1877–79), 1:321.
28. Le Play, *Ouvriers européens* (1855), sec. 9, p. 20.
29. Ibid.
30. Le Play, *Ouvriers européens* (1877–79), "Paysans en communauté et en polygamie de Bousrah (Syria)" [Peasants living in a polygamous community in Bousrah (Syria)], 2:304–97, and "Paysans à famille-souche," 4:445–510.
31. Ibid., "Meunisier de Sheffield," 3:364–99, and "Horloger de Genève," 6:34–73.
32. Ibid., "Maître Blanchisseur," 5:372–423.
33. Le Play apparently could not imagine a situation in which the worker might prefer renting a home to owning one. The 1877–79 edition of *Ouvriers européens* provides monographic studies of "model" workers in Russia ("Paysans, portefaix et bateliers émigrants," 2:179–230), the Netherlands ("Pecheur côtier: Maître de barques de l'ile de Marken" [Coast fisherman: captain from Marken], 3:204–72), Germany ("Mineur du Haut-Hartz," 3:99–152), Spain ("Métayer de la Vielle Castille," 4:247–90), and France ("Paysan-Savonnier de la Basse-Provence" [Peasant soapworker of Basse-Provence], 4:390–433 and "Paysans à famille-souche," 4:445–512).
34. See Le Play, *Ouvriers européens* (1877–79), "Sur les habitudes des ouvriers sédentaires dans la ville de Paris" [On the habits of sedentary workers in the city of Paris], 6:291–96. See also pp. 218–28 in this volume.
35. See, for example, Le Play, *Ouvriers européens* (1877–79), "Coutelier de Sheffield," 3:318–63, and "Débardeur de Port-Marly (Banlieus de Paris)" [Stevedore of Port-Marly (outskirts of Paris)], 6:442–94.
36. Ibid., 6:292.
37. Ibid., "Chiffonier de Paris," 6:293–302.
38. Ibid., 6:291–96; and "Conditions of Social Mobility" in this volume (IV, 15).
39. Le Play, *Ouvriers européens* (1877–79), 1:357.
40. Ibid., 1:353.
41. Ibid., "Coutelier de Londres," 3:273–76.
42. Ibid., "Bordier émigrant de Laonnais," 6:84–142.

43. For an analysis of the role of religion in Le Play's monographs, see Dion, "Science sociale et religion chez Le Play," *Archives de sociologie des religions* 24 (1967):83–101, and Le Play, *Ouvriers européens* (1877–79), "Chiffonier de Paris," 6:259–60.
44. Le Play, *Ouvriers européens* (1877–79), 1:357.
45. Ibid., "Maître Blanchisseur," 5:374–75.
46. Ibid., "L'Armurier de Solingen," 3:153–203.
47. Quoted in Cochin, *Les Ouvriers européens: Résumé de la méthode*, p. 53.
48. Le Play, *Ouvriers européens* (1877–79), 1:355–57 and 5:374–75.
49. See his discussion of women's role, ibid., 1:270–75.
50. See, for example, ibid., "Paysans et charrons à corvée des steppes d'Orenbourg" [Serfs and serf-wheelwrights of the Ourenbourg Steppes], 2:47–98, especially p. 59. See also the study "Bachkirs de l'Oural," ibid., 2:1–46.
51. "The basis for any improvement in the condition of the working classes is the moral education of household members." Le Play, *Ouvriers européens* (1877–79), 1:274.
52. Ibid., "Paysans de Bousrah," 2:305–97, and "Fondeur de Buskerud," 3:54–98.
53. Ibid., 5:385. See also ibid., "Mineur de Pontgibaud," 5:162–63.
54. Le Play, *Ouvriers européens* (1855), p. 28.
55. Le Play believed that women's greatest economic contributions were in the household. However, this position was not linked with a conservative view of women and women's work. Le Play campaigned for the rights of unmarried mothers and against a law which forbade searches for the fathers of illegitimate children. He stressed the importance of good working conditions for those women who had to work. Women were admitted as full members in the Société d'économie sociale. See Brooke, *Le Play*, p. 108.
56. Le Play criticized seduction laws contained in the French penal code of September 25, 1871. These laws treated sixteen-year-old girls as consenting agents. See *Ouvriers européens* (1877–79), 6:316–26.
57. Le Play, *Ouvriers européens* (1855), p. 18. See also "Family Organization in the Four Social Systems of Europe" in this volume (VI, 20).
58. Le Play, *Ouvriers européens* (1855), "L'Organisation du patronage," p. 19. See also "Les Institutions et les coûtumes qui gouvernant l'assistance et la direction des classes imprévoyantes" [The institutions and customs governing the assistance and guidance of the improvident], ibid., pp. 285–86.
59. Ibid., sec. 3, p. 11.
60. This period was characterized by the weakening of the state and the resurgence of localism. It was also a period of economic stagnation. For a discussion of localism, see Tudesq, *Les Grands notables,* 2:1241.

61. Le Play, *Ouvriers européens* (1877–79), 3:198–99.
62. Tudesq, *Les Grands notables*, 2:1231–1327.
63. Le Play, *Ouvriers européens* (1855), pp. 19–20.

Theory of Social Change

1. Nisbet, *The Sociological Tradition*, pp. 61–67; and Charles Gide and Charles Rist, *A History of Economic Doctrines*, trans. R. Richards, p. 525.
2. C. Wright Mills, *The Sociological Imagination*, pp. 51ff.
3. Robert K. Merton, *Social Theory and Social Structure*, pp. 85–99.
4. See "Social Systems and Social Change" in this volume (V, 16).
5. Le Play, *Ouvriers européens* (1855), Foreword, p. 4.
6. Le Play, *Ouvriers européens* (1877–79), 1:vii.
7. Le Play, *Ouvriers européens* (1855), p. 26.
8. Sorokin, *Contemporary Sociological Theories*, chap. 3; and Zimmerman, "Frédéric Le Play as a Social Change Theorist," *Recueil d'études sociales*, pp. 99–107. See also Brooke, *Le Play*, pp. 20–21, 100–106.
9. See "An Analysis of Social Trends" in this volume (V, 17).
10. Le Play, *Ouvriers européens* (1855), p. 17. Each system was defined along comparable dimensions. See pp. 98–99.
11. "Worker-owner" refers to workers who own a house but are employed by someone else.
12. "Owner-worker" refers to workers who exploit their own property as a source of livelihood.
13. Le Play, *Ouvriers européens* (1855), p. 282.
14. Ibid.
15. Quoted in Cochin, *Les Ouvriers européens: Résumé de la méthode et des observations de Frédéric Le Play*, p. 53.
16. Le Play, *Ouvriers européens* (1855), sec. 43, p. 282.
17. Unlike Marx, Le Play believed that social antagonisms did not exist in social and economic regimes that preceded the industrial revolution. He saw the revolts that erupted against the ancien régime as reactions to the irresponsibility and corruption of the elites. Le Play thought that class antagonisms emerged only after the Revolution of 1789 had destroyed ancient customs and mores and brought about the "extinction of the national tradition." See *Réforme sociale* (1878), 1:9–32.
18. Le Play, *Ouvriers européens* (1855), Appendix, sec. 43, p. 283.
19. It should be pointed out that Condorcet, Montesquieu, and other philosophers of the Enlightenment accepted both the inevitability of progress and the role of men in shaping history, and they believed that rational choices directed human action. See Peter Gay, *The Enlightenment*, p. 108.
20. Le Play, *Ouvriers européens* (1877–79), 1:184–92.
21. An abstract concept of freedom was at the center of the philosophy

of the Enlightenment. Le Play argued that the use of the concept of Freedom with a capital "F" led to the limitation of concrete freedoms.

22. Le Play, *Ouvriers européens* (1855), sec. 43, p. 282.
23. See "Social Systems and Social Change" in this volume (V, 16).
24. The term "corporation" as used by Le Play refers neither to modern economic institutions nor to the old corporative system of the ancien régime. The term describes a form of economic institution based on a contract but which had many features in common with the old corporations. After the 1848 revolution, it became a popular term, invested with a new meaning, different from that of the old corporations. See "Defining 'Workers,' 'Associations,' and 'Social Systems,' " in this volume (II, 7).
25. Le Play, *Ouvriers européens* (1877–79), 2:xxviii.
26. Ibid., Introduction, p. 10.
27. Ibid., "Tailleur de Paris," 6:387–441.
28. Le Play, *Ouvriers européens* (1855), p. 18.
29. Ibid., p. 19.
30. Le Play discusses land societies in "Menuisier de Sheffield," *Ouvriers européens* (1877–79), 3:376–77, 397–99. He discusses workers' associations in "Tisserand de Mamers" [Weaver of Mamers], 6:245–47.
31. Ibid., 2:258.
32. Ibid., 1:256–60.
33. Ibid., "Compositeur-typographe de Bruxelles" [Typesetter of Brussels], 5:142–47.
34. Ibid., 1:260.
35. Le Play, *Ouvriers européens* (1855), sec. 6, p. 18.
36. Ibid. See also *Ouvriers européens* (1877–79), "Manoeuvre-Agriculteur de Morvan," 5:259–322, and "Chiffonier de Paris," 6:257–326.
37. See "Inheritance Laws, Family Organization, and Social Reform" in this volume (VI, 21).
38. Le Play, *Ouvriers européens* (1855), sec. 45, p. 286.
39. See "Inheritance Laws, Family Organization, and Social Reform" in this volume (VI, 21).
40. Le Play rejected a linear theory of change and did not believe in the inevitable progress or decline of nations. See *Ouvriers européens* (1877–79), 1:72.
41. Le Play mentioned Vico several times in his writings. Emile Cheysson, Le Play's friend and disciple, related that Le Play frequently quoted Vico in conversation. See Brooke, *Le Play,* p. 99.
42. Le Play, *Constitution essentielle,* p. 131.
43. St. Augustine, *Confessions,* I, VII, 19.
44. Le Play, *Ouvriers européens* (1877–79), 1:186.
45. Le Play, *Réforme sociale* (1872), 2:85.
46. Nathan Rotenstreich, "The Idea of Historical Progress and Its Assumptions," *History and Theory* 10 (1971), quoted in Kellner, "Frédéric Le Play," p. 183.

47. Le Play, *Constitution essentielle*, pp. 103–35; 136–203.
48. Le Play, *Ouvriers européens* (1877–79), 1:70.
49. Of all the evils created through the abuse of power, Le Play especially deplored the use of armed force to conquer other nations. He considered military men even more dangerous to society than men of letters *(lettrés):* "Large nations, rich and cultured, establish themselves, and the men who govern them abuse their power by invading the territory of their neighbors. Under this pressure, armies multiply. Finally, the success of the men of war excites the arrogance of the population, stimulates error and vice, and brings on the nation's ruin!" Ibid., 1:72.
50. Le Play, *Réforme sociale* (1878), 1:124–41; and *Constitution essentielle*, pp. 104–203.
51. This law, of June 1791, which prohibited any association between masters and workers, was later reinforced by the Napoleonic Civil Code. It was used to break many strikes between 1815 and 1848.
52. Le Play, *Réforme sociale* (1878), 1:73–108 and 4:98–153.
53. Le Play, *Constitution essentielle*, p. 89.
54. Ibid., pp. 11–12. See also the part "Social Reform" in this volume (VII).
55. Le Play, *Ouvriers européens* (1877–79), 1:579–82; and *Constitution essentielle*, pp. 53–80.
56. Le Play, *Constitution essentielle*, p. 48.
57. See "The Three Ages of Work" in this volume (V, 18).
58. Le Play, *Ouvriers européens* (1855), p. 294.
59. Ibid.
60. Ibid., p. 129.
61. Le Play, *Ouvriers européens* (1877–79), 1:132–33.
62. See pp. 123–24 of this volume.
63. Lazarsfeld, "Notes on the History of Quantification," pp. 315–18.

Le Play's Followers

1. Henri de Tourville, Edmond Demolins, Paul de Rousiers, Robert Pinot, and other disciples taught method courses, including a field research course called "L'Ecole des voyages." See Catherine Bodard, "A Contribution to the History of Empirical Social Research in France: The Study of the School 'La Science sociale,'" pp. 7–20.
2. The full title is: *Les Ouvriers des deux mondes: Etude sur le travail, la vie familiale, et la condition morale des ouvriers de divers pays et des liens qui les lient aux autres classes* [Workers of two worlds: studies on the work, family life, and moral condition of the workers of different countries and of the bonds which link them to other classes]. In their weekly meetings, the group attracted a variety of people, especially Saint-Simonians. Those who came to debate social issues included: Arago, Lamartine, Montalembert, Carnot, de Tocqueville, Sainte-Beuve, Abbé Dupanloup, J. B. Dumas, Thiers, Reynaud, Chevalier, and de Lesseps. See Auburtin, *Frédéric Le Play d'après lui-même* [Frédéric Le Play according to himself], pp. 26–27.

3. The six conditions were: "(1) permanent reciprocal commitments between the employer and the worker; (2) complete agreement about salaries; (3) complementarity between home industries, rural enterprise, and crafts; (4) the habit of thrift; (5) an indissoluble link between a family and its home; (6) respect and protection provided to the wife."

4. For a detailed analysis of the split between the two groups, see Catherine Bodard, "A Contribution to the History of Empirical Social Research in France," pp. 7–20.

5. De Tourville, "La Science sociale est-elle une science?" [Is social science a science?], *La Science sociale* 1 (1886):9–109, 289–304; 2 (1886):493–516.

6. Bodard, "A Contribution to the History of Empirical Social Research in France," pp. 21–41.

7. Clark, "De Tourville," *International Encyclopedia of the Social Sciences,* 16:113–14. See also Marie-André Dieux, *Ordre et Liberté* [Order and freedom].

8. De Rousiers, "Demolins," *La Science sociale* (August–September 1907).

9. Members of *La Science sociale* held the following academic positions: de Rousiers became a professor at the Ecole libre des sciences politiques and also gave courses at the Institut des hautes études commerciales, a business school; Pinot, who also taught a course at the Institut des hautes études commerciales, became a member of the Académie des sciences morales et politiques; Leon Gérin, a Canadian, became a professor at the University of Montreal and at Laval University; Descamps taught for several years at the University of Coimbra in Portugal; Melin taught a course in social science at the University of Nancy; Bureau taught for 20 years at the Faculté libre de droit de Paris, a Catholic law school; Babelon was a history professor.

10. Clark, *Prophets and Patrons,* pp. 163–95.

11. Edmond Demolins, "La Classification sociale" [Social classification], *La Science sociale,* nos. 10 and 11 (1905), pp. 3–160.

12. These ideas are set forth most clearly in de Tourville's *Histoire de la formation particulariste: L'origine des grands peuples actuels* [History of particularist formation: the origins of modern nations], 1904.

13. Demolins, "Comment on analyse et comment on classe les types sociaux" [How to analyse and classify social types], *La Science sociale,* no. 1 (1904), pp. 65–92.

14. Sorokin, *Contemporary Sociological Theories,* pp. 72–73.

15. Demolins, *Comment la route crée le type social* [How the route creates social types], p. 114.

16. Demolins, "La Classification sociale," *La Science sociale,* no. 10 (January 1905), chaps. 6–9.

17. Le Play's followers replaced the concept of the stem family with a new type of family—the "particularist" family.

18. Gérin, "La Science sociale en histoire" [Social science in history], *Revue trimestrielle canadienne*, December 1925, pp. 6–14.

19. Paul Roux, "Guide pratique de science sociale" [Practical guide to social science], *La Science sociale*, no. 102 (March 1913), pp. 3–73.

20. Roux, *Précis de science sociale* [Summary of social science], (1914).

21. Paul de Rousiers, *La Vie américaine* [American life], (1891), and *La question ouvrière en Angleterre* [The labor question in England], (1895). Pierre du Maroussen, another disciple of Le Play, undertook monographs of department stores and crafts and workers' associations. See du Maroussen, "Soixante années d'enquêtes et de doctrine" [Sixty years of investigations and of doctrine], *La Réforme sociale* 73 (1917):37–73, and *Les Enquêtes, pratique et théorie* [Investigations, theory and practice].

22. Fernand Butel, "La Vallée d'Ossau" [The Ossau Valley], serialized in *La Science sociale*, 13 (1892), 14 (1892). See also Robert Pinot, "Monographie du Jura Bernois" [The Bernese Jura region], serialized in *La Science sociale*, 3 (1887), 4 (1887), 6 (1888), 7 (1889), and 8 (1889). For more details on both of these works, see the Bibliography.

23. Paul Bureau, *Introduction à la méthode sociologique* [Introduction to sociological method].

24. For further analysis of Le Play's influence in England, see Brooke, *Le Play*, pp. 120–36.

25. Victor Branford and Patrick Geddes, *The Making of the Future: The Coming Polity* (1919); Victor S. Branford, *An Introduction to Regional Surveys* (1924); and Lewis Mumford, "Patrick Geddes, Victor Branford, and Applied Sociology in England: The Social Survey, Regionalism, and Urban Planning," in H. E. Barnes, ed., *An Introduction to the History of Sociology*, pp. 677–95.

26. Charles Booth, *Journal of the Royal Statistical Society* (London, 1893), pp. 255–68. Despite Booth's acknowledgment of Le Play's work, neither his biographies (such as those by T. S. Simey and M. B. Simey), nor his autobiography (written with Beatrice Webb) show any evidence that Booth had read Le Play before undertaking his study of the people of London.

27. Paul de Rousiers, "Le Play and Social Science," *Annals of the American Academy of Political and Social Science* 4 (1893–94):620–46.

28. Sorokin, *Contemporary Sociological Theories*, and Carle C. Zimmerman and Merle E. Frampton, *Family and Society: A Study of the Sociology of Reconstruction*.

29. *Recueil d'études sociales à la mémoire de Le Play*, pp. 29–48.

30. Vidal de la Blache, *Principes de géographie humaine* [Principles of human geography], trans. M. T. Bingham (1926); Jean Brunhes, *La Géographie humaine: essaie de classification positive* [Human geography: essay on classification] (1912); and Henri Mendras, *Etudes de*

sociologie rurale [Studies in rural sociology] (1953).
   31. Branford and Geddes, *The Making of the Future;* and Branford, *An Introduction to Regional Surveys.*
   32. Halbwachs, *La Classe ouvrière et les niveaux de vie.*
   33. Conrad Arensberg, *Culture and Community* (1965), pp. 97–116.
   34. Philippe Ariès, *Histoire des populations française,* and *Centuries of Childhood.*

Conclusion
   1. The major effort of categorization made by Le Play and his followers started a sociological tradition which culminates in the Parsonian system of patterned variables.
   2. Dion has already stressed the continuity between Le Play and Durkheim. See "La généralisation théorique dans l'oeuvre de Le Play et dans *La Division du travail social* de Durkheim" [Theoretical generalization in Le Play's work and in Durkheim's *Division of Labor*]. Paper presented at the Seventh World Congress of Sociology, Varna, Bulgaria, 14–19 September 1970.
   3. Merton, *On Theoretical Sociology,* p. 3. See also Robert L. Geiger, "The Institutionalization of Sociological Paradigms: Three Examples from Early French Sociology."
   4. Raymond Boudon, "A propos d'un livre imaginaire" [On an imaginary book], in P. Lazarsfeld, ed., *La Philosophie des sciences sociales* [Philosophy of the social sciences] (Paris, 1970), pp. 7–72.
   5. Durkheim, *De la division du travail social,* pp. 237–90.
   6. Giddens's preface to *Emile Durkheim: Selected Writings,* ed. Anthony Giddens, pp. 1–48.
   7. Ibid., p. 42.
   8. Le Play, *Constitution essentielle,* p. 175.
   9. Durkheim, *De la division du travail social,* pp. 391–406.
   10. Like Saint-Simon, Le Play thought that the family was an institution to which the laws of the market did not apply and that the family should therefore be reinforced. See Le Play, *Organisation de la famille,* p. 258.
   11. Georges Sorel, *The Illusions of Progress,* p. xxxv.
   12. Le Play, *Constitution essentielle,* pp. 30–36.
   13. Morris Janowitz, "Sociological Theory and Social Control," *American Journal of Sociology* 81, no. 1:88.
   14. A concrete example of this type of analysis can be found in *Ouvriers européens* (1877–79), "Paysans de Bousrah," 2:368–76.
   15. Levasseur, *Histoire des classes ouvrières,* pp. 479–523. See also Peter Stearns, *Lives of Labor: Work in Maturing Industrial Society,* pp. 173–75.
   16. Morazé, *The Triumph of the Middle Classes,* pp. 152–91.
   17. Le Play, *Ouvriers européens* (1855), sec. 48, pp. 291–92. See also

"The Science of Society as a Theory of Social Reform" in this volume (VII, 22). See also Le Play, *Constitution essentielle*, p. 228.

18. Thomas Kuhn emphasizes the importance of consensus in science, the role of shared "paradigms" which commit those in a scientific discipline to the same rules and standards of scientific behavior. See his *The Structure of Scientific Revolutions*, p. 45.

19. Le Play's ideas on this subject overlap with those of Georges Sorel, who criticized social scientists for the separation they introduced between thought and action. See Sorel, *The Illusions of Progress*, p. 140.

20. Le Play, *Réforme sociale* (1872), pp. xviii–xix.

21. Ibid., 3:391.

22. Some of these themes have been the focus of interest among recent radical sociologists whose vision of sociology is at once theoretical, empirical, and political. See, for example, T. B. Bottomore, *Sociology as Social Criticism*, pp. 11–16.

BIBLIOGRAPHY

Works by Frédéric Le Play

La Constitution essentielle de l'humanité: Exposé des principes et des coûtumes que créent la prosperité ou la souffrance des nations. Tours: Mame, 1881. Second edition, 1893.

Descriptions des procédés métallurgiques employés dans le pays de Galles pour la fabrication du cuivre et recherches sur l'état actuel et sur l'avenir probable de la production et du commerce de ce métal. Paris: Carilian-Goeury, 1848.

Instruction sur la méthode d'observation dite des monographies de famille. Paris, 1862. New edition, revised by A. J. Focillon, Paris, 1887.

"Instruction in the Observation of Social Facts According to the Le Play Method." Translated and edited by C. A. Ellwood, *American Journal of Sociology* 2 (1897):662–79.

La Méthode de la science sociale. Tours: Mame, 1879.

Observations sur l'histoire naturelle et la richesse minérale de l'Espagne. Paris: Carilian-Goeury, 1834.

Observations sur le mouvement commercial des principales substances minérales entre la France et les puissances étrangères pendant les douze dernières années et particulièrement pendant les années 1829, 1830, et 1831. Paris: Carilian-Goeury, 1832.

L'Organisation de la famille, selon le vrai modèle signalé par l'histoire de toutes les races et de tous les temps. Tours: Mame, 1871. Third edition, 1884.

L'Organisation du travail, selon la coûtume des ateliers et la loi du Décalogue, avec un précis d'observations comparées sur la distinction du bien et du mal dans le régime du travail, les causes du mal actuel et les moyens de réforme, les objections et les réponses, les difficultés et les solutions. Tours: Mame, 1870.

Les Ouvriers européens: Etudes sur les travaux, la vie domestique et la condition morale des populations ouvrières de l'Europe, et leur relations avec les autres classes, précédé d'un exposé de la méthode d'observation. Paris: Imprimerie Impériale, 1855. Second edition, 6 volumes. Tours: Mame, 1877–79.

Les Ouvriers des deux mondes. This series of monographs was started by Le Play. He edited and contributed to the first four volumes: 1, 1857; 2, 1858; 3, 1861; 4, 1862. The later volumes appeared as follows (after Le Play's death): 5, 1885; second series—1, 1887; 2, 1890; 3, 1892; 4, 1895; 5, 1899; third series—1, 1904; 2, 1908; 3, 1912 (also issued in separate parts).

La Paix sociale après le désastre. Tours: Mame, 1871. Second edition, Tours, 1876.

Preface to *Programme de gouvernement et d'organisation sociale d'après l'observation comparée de divers peuples.* Paris: Maurice Tardieu, 1881.

Recherches statistiques sur la production et l'élaboration de la soie en France. Paris: Bourgogne et Martinet, 1839.

La Réforme sociale en France, déduite de l'observation comparée des peuples européens. Two volumes. Tours: Mame, 1864. Fourth edition, 1872. Sixth edition, 1878.

La Réforme en Europe et le salut en France. Tours: Mane, 1876. This book contains the program of the Unions de la paix sociale.

Vues générales sur la statistique. Paris: 1840. Reprint from *L'Encyclopédie nouvelle.*

With Alexis Delaire. *La Constitution d'Angleterre considerée dans ses rapports avec la loi de Dieu et les coûtumes de la paix sociale, précédée d'aperçus sommaires sur la nature du sol et l'histoire de la race.* Two volumes. Tours: Mame, 1875.

Periodicals and annuals

Bulletin de la Société internationale des études pratiques d'économie sociale, Paris, 1864–83. Edited by Alexis Chevalier, this bulletin contained the minutes of the meetings of the Society. Summaries of these minutes are also to be found in the earlier volumes of *Les Ouvriers des deux mondes.*

La Réforme sociale. Paris bimonthly, founded by Le Play in 1881. In 1931 it became *La Revue d'économie sociale et rurale.* In 1936 it merged with *La Science sociale* (founded by one group of Le Play's followers in 1886) to become *Les Etudes sociales,* published irregularly. Another periodical of the Le Play school was *Le Mouvement social,* founded in 1892, which merged with *La Science sociale* in 1896.

Les Unions de la paix sociale. Annually. Paris, 1875–80. Each volume begins with an article by Le Play on current affairs.

Leçons (Lecture notes at the Ecole des Mines). Three volumes. Paris: 1840–56, *Bibliothèque de l'Ecole des Mines.* The Le Play family also has a copy of the notes taken by one of Le Play's students.

Le Play's unpublished correspondence is to be found in La Bibliothèque de l'Institut de France and in Les Archives nationales (with his official dossier).

Secondary Sources

Abrams, Philip. *The Origins of British Sociology.* Chicago: University of Chicago Press, 1968.
Allard, Paul. "Frédéric Le Play et la Normandie," *Revue catholique de Normandie* 16 (1906).
Anderson, Michael. "Family, Household, and Industrial Revolution." In *The American Family in Social-Historical Perspective,* edited by Michael Gordon. New York: St. Martin's Press, 1973.
———. *Family Structure in 19th Century Lancashire.* London: Cambridge University Press, 1970.
Arensberg, Conrad. *Culture and Community.* New York: Harcourt, Brace and World, 1965.
Ariès, Philippe. *Centuries of Childhood.* Translated by Robert Baldick. London: Jonathan Cape, 1962.
———. *Histoire des populations françaises et de leurs attitudes durant la vie depuis le 18ᵉ siècle.* Paris: Editions du Seuil, 1971.
Aron, Raymond. *Main Currents in Sociological Thought.* Vol. 1. Garden City: Doubleday, 1968.
Auburtin, Fernand. *Frédéric Le Play d'après lui-même. Vie, méthode, doctrine.* Paris: Giard et Brière, 1906.
Audiganne, Armand. *Les Populations ouvrières et les industries en France.* 2 vols. Paris: Capelle, 1854.
———. *Les Ouvriers d'à présent et la nouvelle économie du travail.* Paris: Lacroix, 1865.
St. Augustine. *Confessions.* Translated by Edward B. Pusey. New York: Collier Books, 1961.
Baudin, Louis, ed. *Le Play: Textes choisis.* Paris: Dalloz, 1947.
Baussan, George. *De Frédéric Le Play à Paul Bourget.* Paris: Flammarion, 1935.
Becker, Howard, and Elmer Barnes. *Social Thought from Lore to Science.* New York: Dover, 1961.
Berkner, Lutz K. "Recent Research on the History of the Family in 19th Century Europe." *Journal of Marriage and the Family* 35 (1973):395–405.
Bodard, Catherine. "A Contribution to the History of Empirical Social

Research in France: The Study of the School 'La Science Sociale.'" Mimeo. Master's essay, Bureau of Applied Social Research, Columbia University, New York, 1966.

Bonald, Vicomte Louis Gabriel Ambroise de. *Oeuvres complètes*. 3 vols. Paris: Migne, 1864.

Booth, Charles. *Life and Labour of the People in London*. 17 vols. London: Macmillan, 1902–3.

———. *Journal of the Royal Statistical Society*. London, 1893:255–68.

Bossy, John. "The Counter-Reformation and the People of Catholic Europe." *Past and Present* 47 (1970):51–70.

Bottomore, T. B. *Sociology as Social Criticism*. New York: Pantheon Books, 1975.

Boudon, Raymond. "A propos d'un livre imaginaire." In *Philosophie des sciencies sociales,* edited by Paul Lazarsfeld. Paris: Gallimard, 1970.

Bourgin, Georges, and Hubert Bourgin, eds. *Les Patrons, les ouvriers et l'état: Le Régime de l'industrie en France de 1814 à 1848*. 3 vols. Paris: Picard, 1912–14.

Bouthoul, Gaston. *Traité de sociologie*. 2 vols. 3d ed. Paris: Payot, 1959.

Branford, Victor S. *An Introduction to Regional Surveys*. Westminster: Le Play House Press, 1924.

———, and Patrick Geddes. *The Making of the Future: The Coming Polity*. 2d ed., enlarged. London: Williams, 1919.

Brants, Victor. "Les Etudes pratiques d'économie sociale." *Revue catholique de Louvain* (January 1882).

Brooke, Michael Z. "La Théorie de Le Play sur les relations industrielles." *Etudes sociales,* nos. 64–65 (1965):1–11.

———. *Le Play, Engineer and Social Scientist: The Life and Work of Frédéric Le Play*. Harlow (UK): Longmans, 1970.

Brunhes, Jean. *La Géographie humaine: Essaie de classification positive*. Paris: F. Alcan, 1912.

Buchner, Ludwig. *Darwinismus und Sozialismus*. Leipzig: E. Gunther, 1894.

Bureau, Paul. *Introduction à la méthode sociologique*. Paris: Bloud et Gay, 1923.

Buret, Emile. *De la misère des classes ouvrières en Angleterre et en France*. Paris: Paulin, 1840.

Burke, Edmund. *Selected Writings and Speeches*. Edited by P. Stanlis. Garden City: Dubleday, 1961.

Burke, John G. "Mineral Classification in the Early 19th Century." In *Toward a History of Geology,* edited by Cecil Schneer. Cambridge: M.I.T. Press, 1969.

Butel, Fernand. "La Vallée d'Ossau." Serialized in *La Science sociale,* 13 (1892):308–20, 457–72; 14 (1892):205–18; 15 (1893):119–32, 182–93, 276–84, 447–62.

Champault, Philippe. "La Science sociale d'après Le Play et de Tourville." *La Science sociale*, no. 109 (1913):5–127.
———. "Les Types familiaux: Fonction et classification valeur éducatrice, natalité." *La Science sociale*, no. 76 (1910):1–104.
Charléty, Sebastian. *Histoire de Saint-Simonisme*. Paris: Gonthier, 1931.
Chevalier, Louis. *Laboring Classes and Dangerous Classes in Paris during the First Half of the Nineteenth Century*. Translated by Frank Jellinek. New York: H. Fertig, 1973.
Cheysson, Emile. "Frédéric Le Play, sa méthode, sa doctrine, son école." In *Compte rendus de l'Académie des sciences morales et politiques*. Paris, 1905. Reprinted in *Oeuvres choisies*. Paris, 1911, vol. 2, chap. 8. See also chap. 1, "Mon Testament social."
———. Epilogue to Le Play, *L'Organisation de la Famille*. Tours: Mame, 1844.
Chulliat, Christian. "Le Play et Durkheim: Essai de synthèse." In *Recueil d'études sociales publié à la mémoire de Frédéric Le Play*, pp. 15–22. Paris: A. et J. Picard, 1956.
Clapham, Sir John H. *The Economic Development of France and Germany, 1815–1914*. 4th ed. Cambridge: Cambridge University Press, 1951.
Clark, Terry N. "Discontinuities in Social Research: The Case of the *Cours élémentaire de statistique administrative*." *History of Behavioral Sciences* 3 (1967):3–16.
———. "De Tourville." In *International Encyclopedia of the Social Sciences*, 16:113–14.
———. "Emile Durkheim and the Institutionalization of Sociology in the French University System." *Archives européennes de sociologie* 9 (1968):37–71.
———. *Prophets and Patrons: The French University and the Emergence of the Social Sciences*. Cambridge: Harvard University Press, 1973.
Cohen, D. K. "The Vicomte de Bonald's Critique of Industrialism." *Journal of Modern History* 41 (1969):475–84.
Cochin, Augustin. *Les Ouvriers européens: Résumé de la méthode et des observations de Le Play*. Paris: Douniol, 1856.
Comte, Auguste. *Système de Politique Positive*. Paris: Le Roux, 1882.
Coser, Lewis. *Masters of Sociological Thought*. New York: Harcourt Brace Jovanovich, 1971.
Crozier, Michel. *The Bureaucratic Phenomenon*. Chicago: University of Chicago Press, 1964.
Cullen, Michael J. *The Statistical Movement in Early Victorian Britain*. New York: Harvester Press, 1975.
Cuvillier, Armand. "Les Antagonismes de classes dans la littérature française de Saint-Simon à 1840." *International Review of Social History* 1 (1956):353–63.

———. *Les Doctrines sociales de 1840*. Paris: Marcel Rivière, 1956.
Delaire, Alexis. *F. Le Play et la science sociale*. Paris: Bureau de la Réforme Sociale, 1892.
———. "Le Play et la science sociale." *La Nouvelle revue* 98 (1896):680–99.
Demolins, Edmond. "L'Etat de la science sociale." *La Science sociale* 15 (1893):5–20.
———. "M. Le Play et son oeuvre de réforme sociale." *Le Correspondant* (Paris), n.s., no. 81 (1879):851–70.
———. "La Science sociale depuis F. Le Play: Classification sociale." *La Science sociale*, nos. 10 and 11 (1905):3–160.
———. *Comment la route crée le type social*. Paris: Firmin Didot, 1901.
———. "Comment on analyse et comment on classe les types sociaux." *La Science sociale*, no. 1 (1904):65–92.
———, with Robert Pinot and Paul de Rousiers. "La Méthode sociale." *La Science sociale*, no. 1 (1904):1–92.
Deniel, Raymond. *Une Image de la famille et de la société sous la Restauration*. Paris: Les Editions Ouvrières, 1965.
Descamps, Paul. *La Sociologie expérimentale*. Paris: Marcel Rivière, 1933.
Dieux, Marie-André. *Ordre et Liberté*. Paris: Bloud et Gay, 1926.
———. *L'Abbé de Tourville*. Paris: Flammarion, 1931.
Dion, Michel. "Les Enquêtes de Buret et de Villermé." Mimeo. Paris: Centre national de la recherche scientifique, 1962.
———. "La généralisation théorique dans l'oeuvre de Le Play et dans *La Division du travail social* de Durkheim." Paper presented at the Seventh World Congress of Sociology, Varna, Bulgaria, 14–19 September 1970.
———. "Science sociale et religion chez Le Play." *Archives de sociologie des religions* 24 (1967):83–101.
Dolléans, Eduard. *Histoire du mouvement ouvrier*. Vol. I: *1830–1871*. Paris: Colin, 1967.
Ducpétiaux, M. *Budgets économiques des classes ouvrières en Belgique: Subsistances, salaires, population*. Brussels: M. Hayez, imp. de la Commission centrale de statistique, 1855.
Dunham, Arthur Louis. *La Révolution industrielle en France, 1815–1848*. Paris: Marcel Rivière, 1953.
Dupin, Baron Charles. "Séance publique de l'Académie des sciences." 28 January 1856.
Durkheim, Emile. *De la division du travail social*. Paris: Presses universitaires de France, 1960.
———. *Rules of Sociological Method*. Translated by Sarah A. Soloway and John H. Mueller. George E. Catlin, editor. Glencoe: The Free Press, 1966.
———. *Le Socialisme*. Paris: Alcan, 1928.

———. "La Sociologie en France pendant le 19ᶜ siècle." *Revue politique et parlementaire* 19 (May 1900):651ff.
Duroselle, Jean-Baptiste. *Les Débuts du catholicisme social en France, 1822–1870*. Paris: Presses universitaires de France, 1951.
Duveau, Georges. *La Vie ouvrière en France sous le Second Empire*. Paris: Presses universitaires de France, 1946.
Einaudi, Luigi. "The Doctrine of Original Sin and the Theory of the Elite in the Writings of Frederic Le Play." In *Essays in European Economic Thought*, translated and edited by Louise Sommer. Princeton: Princeton University Press, 1960.
Elesh, David. "The Manchester Statistical Society: A Case Study of Discontinuity in the History of Empirical Research." In *The Establishment of Empirical Sociology*, edited by Anthony Oberschall. New York: Harper and Row, 1972.
Eliot, Thomas D., et al. *Norway's Families*. Philadelphia: University of Pennsylvania Press, 1960.
Ellwood, C. A., translator and editor. "Instruction in the Observation of Social Facts According to the Le Play Method of Family Monographs" *American Journal of Sociology* 2 (1897):662–79.
Engel, Ernst, ed. *International Statistical Congress (1853–1860)*. Berlin: Imprimerie Royale.
Engels, Friedrich. *The Condition of the Working Class in England in 1844*. London: Panther, 1969.
Evans, David O. *Social Romanticism in France, 1830–1848*. Oxford: Clarendon, 1951.
Farmer, Paul. "The Social Theory of Frédric Le Play." In *Teaching of History: Essays in Honor of Lawrence Bradford Packer*, edited by H. S. Hughes et al. Ithaca: Cornell University Press, 1954.
Festy, Octave. *Le Mouvement ouvrier au début de la Monarchie de Juillet (1830–1848)*. Paris: E. Cornély, 1908.
Finch, James K. *The Story of Engineering*. New York: Doubleday, 1960.
Fletcher, Ronald. "Frederic Le Play." In *The Founding Fathers of Social Science*, edited by Timothy Raison. London: Penguin Books, 1969.
Focillon, Adolphe-Jean. "Le Play, le fondateur de l'Ecole de la paix sociale." *Le Réforme sociale* (1882):474–82.
———. "La Méthode scientifique d'observation et la question sociale en Occident." *Revue des questions scientifiques* 6 (July 1879):234–80.
Frégier, Henri A. *Des classes dangereuses de la population dans les grandes villes et des moyens de les rendre meilleures*. 2 vols. Paris: Baillière, 1840.
Gay, Peter. *The Enlightenment: An Interpretation*. 2 vols. New York: Knopf, 1969.
Geiger, Robert L. "The Institutionalization of Sociological Paradigms: Three Examples from Early French Sociology." Paper presented at the International Society for the History of the Behavioral and Social

Sciences, Durham, New Hampshire, June 2, 1974.
Gérando, Comte J. M. de. *De la bienfaisance publique*. 4 vols. Paris: Renouard, 1849.
Gérin, Léon. "Trois types de l'habitat Canadien-Français," *La Science sociale* 28 (1899):96–115.
———. *Le Type economique et social des Canadiens*. Montreal: Edition de l'E.F.P., 1938.
———. "La Science sociale en histoire." *Revue trimestrielle canadienne* (December 1925):6–14.
Giddens, Anthony. *Positivism and Sociology*. London: Heinemann, 1974.
———, ed. *Emile Durkheim: Selected Writings*. Cambridge: Cambridge University Press, 1972.
Gide, Charles, and Charles Rist. *A History of Economic Doctrines from the Time of the Physiocrats to the Present Day*, trans. R. Richards. New York: Heath, 1948.
Gille, Bertrand. *Les Sources statistiques de l'histoire de France des enquêtes du 17e siècle à 1870*. Geneva: Droz, 1964.
Glazer, Nathan. "The Rise of Social Research in Europe." In *The Human Meaning of the Social Sciences*, edited by Daniel Lerner. Cleveland: World Publishing Co., 1959.
Goldfrank, Walter. "Reappraising Le Play." In *The Establishment of Empirical Sociology: Studies in Continuity, Discontinuity and Institutionalization*, edited by Anthony Oberschall, pp. 130–51.
———. "Working Paper on Le Play and His Followers." Seminar paper, Columbia University, New York, 1965.
Gossez, Rémi. "La Diversité des antagonismes sociaux vers le milieu du 19e siécle." *Revue économique* no. 3 (1956):439–57.
Gouldner, Alvin W. *The Coming Crisis in Western Sociology*. New York: Basic Books, 1970.
Guérry, Ange-Michel. *Essai sur la statistique morale de la France*. Paris: Crochard, 1833.
Gurvitch, Georges. "Brève esquisse de l'histoire de la sociologie." In *Traité de sociologie*, edited by G. Gurvitch. Paris: Presses universitaires de France, 1958.
Habakkuk, H. J. "Family Structure and Economic Change in Nineteenth-Century Europe." *Journal of Economic History* 1 (1955):1–12.
Halbwachs, Maurice. *La Classe ouvrière et les niveaux de vie*. Paris: Alcan, 1912.
Hayek, Friedrich A. von. *The Counter-Revolution of Science: Studies in the Abuse of Reason*. Glencoe: The Free Press, 1964.
Herbertson, Dorothy. *The Life of Frédéric Le Play*. Edited by V. V. Branford and A. Farquharson. Ledbury: 1950. Chaps. 1–4 were printed in the *Sociological Review* 12 (1920) and 13 (1921), and the whole was printed in ibid. 38 (1946).

Higgs, Henri. "Frédéric Le Play." *Quarterly Journal of Economics* 4 (1890):408–33.
Hohenberg, Paul. "Change in Rural France in the Period of Industrialization." *Journal of Economic History* 32 (1972):219–40.
Homans, George. *English Villagers of the Thirteenth Century*. Cambridge: Cambridge University Press, 1941.
Hudson, Nora. *Ultra-Royalism and the French Restoration*. Cambridge: Cambridge University Press, 1936.
Ibarrola, Jesus. *Structure sociale et fortune dans la campagne proche de Grenoble en 1847*. Paris: Mouton, 1966.
Iribarne, Manuel Fraga. "La influencia de Le Play en la sociologia española del siglo xix." In *Recueil d'études sociales publié à la mémoire de Frédéric Le Play*, pp. 29–34. Paris: A. et J. Picard, 1956.
Isambert, François A. "Epoques critiques et époques organiques: Une contribution de Buchez à l'élaboration de la théorie sociale des Saint-Simoniens." *Cahiers internationaux de sociologie* 27 (1969):131–52.
———. "Les recherches statistiques d'Ange-Michel Guérry (1802–1866)." *Cahiers internationaux de sociologie* 47 (1969):35–44.
Janowitz, Morris. "Sociological Theory and Social Control." *American Journal of Sociology* 81, no. 1:82–108.
Joly, Henri. "Auguste Comte et Frédéric Le Play." *La Réforme sociale* 39 (1900):901–26.
Julhiet, Eduard. "Le Mineur du Hartz 50 années après Le Play." *La Réforme sociale* 33 (1897):73–84.
Kellner, Hans D. "Frédéric Le Play and the Development of Modern Sociology." Ph.D. dissertation, University of Rochester, 1972.
Kindleberger, Charles P. *Economic Growth in France and Britain, 1851–1950*. Cambridge: Harvard University Press, 1964.
Kosemihal, N. S. "L'Ecole de Le Play et son influence en Turquie." In *Recueil d'études sociales publié à la mémoire de Frédéric Le Play*, pp. 35–47. Paris: A. et J. Picard, 1956.
Kuhn, Thomas. *The Structure of Scientific Revolutions*. 2d ed. rev. Chicago: University of Chicago Press, 1970.
Landes, David. *The Unbounded Prometheus: Technological Change and Industrial Development in Western Europe from 1750 to the Present*. London: Cambridge University Press, 1969.
Lazarsfeld, Paul. Foreword to *The Establishment of Empirical Sociology: Studies in Continuity, Discontinuity and Institutionalization*, edited by Anthony Oberschall. New York: Harper and Row, 1972.
———. "Notes on the History of Quantification in Sociology." *Isis* 52 (pt. 2) (1961):277–333.
———. *La Philosophie des sciences sociales*. Paris: Gallimard, 1970.
Leclerc, Gérard. *Observation de l'homme*. Paris: Alcan, 1978.
Lécuyer, Bernard, and Anthony Oberschall. "The Early History of Social Research." In *International Encyclopedia of the Social Sciences*, 15:36–53. New York: Macmillan, 1968.

Le Play, Albert. "Souvenirs sur Frédéric Le Play." *Recueil d'études sociales publié à mémoire de Frédéric Le Play*, pp. 3–14. Paris: A. et J. Picard, 1956.
Lerner, Daniel, ed. *The Human Meaning of the Social Sciences*. New York: World Publishing Co., 1962.
Leroy, Maxime. *Histoire des idées sociales en France*. 3 vols. Paris: Gallimard, 1954.
Levasseur, Emile. *L'Histoire des classes ouvrières en France depuis 1789 jusqu'à nos jours*. 2 vols. Paris: Hachette, 1867.
Lhomme, Jean. *La Grande bourgeoisie au pouvoir (1830–1880)*. Paris: Presses universitaires de France, 1960.
Locke, Robert R. *French Legitimists and the Politics of Moral Order in the Early Third Republic*. Princeton: Princeton University Press, 1974.
Lodin, Arthur. "Les travaux métallurgiques de F. Le Play." *La Réforme sociale* 52 (1906):122–26.
Lottin, Joseph. *Quetelet, statisticien et sociologue*. New York: Burt Franklin, 1969.
Madge, John. *The Origin of Scientific Sociology*. New York: The Free Press, 1962.
Mannheim, Karl. *Ideology and Utopia*. London: Routledge & Kegan Paul, 1960.
Manuel, Frank E. *The Prophets of Paris*. Cambridge: Harvard University Press, 1962.
Maroussem, Pierre du. "Soixante années d'enquêtes et de doctrine." *La Réforme sociale* 73 (1917):37–73.
―――. *Les Enquêtes, pratique et théorie*. Paris: Alcan, 1900.
Marshall, Alfred. *Principles of Economics*. 8th ed. London: Macmillan, 1920.
Mayo, Elton. *The Human Problems of an Industrial Civilization*. New York: Macmillan, 1933.
Medick, Hans. "The Proto-Industrial Family Economy: The Structural Function of Household and Family during the Transition from Peasant Society to Industrial Capitalism." *Social History* 3 (1976):291–316.
Méline, Pierre. *F. Le Play: L'Oeuvre de science*. Paris: Bloud et Gay, 1912.
Mendras, Henri. *Eléments de sociologie*. Paris: Colin, 1967.
―――. *Sociologie de la campagne française*. Paris: Presses universitaires de France, 1959.
―――. *Etudes de sociologie rurale*. Paris: A. Colin, 1953.
Merton, Robert K. *On Theoretical Sociology*. New York: The Free Press, 1967.
―――. "Recent French Sociology." *Social Forces* 12 (1934):537–45.
―――. *Social Theory and Social Structure*. Glencoe: The Free Press, 1961.
Michel, Andrée. "Les Cadres sociaux de la doctrine morale de Frédéric Le Play." *Cahiers internationaux de sociologie* 34 (1963):47–68.

Mills, C. Wright. *The Sociological Imagination.* New York: Grove Press, 1961.
Mogey, John. "La 'Science sociale' en Angleterre." In *Recueil d'études sociales publié à la mémoire de Frédéric Le Play,* pp. 57–64. Paris: A. et J. Picard, 1956.
Montesquiou, Comte Léon de. *L'Oeuvre de Frédéric Le Play.* Paris: Nouvelle librairie nationale, 1912.
Moody, Joseph N. "The Dechristianization of the French Working Class." *Review of Politics* 20 (1958):46–69.
Moon, Parker T. *The Labor Problem and the Social Catholic Movement in France.* New York: Macmillan, 1921.
Morazé, Charles. *The Triumph of the Middle Classes: A Study of European Values in the 19th Century.* London: Weidenfeld and Nicolson, 1966.
Morogues, Baron Bigot de. *Recherches sur les causes de la richesse et de la misère des peuples civilisés.* Paris: Delarue, 1834.
Mumford, Lewis. "Patrick Geddes, Victor Branford, and Applied Sociology in England: The Social Survey, Regionalism, and Urban Planning." In *An Introduction to the History of Sociology,* edited by Harry E. Barnes. Chicago: University of Chicago Press, 1948.
Nisbet, Robert. *Social Change and History.* London: Oxford University Press, 1969.
———, *The Sociological Tradition.* New York: Basic Books, 1966.
———. *Tradition and Revolt.* New York: Vintage, 1970.
Noilhan, Henri. "Actualité de la méthode d'observation." In *Recueil d'études sociales publié à la mémoire de Frédéric Le Play,* pp. 65–72. Paris: A. et J. Picard, 1956.
Nolte, E. *Three Faces of Fascism: Action Française, Italian Fascism, National Socialism.* New York: Holt, Rinehart and Winston, 1966.
Oberschall, Anthony, ed. *The Establishment of Empirical Sociology: Studies in Continuity, Discontinuity, and Institutionalization.* New York: Harper & Row, 1972.
Paillat, Paul. "Les Salaires et la condition ouvrière en France à l'aube du machinisme." *Revue économique,* no. 6 (1951):766–77.
Palmade, Guy de. *Capitalisme français au 19e siècle.* Paris: Armand Colin, 1962.
Parent-Duchâtelet, Alexandre Jean Baptiste. *De la prostitution dans la ville de Paris.* 2 vols. 3d ed. Paris: Baillière et fils, 1857.
Pareto, Vilfredo. *The Mind and Society.* New York: Harcourt, Brace and Co., 1935.
Parsons, Talcott; Edward Shils; Kaspar Naegele; and Jesse R. Pitts, eds. *Theories of Society.* New York: The Free Press, 1965.
Périer, Philippe. "L'Ecole sociologique de Le Play et la statistique." *Les Etudes sociales,* nos. 69–70 (1966):60–62.
Pinet, G. *Ecrivains et penseurs polytechniciens.* Paris: Ollendorf, 1898.
Pinot, Robert. "Monographie du Jura Bernois." Serialized in *La Science*

sociale 3 (1887):295–312, 384–412, 485–516, 594–614; 4 (1887):372–88, 468–96, 591–631; 6 (1888): 158–76, 249–64, 525–41; 7 (1889):90–105, 367–80; 8 (1889):79–100, 271–88, 427–68.

———. "La Classification des espèces de famille établie par Le Play est-elle exacte?" *La Science sociale,* no. 1 (1904):44–64.

Pitts, Jesse R. "Le Play, Frédéric." *International Encyclopedia of the Social Sciences,* 9:84–91. New York: Macmillan, 1968.

Polanyi, Karl. *The Great Transformation.* Boston: Beacon Press, 1957.

Pollard, Sidney. *History of Labour in Sheffield.* Liverpool: Liverpool University Press, 1959.

Ponteil, François. *Les Classes bourgeoises et l'avènement de la démocratie.* Paris: Albin Michel, 1968.

Proudhon, Pierre Joseph. *De la justice dans la révolution et dans l'église.* 3 vols. Paris: Garnier frères, 1858.

Quetelet, Adolphe. *De l'homme et du developpement de ses qualités: Physique sociale.* 2 vols. Brussels: Hauman et Comp., 1836.

Recueil d'études sociales publié à la mémoire de Frédéric Le Play. Foreword by Roger Grand. Paris: A. et J. Picard, 1956. This collection of studies, published at the time of the centenary of the Société d'économie sociale, contains some of the most interesting printed studies of the life and work of Le Play. The articles are listed here under the names of their authors.

Rémond, René. *La Droit en France, 1815–1848.* Paris: Aubier, 1963.

Reuss, Alfons. *Frédéric Le Play in einer Bedeutung für die Entwicklung der sozialwissenschaftlichen Methode.* Jena: Gustav Fischer, 1913.

Ribbe, Charles de. *Le Play, d'après sa correspondance.* Paris: Firmin Didot, 1884.

Ribot, Paul. *Du role social des idées chrétiennes suivi d'un exposée critique des doctrines sociales de M. Le Play.* Paris: Plon, 1882.

Riche, L'Abbé A. *Frédéric Le Play.* Paris: C. Poussielgue, 1891.

Riley, Matilda White. *Sociological Research.* New York: Harcourt and Brace, 1963.

Rogers, Lois H. "Frédéric Le Play." M.A. Thesis, Department of History, Columbia University, 1950.

Rotenstreich, Nathan. "The Idea of Historical Progress and Its Assumptions." *History and Theory* 10 (1971):197–221.

Rousiers, Paul de. "Le Play and Social Science," *Annals of the American Academy of Political and Social Science* 4 (1893–94):620–46.

———. *La Question ouvrière en Angleterre.* Paris: Firmin Didot, 1895.

———. *La Vie américaine.* Paris: Firmin Didot, 1891.

———. "Demolins." *La Science sociale* (August–September 1907).

Roux, Paul. *Précis de science sociale.* Paris: Giard et Bière, 1914.

———. "Guide pratique de science sociale." *La Science sociale,* no. 102 (March 1913):3–73.

Ruggiero, Guido. "Positivism." In *Encyclopedia of the Social Sciences,* 12:260–66. New York: Macmillan, 1930.

Sainte-Beuve, C. A. "La Réforme sociale en France." *Les Nouveaux Lundis* (Paris) 9 (1867):161–201.
Saint-Simon, Claude-Henri, Comte de. *Mémoire sur la science de l'homme.* In *Oeuvres de Claude-Henri de Saint-Simon*, vol. 5. Paris: Editions Anthropos, 1966.
Schäffle, A. E. F. *Das Gesellschaftliche System der menschlichen Wirtschaft: ein lehr-und Handbuch der Nationalökonomie.* Tubingen, 1867.
Sée, Henri. *Histoire économique de la France des temps modernes, 1789–1914.* Paris: Armand Colin, 1951.
———. "Quelques aperçus sur la condition de la classe ouvrière et sur le mouvement ouvrier en France de 1815 à 1848." *Revue d'histoire économique et sociale* 12 (1924):493–521.
———. *La Vie économique de la France sous la monarchie censitaire, 1815–1848.* Paris: Alcan, 1927.
Simiand, François. *Le Salaire, l'évolution sociale et la monnaie.* 3 vols. Paris: Alcan, 1932.
Small, Albion W., and George E. Vincent. *An Introduction to the Study of Society.* New York: American Book Co., 1894.
Smelser, Neil J. *Social Change and the Industrial Revolution.* Chicago: University of Chicago Press, 1959.
Smith, Harvey. "Work Routine and Social Structure in a French Village: Cruzy (Hérault) in the 19th Century." Paper read at the Brockport Conference, Brockport College, State University of New York, September 29, 1972.
Sorel, Georges. *The Illusions of Progress.* Translated by J. and C. Stanley. Berkeley: University of California Press, 1969.
Sorokin, Pitirim A. *Contemporary Sociological Theories.* New York: Harper, 1928.
Stearns, Peter. *Lives of Labor: Work in Maturing Industrial Society.* New York: Holmes and Meier, 1975.
Thomas, Louis. *Frédéric Le Play.* Paris: Mercure de France, 1943.
Tilly, Louise A., and Joan W. Scott. *Women, Work and Family.* New York: Holt, Rinehart and Winston, 1978.
Timasheff, Nicholas S. *Sociological Theory: Its Nature and Growth.* Rev. ed. New York: Random House, 1959.
Tocqueville, Alexis de. *Democracy in America.* Translated by George Lawrence. Edited by J. P. Mayer. Garden City: Doubleday, 1969.
———. *The Old Régime and the French Revolution.* Translated by Stuart Gilbert. Garden City: Doubleday, 1955.
Tourville, Henri de. *Histoire de la formation particulariste: L'origine des grands peuples actuels.* Paris: Firmin Didot, 1904.
———. "La Science sociale est-elle une science?" *La Science sociale* 1 (1886):9–21, 97–109, 289–304; 2 (1886):493–516.
———. "La Science sociale se confond-t-elle avec la science de la morale?" *Le Mouvement social* (May–June 1894).

Tudesq, A. J. *Les Grands notables en France, 1840–1849: Etude historique d'une psychologie sociale*. 2 vols. Bordeaux: Delmas, 1964.

———, and André J. Jadin. *La France des notables, 1815–1848*. 2 vols. Paris: Editions du Seuil, 1973.

Vidal de la Blache, Paul. *Principes de géographie humaine*. Paris: A. Colin, 1922.

———. *Principles of Human Geography*. Trans. by Millicent Todd Bingham. New York: H. Holt & Co., 1926.

Vignes, J.-B.-M. *La Science sociale d'après les principes de Le Play et de ses continuateurs*. 2 vols. Paris: Biard et Brière, 1897.

Villeneuve-Bargemont, Vicomte Alban de. *Economie politique chrétienne, ou recherches sur la nature et les causes du paupérisme en France et en Europe et sur les moyens de les soulager et de les prévenir*. Brussels: Méline, 1837.

Villermé, Louis René. *Tableau de l'état physique et moral des ouvriers employés dans les manufactures de coton, de laine, et de soie*. 2 vols. Paris: Renouard, 1840.

Weber, Max. *Economy and Society*. Translated by Ephraim Fischoff and others. Edited by Guenther Roth and Claus Wittich. 3 vols. New York: Bedminster, 1968.

Weiss-Rigaudias, Hilda. *Les Enquêtes ouvrières en France entre 1830 et 1848*. Paris: Alcan, 1936.

Zeldin, Theodore. *France, 1845–1945*. 2 vols. London: Oxford University Press, 1973.

Zimmerman, Carle C. "Frédéric Le Play as a Social Change Theorist." In *Recueil d'études sociales publié à la mémoire de Frédéric Le Play*, pp. 99–107. Paris: A. et J. Picard, 1956.

———. "Quelques remarques sur Frédéric Le Play." *Les Etudes sociales* 29 (1955):12–14.

———, and Merle E. Frampton. *Family and Society: A Study of the Sociology of Reconstruction*. New York: Van Nostrand, 1935.